PRAISE FOR *THE FANTASY FILM*

"*The Fantasy Film* is an exciting and readable adventure into the formulas and pleasures of films unjustly neglected in favor of their genre kin. This book will help remedy that." *Janet Staiger, University of Texas*

"Fowkes's book provides a lively, informed and accessible introduction to the important area of fantasy film. The author's enthusiasm for her subject is unmistakeable as she moves from classics such as *The Wizard of Oz* to contemporary fantasy blockbusters such as the *Lord of the Rings* trilogy and the Harry Potter movies." *Peter Hutchings, Northumbria University*

"An illuminating analysis of key American fantasy films, from *The Wizard of Oz* to *The Lord of the Rings*. This study has a keen eye for the literary antecedents and the many guises of fantasy, including comics and animation film." *Ernest Mathijs, University of British Columbia*

"Meticulously researched, elegantly written, and filled with insight, this is a graceful tribute to an important but elusive genre that is often over-looked. Katherine Fowkes has a deep and wise appreciation for these films that will enlighten those who know them well and inspire those who have not seen them to fire up their Netflix queue and start watching." *Nell Minow, Beliefnet Movie Critic*

NEW APPROACHES TO FILM GENRE

Series Editor: Barry Keith Grant

New Approaches to Film Genre provides students and teachers with original, insightful, and entertaining overviews of major film genres. Each book in the series gives an historical appreciation of its topic, from its origins to the present day, and identifies and discusses the important films, directors, trends, and cycles. Authors articulate their own critical perspective, placing the genre's development in relevant social, historical, and cultural contexts. For students, scholars, and film buffs alike, these represent the most concise and illuminating texts on the study of film genre.

THE FANTASY FILM

Katherine A. Fowkes

A John Wiley & Sons, Ltd., Publication

In loving memory of my father, Conard Fowkes (1933–2009): Actor, film lover, and tireless champion of the performing arts.

CONTENTS

LIST OF PLATES

ACKNOWLEDGEMENTS

I wish to thank a number of people, including series editor Barry Keith Grant, who has been a pleasure to work with and whose close reading of the proposal and penultimate draft have been invaluable. Thanks to the incomparable Nell Minow for also reading the penultimate draft, and to Jayne Fargnoli and Margot Morse at Wiley-Blackwell for their enthusiasm, and for being so wonderful to work with! And special thanks to my fabulous project manager and crack-commando copy-editor, Justin Dyer.

Thanks to Dennis Carroll, Carole Stoneking, Wilfred Tremblay, and Nido Qubein for all their support. Thanks also to my students Andrew Tzvaras and Matt Wells. And on a personal note, thanks to my sister Cly Fowkes, Dr Holly Lee, Dr Lewis Lipsey, Kirby and Carmen, and Michelle Bishop.

Finally, my deepest thanks goes to the love of my life and best friend, Pranab Das, for sticking with me, for tech support, for help with editing, and for all the many ways in which he brings me joy.

CHAPTER 1

WHAT'S IN A NAME
Defining the Elusive Fantasy Genre

Names and labels have a sneaky way of influencing our physical reality. Words form the prism through which we understand the world, and genre identifications help to shape expectations for what we find at the local cinema (or in our DVD players or computers). In the real world, we say that sticks and stones may break our bones, but words will never hurt us. But denizens of fantasy worlds might beg to differ. In *The Lord of the Rings* trilogy (2001–3), *The Chronicles of Narnia* (2005, 2008), and many other fantasy stories, great importance is given to words. In the *Harry Potter* films (2001–9) it is anathema to say the name "Voldemort" out loud. And making magic often depends upon correctly using names and language. The ridiculous and sometimes catastrophic results of poor diction in the *Potter* films illustrate the importance of precise language in casting magic "spells." In fantasy, to know a thing's true name is to have power over it.

If words become spells that harm or charm, then the word "fantasy" has itself cast a negative spell on a number of movies in the real world. The label "fantasy" has often been pejorative, applied to films seen to be trivial or childish, or said to seduce us with unrealistic wish-fulfillment. Until recently the film industry has considered fantasy "box-office poison" (Thompson 2007, 55). The tide seems to have turned, and yet "fantasy" is still a genre struggling to be taken seriously. Although it has been notoriously difficult to pin down the genre, one central aspect of fantasy stories is that they each feature a fundamental break with our sense of reality. This break, an "ontological rupture," is one of the hallmarks of the genre, but one whose subtleties bear exploring with regard to neighboring genres.

It is generally agreed that fantasies tell stories that would be impossible in the real world. They frequently concern mythical creatures or involve events that circumvent physical laws. But looking more closely, we see that fantasy's generic boundaries are rarely hard and fast. *Splash* (1984) is both a fantasy *and* a romantic comedy, *The Wizard of Oz* (1939) is *also* a musical, and *Shrek* (2001) is an animated, comic, fairy tale. This tendency toward hybrids may at first seem to militate against designating fantasy as a discrete genre, particularly in light of the wide difference in tone among fantasy movies (ranging from films like *Pan's Labyrinth*, 2006, to *Beetlejuice*, 1988, for example). The problem intensifies when we consider fantasy's relation to science fiction and horror, two types of film intimately related to fantasy. *The Terminator* (1984) is usually considered to be sci-fi, and *Dracula* (1931) horror, but isn't each also a kind of fantasy? If "fantasy" is to be an overarching term that includes sci-fi and horror, then we must ask why we don't also have a unique designation for films that don't qualify as *either* sci-fi or horror (*The Santa Clause*, 1994, for example, certainly doesn't belong to either of those categories).

This has left us with a kind of negative definition – fantasy films that are neither horror nor sci-fi get lumped into one big pool merely by virtue of *not* fitting one of those two categories. "Fantastic" might be more useful as an umbrella category to describe this overall "mode" of fiction, thus reserving the term "fantasy" as a designation related to, but distinct from, science fiction and horror. (This is essentially Brian Attebery's approach [11]. Note, however, Tzvetan Todorov's very different use of the term "fantastic," described in Ch. 3.) Although the three strands of "fantastic" cinema are related, each has come to be associated with specific types of stories. Classic or Gothic horror is distinguished from sci-fi and fantasy by its attempt to scare us, but may also announce itself through certain themes and iconography – dark and stormy nights, monsters, vampires, etc. (Modern horror may not feature supernatural elements at all, and thus represents a subset less relevant to this discussion.) Science fiction usually refers to stories that extrapolate from rational and scientific principles, and here again we expect a certain iconography – spaceships, robots, advanced technology, etc. But there is a great deal of overlap between all three of these categories. In combining a horrific and deadly monster with

PLATE 1 *E.T.: The Extra-terrestrial* (1982 Universal): Science fiction or fantasy? (Courtesy of Photofest.)

a futuristic outer-space setting, *Alien* (1979) is arguably both horror and sci-fi. And with its space alien, *E.T.: The Extra-terrestrial* (1982) is certainly science fiction, but shades into fantasy in its homage to other classics in the genre such as *The Wizard of Oz* (see Ch. 4) and *Peter Pan* – a story explicitly referenced in the film and also echoed through a delight in spontaneous flight (the famous bicycle scene) and through an emphasis on *belief* when encountering fantastic phenomena (Plate 1).

So, is there really such a thing as the fantasy genre, or is it a figment of this author's imagination – a fantasy itself, if you will? If conceptualizing fantasy as a genre proves elusive and messy at times, it may say as much about the concept of genre as it does about fantasy. As it turns out, many scholars agree that generic mixing is neither a new nor an isolated phenomenon. "The closer we look at individual genres and their histories, the less straightforward they become. . . . Genre labels are flags of convenience more than markers of entirely distinct territories" (King, 141–2). And precisely *because* so many critics and scholars *already* conceive of science fiction and horror as distinct from other fantasy films, it is convenient here to devise a study which examines some of the films left out of those discussions, even though their range is unusually eclectic.

Despite their differences, movies as varied as the comedic *Liar, Liar* (1997) and the epic *Beowulf* (2007) may be categorized as fantasy, thereby distinguishing them from horror and science fiction, but also reflecting a duality that seems to separate all fantastic or "fantasy" from other fictional films. "Dogmas of realism" have shaped our conception of cinema, creating a binary that privileges codes of realism and mimesis (the representation of reality) over more fantastic stories (Singer, 43). This duality has haunted art in general but also informs our understanding of the nature of cinema, influencing our evaluation of individual films. While it would be rare to hear that a movie was flawed because it was "too realistic," many are criticized for the opposite reason: "It was so unrealistic." "That could never happen." "It was implausible." Yet this long-standing tradition favoring mimesis and realism has, ironically, helped to obscure the relative "fantasy" nature of all fiction. Fantasy and mimesis are not actually opposites. "Mimesis without fantasy would be nothing but reporting one's perceptions of actual events. Fantasy without mimesis would be a purely artificial invention, without recognizable objects or actions" (Attebery, 3).

Assessments of the realism of a film often have little to do with actual reality but more to do with the specific conventions of realism and storytelling as we have come to know them through an accretion of Hollywood movies. The conventions for depicting time, space, and causality in Hollywood films help them tell coherent stories that seem internally consistent, regardless of whether they are realistic *per se*. Our sense of realism in a given film depends upon a number of factors, including sequences of cause and effect and our expectations for the conventions of genre (Bordwell et al., 12–20). When Gene Kelly sings and dances in the rain, we don't complain that it's unrealistic – it's realistic in a musical, in much the same way that aliens might seem "realistic" in a science-fiction movie. So if fantasy films don't resonate with viewers it's not necessarily because they feature unrealistic scenarios. Rather, a film is more likely to be criticized for failing to be internally consistent, hence thwarting coherence and meaning. In fantasy, the use of magic may subvert the normal circuits of cause and effect, but this in no way implies a lack of logic or coherence in the rest of the story. Instead, as a trope of fantasy, magic *stands in* for causality – its rejection of realistic causality is precisely its point.

If we are going to criticize fantasy films for offering up "unrealistic," wish-fulfillment scenarios, then shouldn't we at least acknowledge that films like *Rocky* (1976) are also fantasies of a sort? Yes! But of course that is clearly *not* what most people mean when they speak of fantasy film. Instead, they most likely mean a type of movie that departs *so* significantly from our understanding of reality that we feel comfortable bracketing it off from other fictional films. At the other extreme, films that are so experimental as to elude any possibility of a mimetic or realist interpretation have usually not been called fantasy. Instead, the terms "surrealism," "magical realism," "impressionism," "avant-garde," etc., are often applied. For my purposes then, the term "fantasy film" is most usefully restricted to mainstream cinema. The further we move away from classical Hollywood storytelling conventions and techniques, the more likely we are to abandon the term "fantasy" for one that evokes art with a capital "A" or denotes more subversive, experimental modes of cinema.

Using the term "fantasy" to describe a film does not *necessarily* force us to fall back on the same old binary of fantasy versus reality. Rather, within the context of mainstream cinema, the term could be understood to refer to "fantastic" story elements that are integral to the film's story-world. Brian Attebery's approach to fantasy literature (although not fantasy *film*) relies on the notion of fuzzy sets in which not all members of the set will feature all of the elements that define it. More likely, a core of fantasy themes and ideas exists at some metaphorical center, and movies may share many or few of these commonalities such as magic, physical transformations, or the ability to fly. A host of iconography helps to distinguish fantasy from other genres, particularly science fiction and horror, so that when we encounter wizards, crystal balls, flying brooms, fairies, magic talismans, or talking animals, we tend to assume fantasy unless otherwise informed. But a movie doesn't necessarily need to feature any or all of these to be considered fantasy.

My own definition is that that the audience must at the very least perceive an "ontological rupture" – a break between what the audience agrees is "reality" and the fantastic phenomena that define the narrative world. The word "rupture" distinguishes the fantastic elements in fantasy from those in science fiction, where fantastic phenomena are ostensibly *extrapolations* or extensions of rational, scientific principles. Thus in science fiction, the ability to instantly transport oneself to a distant location will be justified by extrapolating from scientific or quasi-scientific principles ("beam me up, Scotty"), while in fantasy it may be attributed to magic, as in the *Harry Potter* movies, where characters skilled in magic can use an old boot to "disapparate" from one place to another. The term "ontological" denotes the fact that fantastic phenomena are understood to really exist *within* the story-world – an existence as real as the reference world from which they break. This contrasts with movies that feature hoaxes, or hinge on characters' hallucinations or delusions. Although the premise of some fantasies concerns this very distinction, fantasy tends to discourage a solely psychological interpretation of events, or at least minimize its impact on the viewer's experience (*The Wizard of Oz*, for example). Supernatural horror may share in fantasy's rupture, but is distinguished from fantasy by its express purpose to frighten viewers with its alternate realities or impossible phenomena.

Fantasy's ontological rupture must be inherent in the premise of the movie or be otherwise integral to the story. Movies that feature only brief moments of weirdness or a single miraculous coincidence may not qualify. Occasional over-the-top violence in a slapstick comedy or a series of outrageous physical stunts in an action film may well be impossible in the real world, yet these are mostly not ontological breaks, but *exaggerations* of the possible in service of the genre in which they appear – humor in the case of a comedy, thrills in the case of an action film. Scary moments may be featured in fantasy, but they are necessarily part of a larger narrative and not the main point of the movie, as in horror. As a rule, fantasy tends to favor happy endings, and eschews not only tragedy, but cynicism, providing solace and redemption in a world of evil and violence.

J.R.R. Tolkien characterized fantasy as a literature of *hope*, a sentiment echoed by numerous fantasy scholars, and widely celebrated by fans of the genre. This emphasis on hope, happy endings, and a rejection of cynicism has only encouraged scholars and critics to ignore or vilify fantasy. But this impulse is contradictory. While fantasy is often accused of being "mere" escapism and therefore trivial, this very escapism is often the source of its alleged harm – supposedly encouraging audiences to abandon real-world problems and solutions for (usually) nostalgic and conservative illusions. Ideologically loaded terms associated with fantasy such as "naïve" and "childish" are usually assumed to be pejorative. Yet it behooves us to consider not only *why* these terms seem so negative but also whether they might also be considered in a positive light. In fact when we identify some of the recurring critiques of fantasy film, we find that many of these concepts actually form the basis of fantasy film content.

One important notion of film genre relies on the type of pleasure offered the viewer, almost always opposed in some way to social norms. Genres (by definition) "sequentially promote two different value systems, each providing pleasure by virtue of its difference from the other" (Altman, 156). The rhetoric surrounding fantasy film illuminates a host of contradictions and contrasting attitudes regarding work vs play and leisure, rationality vs imagination, adults vs children, nostalgia vs progress, etc., and these are some of the themes to which fantasy repeatedly returns. The negative reading of escapism is both pejorative and defining: calling attention to what it is *not* (like the fantasy genre itself) – not productive, not serious. The conventional wisdom is that escapist literature '"aims at no higher purpose than amusement"' (Rabkin, 44). Fantasy films lie at the extreme of such critiques because with fantasy we do, in effect, vicariously escape to a completely different world. But is this a bad thing? Eric S. Rabkin disputes what he sees as a false dichotomy between escapist and so-called "serious" literature, noting two misconceptions: "first that 'seriousness' is better than 'escape'; second, that escape is an indiscriminate rejection of order" (44). If, as Altman says, genres concern themselves with cultural interdictions, then one of fantasy's key interdictions is also integral to the pleasure we take from watching movies in the first place. No matter what the genre, we put aside other activities when we go to the movies and escape into another world for a few hours.

Viewers may not be consciously aware that they have escaped into an "alternate universe" when watching an action movie (for example), but that's exactly what they are doing. Fantasy just exaggerates aspects of this pleasure and makes it explicit in its *content*. Hence, in *The Wizard of Oz*, Dorothy escapes boredom, neglect, and persecution, as does Harry Potter, who escapes the oppressive and unimaginative Muggle world. The children in *The Chronicles of Narnia* escape boredom and loneliness in the first film, and school and bullies in the second. Again, is this a bad thing? Many proponents of fantasy would say "no." In part, this is because we are not just escaping *from* something, we are also escaping *into* something, and therefore the quality of the escape rests on the quality of the fantasy.

As is true of all movie genres, poor-quality fantasy films can easily be found, yet this doesn't necessarily explain why escape itself is so vilified. As noted, some genre scholars, including John G. Cawelti, W.R. Irwin, and others, see our engagement with genres as a kind of game between readers (or viewers) and texts. "Each genre game begins by positing a cultural norm, in order to permit the construction of generic pleasure as in some way contradicting that norm" (Altman, 157). As we shall see, a number of fantasy films explicitly or implicitly position themselves as imaginative and playful in contrast to a world of rationality, work, and conformity. The binaries reveal a conflicted attitude but one which, upon examination, reveals a need to justify our desire to fantasize, to play, to escape, or to engage in imaginative pursuits. It's not uncommon to question the value of escape or leisure, but it is far less common to question the value of work. Many films critique its *abuse* – work in excess, for example, or work for "the wrong reasons" (for greed or glory) – but the work ethic itself is not usually suspect. Play and other sorts of leisure, however, often seem worthless when characterized as the antitheses of productive society, often seen as "childish" distractions from important adult duties. Dreams, daydreams, and fantasizing also tend to be suspect unless a useful purpose can be ascribed to them. But as Roger Caillois argues, isn't "play" defined precisely as non–utilitarian and "unproductive?" (10). And if we concede that movies can be considered a type of play, as both Brian Sutton-Smith (145) and Caillois would (41), then it's interesting that critics would alternately celebrate movies for being entertaining, but at the same time insist upon movies being "useful." An argument can certainly be made that the "trivialness" of any given movie should be of less concern than the sheer amount of time spent engaging in the many "trivial pursuits" that distract us from more important things. On the other hand, if any sort of play or imaginative activity (escape, entertainment) is conceived of primarily in this light, it then seems off–limits to adults except as a guilty pleasure, a distraction from the "work of adulthood."

Sutton-Smith rejects the notion that any sort of play is frivolous (208), and certainly the movie industry would have to agree, but perhaps for different reasons. A consumer society predicated on leisure spending (an "indulgence" often conceived of as relief from work) can't afford for hard-working adults to stop spending big bucks on leisure pursuits, whether they be vicarious spectator events like movies or more active, but expensive, pursuits like skiing. That would be throwing the baby out with the bathwater. But as Josef Pieper argues, playful pursuits and leisure need not be seen as idleness, but can be viewed as essential aspects of humanity and culture. "Leisure lives on affirmation." It is not the same as the absence of activity (33). Rather than see work and leisure as antagonistic (the "Thank God it's Friday" syndrome), a vibrant culture would seek a more holistic approach. In Pieper's view, the proper attitude toward leisure is one of joy, best expressed by the concept of "festival," where humanity actively affirms and celebrates life and community. Such a perspective is dramatized and then threatened in *Rings* through the Hobbit's lifestyle in the Shire, where joyful work goes hand in hand with a love of gathering with others for music, food, and merriment. In fantasies such as *Harvey* (1950), *Big* (1998), and *Groundhog Day* (1993), the tension between work and leisure finds no such happy integration, but instead forms the basis of conflict underlying the fantasy narratives themselves.

The need to justify leisure, play, and flights of imagination helps to explain why so many fantasies are either aimed at children, or feature child characters. Childhood becomes the "place" where play is permitted and even encouraged. And we may be more likely to accept escapist stories when not constantly reminded that the "serious" world is being left behind by adult characters. In any case, both the content of fantasy film and the reactions that characterize such films as childlike or escapist point to a culture that is intensely conflicted about its relationship with work and utility in the face of guilty desire for the participation in and consumption of leisure experiences.

On the other hand, escape and play is often seen as the very work of childhood itself, conceived of as useful when seen as part of a child's normal maturation process. In fact, many fantasies dramatize this process through coming-of-age stories, featuring journeys or quests that result in the protagonist's personal and spiritual growth. Orphans abound in fantasy, untethered from parental authority and free to adventure. Coming-of-age stories are not unique to fantasy, of course, but they dovetail nicely with one of fantasy's central elements in their emphasis on the significant "transformation" of a character. Jack Zipes finds transformation to be a key element of the traditional fairy tale, whether characterized as the actual transformation of physical matter, the transgression of class boundaries, as in *Cinderella*, or coming-of-age transformations where a kid may become a king or a hero (2006, 49). Fairy-tale influences on fantasy movies are obvious through their reliance on stock characters, magical themes, and iconography common to such tales (wizard, wands, etc.), but we also find explicitly *physical* transformations in a variety of films, such as *Ladyhawke* (1985), *Willy Wonka and the Chocolate Factory* (1971), *The Mask* (1994), and comic-book superhero movies.

Despite the many fantasies aimed at or featuring children, proponents of fantasy argue that fantasy is neither childish nor a denial of reality, but an escape into a spiritual or inner journey. Fantasy's appeal may lie in its insistence on engaging us in imaginative experiences that invite us to temporarily transcend our sense of what is possible. If, as Rosemary Jackson writes, "the basic trope of fantasy is the *oxymoron*," (21) (a self-contradiction characteristic of the ontological rupture), then what unites so many fantastic stories (from fairy tales to Gothic horror) is their ability to express and dramatize contradiction so potently. By engaging the reader/viewer on both a psychological and a symbolic level, fantasy provides the opportunity to experience ideas outside of the framework of reason and the boundaries of everyday reality. Like the rabbit/duck illusion (Plate 2), fantasy excels at encouraging multiple and even contradictory readings.

Fantasy's insistence on "imaginative re-visioning" may be one of the things that binds the genre together, on both a thematic and a viewing

PLATE 2 Optical illusion: Rabbit or duck?

level. When viewers adopt a kind of shared vision, they create a virtual group identity, becoming, in Altman's words, a "constellated community." Accepting the

> premises of a genre is to agree to play within a special set of rules, and thus to participate in a community precisely *not* coterminous with society at large. . . . genres do not exist until they become necessary to a lateral communication process, that is until they serve a constellated community. Only when the knowledge that others are viewing similar films similarly becomes a fundamental part of the film-viewing experience does lateral communication exist. (157–62)

Even though Tolkien was wary of adapting *The Lord of the Rings* for film, fans long ago adopted his view of fantasy ("Faerie") in celebration of other fantasy films such as *The Dark Crystal* (1982) and *Labyrinth* (1986). Internet fan sites for such films show evidence that fans embrace them for their examination of the "big questions" and for suggesting a different way of perceiving the world. "There is a whole experience here, a way of sharing and apprehending the world through a newly defined concept of faery" (J. Wood, 292). Longstanding fans of Tolkien's books create a pre-constituted site of reception for the film adaptations, often extending their love of the films to social occasions. Likewise, fans of *Harry Potter* may see themselves as part of a community that forms its identity in opposition to real-world Muggles – those who don't care for the series, and/or anyone who seems to lack imagination.

In their wide-reaching study of movie audiences for *Rings*, Barker and Mathijs have demonstrated the complicated interaction between viewers and the film trilogy. In the general population, variations on the idea of "traditional" fan groups arose worldwide through excitement generated by the films' sophisticated advance publicity (including strategic "blackouts" of information, which stoked suspense), by teasers and trailers, by ancillary materials (which extended to the DVD releases), and by the general excitement and hype surrounding the trilogy. *Rings* became a social phenomenon for enthusiastic newcomers to Tolkien, who, like traditional fans, enjoyed discussing aspects of the films with friends and families. While fans of the books tend to focus on the films as "fantasy" (Mikos et al., 126), many others share the fantasy vision of Tolkien and the films' director, Peter Jackson, through a non-fantasy lens, celebrating the theme of friendship (Biltereyst et al., 57), or variously characterizing the story as epic, as a spiritual journey, adventure, etc. (Barker; Kuipers and De Kloet).

Both casual enthusiasts and traditional fans of fantasy (and other genres) increasingly converse at length in virtual chat rooms, while serious fans may also gather for screenings and conferences, enjoying "the social and communal aspects of fandom" (Klinger, 74). Nevertheless, the constellated communities generated by generic affinities do not depend upon direct communication between individuals. Traditionally, constellated communities have tended to be absent, invisible, or virtual. It is the "fantasized" community, this "invisible bond" between viewers, that becomes important for fans of *any* genre (Altman, 165). For fantasy enthusiasts, it may simply include an attitude open to the possibility of transcending day-to-day material existence, one that encourages us to imaginatively reconsider our sense of reality. For example, the shared "vision" for lovers of *Harvey* (see Ch. 5) might include the winking acceptance of an invisible rabbit. Hence, when strangers encountered Jimmy Stewart in person, it was said that many of them would inquire about how Harvey was doing.

The notion of constellated community also relates to an important aspect of many fantasy films: the theme of home. A variety of myths underlie much of American cinema, including the obvious ones such as happy endings and the idea that love will conquer all. But, "none of these myths is stronger or more persistent than the myth of home as the best possible place in the world" (Selcer). While Elisabeth Bronfen explores the construction of home in a variety of movies, Altman also notes how genres may encourage constellated communities that function as virtual homes, as viewers locate personal memories in the context of favored viewing experiences (187). Selcer points out, however, the inherent ambiguity in the concept of home and how difficult it is to define. "The fact that home cannot be readily defined is probably why it has been the subject of so many movies; it must be depicted rather than defined." If films must construct their own notion of home and their attitude toward it, fantasy may be in a privileged position because home is already an elusive, fantasy-like idea. It is both a physical and a mental/emotional construct, invested with both positive and negative connotations that change over time. Although Selcer argues that home is a distinctly American idea, there is no doubt that the concept also finds resonance with ancient myths and traditional folk and fairy tales through its opposition to adventure and journey. Whereas the house becomes the locus of haunting and repressed evil in Gothic horror, in fantasy it more likely serves as the repository of childhood memories and as a site of safety and nostalgia. But even here, this positive (some would say regressive) idea of home is never stable. It must be constantly re-constructed, re-invented, and re-valued through each narrative, each of which may highlight a variety of related concepts such as the nuclear family, gender roles, capitalism, or patriotism.

While fantasy answers horror in its celebration rather than dread of the supernatural, it answers science fiction by providing an alternative response to our anxiety in the face of technology, rationalism, and alienation. Both science fiction and horror can be seen as concerned with matters of control (McClintock, e.g. 34), and indeed the use or misuse of power is a central theme in a number of fantasy films. As with coming-of-age stories and the preoccupation with home, power struggles are not unique to fantasy or science fiction, but each genre inflects the issues through its own generic lens. So in science fiction, control can be wielded through technology (or via a monster created through technology), but in fantasy, magic often becomes the locus and focus of power. As ever, these tropes may easily be combined, as occurs in *Star Wars* (1977), where science-fiction technology combines with the very fantasy-inflected spiritual dimension of "the Force."

Genres are never stable, and fantasy's themes and motifs, as well as viewers' interpretations, are subject to change over time. Furthermore, we must expect that our notion of what qualifies as science fiction, horror, or fantasy will also change over time. What seems like pure science fiction in one era may actually reflect reality in a later era, and much of what we take for granted in everyday life would seem like magic to earlier generations. Moreover, although many have traced the roots of fantasy and the fantastic back to antiquity, we should be wary of applying modern genre labels to older, and in some cases ancient, texts. As Mark Rose argues:

> Like science fiction, fantasy is a modern, post-enlightenment genre. A spell cast by a sorcerer in a romantic epic of the 1590s simply does not

mean the same thing as one cast by a sorcerer in a fantasy novel of the 1980s. In the sixteenth century the world of objective fact, the empirical world from which fantasy deviates and which it requires as a precondition, had not yet fully emerged. (52)

Rose and others thus see fantasy and science fiction as distinctly modern genres related to, but not synonymous with, earlier fantasy texts.

Just as transformation is a common theme of fantasy, we might also say that "magical" transformation is a hallmark of *all* genres, since they continually mix, merge, evolve, and mutate (Altman, 14). In another vein, we might say that genre itself is a fantasy, one that provides the illusion of stasis in the face of chaos and change. It provides a template for creating but also interpreting texts at a given moment, despite the fact that these *con*texts may change as much as the genre itself, both transmogrifying over time. Furthermore, studios, fans, and critics each use genre labels for their own purposes, and may even do so at cross-purposes. Even as critics and scholars attempt to classify films generically, big studios actually prefer *mixed* genres in order to garner wide audiences, and may shun generic labels altogether in order to establish and protect their own "brands" and franchises (Altman, 99). In that high-stakes Darwinian struggle, the long-denigrated fantasy genre has much to gain, but will continue to be a subject of much debate.

Coming Attractions

The following chapters continue with an exploration of the genre in a short historical overview and a brief review of the critical literature on fantasy. In keeping with the other books in the *New Approaches to Film Genre* series, the focus is on US films (although some examples of non-US cinema can be found in the Historical Overview). Chapters 4 through 13 feature discussions of individual films. With a few exceptions, selection is weighted toward more recent popular films, in part because of the large number of fantasies released in the last few decades, but also because these recent movies are more likely to be familiar to readers. The films are therefore not meant to represent every historical era. Rather these "features" were selected because they have been successful or influential, or because they represent one or more significant thematic trends. In addition, the selections should help reveal commonalities between diverse types of fantasy film, and may help to suggest the variety of stories, themes, and approaches that might be legitimately considered fantasy. For example, *Shrek* is included in part because it exemplifies a type of animated fantasy currently in vogue (computer-generated and appealing to adults as well as children), but also because, in commenting on fairy tales, the film helps to illuminate this strand of the fantasy tradition. *Spider-Man* was chosen to represent the comic-book/superhero fantasy in part because of its enormous popularity, but also because it helps demonstrate the similarities between this subset of fantasy and other, non-comic-book-based fantasies. Finally, the films highlighted here don't significantly overlap with science fiction or horror, well-documented genres which are covered by other books in this series.

Please note that space considerations have required some difficult choices to be made and a number of splendid films have been neglected here. My apologies if your favorite movie doesn't get the attention it deserves.

CHAPTER 2

ONCE UPON A TIME
A Brief Historical Overview

The roots of fantasy fiction tap ancient myths, legends, and folk tales. In the West, stories of wonders and marvel trace all the way back to Homer's *Odyssey*, Ovid's *Metamorphoses*, Lucius Apuleius' *The Golden Ass*, and the chivalric romances of the late Middle Ages. In the East, they draw from epic tales such as the *Mahabharata* and the *Arabian Nights* tales (Kratz). But despite this august lineage, *modern* fantasy is an inheritance of the nineteenth century. The post-Enlightenment era with its increasingly rational and scientific worldview provided a specific moment that influenced the production and consumption of fantasy. Much of it drew on folk and fairy tales that had become popular two hundred years earlier, first as adult parlor entertainment but later as morality tales for children (Zipes 1994, 18).

Fantasy fed on both the sweet and bitter fruits of the Industrial Revolution: the rise of print literature, literacy, and leisure, but also the pollution and mechanization that industry brought. At the same time, changing conceptions of childhood coincided with a reconsideration of the role of imagination as both a mental faculty and an artistic product. As Kath Filmer and others note, nineteenth-century Romantic poets like Wordsworth and Coleridge were influential in re-conceiving the idea of imagination, helping to shift its former association with lying, wishful thinking, or hallucinations to something poetic, beautiful, and essential. Coleridge's coinage the "willing suspension of disbelief" remains a trope for the viewer's acceptance of fiction and fantasy. The Romantics also temporarily revived an appreciation for and interest in mysticism in the face of rationalism, one fueled by the "revulsion" they felt for the "human exploitation and degradation that characterized the early Industrial Revolution" (Filmer, 139). During this era, the Brothers Grimm and Hans Christian Andersen were celebrated for their revisions and adaptations of oral folk tales in print form (138–9). The Grimms had intentionally set out to reshape folk tales for the purpose of creating a kind of modern German mythology. Their aim was to develop a sense of national "community" in Germany (not unlike the notion of constellated communities discussed in the previous chapter). In revising and writing down the tales, however, the Brothers Grimm also laid the groundwork for the worldwide success of fairy tales (Zipes 2006, 82), with stories such as *Snow White*, *Hansel and Gretel*, and *Cinderella* (1812–15). In Denmark, Hans Christian Andersen published a number of tales, such as *The Ugly Duckling* (1845) and *The Little Mermaid* (1837). These soon became so popular and influential that some refer to him as the "father of the modern fairytale" (Clute and Grant, 26). Our vernacular is also rich with other contributions from this century, such as *A Christmas Carol* (1843), penned by Charles Dickens (influenced by Andersen), and *The Adventures of Pinocchio* (1892), by Italian writer Carlo Collodi.

Three British Victorian authors have been credited as the most direct antecedents of modern fantasy. Eric S. Rabkin traces the work of William Morris (1834–96), George MacDonald (1824–1905), and Lewis Carroll (1832–98), invoking the Victorian context as critical to the authors' conceptions of fantasy, as each responded imaginatively to the historical moment. In his story *The Well at the World's End* (1896), Morris used fantasy to confront the era's ambient sense of inevitable progress and civilization. Clute and Grant credit Morris with creating a "united fantasy geography" and for using landscape as an integral part of the story, rather than merely a backdrop (665). J.R.R. Tolkien is clearly indebted to Morris in this regard. MacDonald reacted to religious strictures in fantasies such as *At The Back of the North Wind* (1871), establishing a type of religious fantasy that would later influence Tolkien as well as C.S. Lewis. MacDonald is also known for entwining dream states with fantasy interludes, a much-used trope in fantasy. Lewis Carroll, the best known of the three authors, rebounded off the rising pillars of science and logic with the much-celebrated *Alice's Adventures in Wonderland* in 1865 (Rabkin, 82). Perhaps because its appeal to nonsense and play of verbal logic is ill suited to mainstream movie conventions, experimental approaches, like that taken by Czech filmmaker Jan Svankmajer, have had more success in visually capturing the nonsensical and surreal aspects of the story (see below). However, Tim Burton's upcoming adaptation (2010) suggests that *Alice* may finally enjoy Hollywood popularity.

While Morris, Carroll, and MacDonald all wrote for adults as well as children, Victorians increasingly focused on imagination as an important aspect of childhood development (Filmer, 139). The practical emphasis on development *per se* explains why many fantasies of this era, such as *Alice* and Charles Kingsley's *The Water-Babies* (1863), were supposedly written for a particular child, a tradition continued with later works such as P.L. Travers' *Mary Poppins* (1934), A.A. Milne's *Winnie the Pooh* (1926), and C.S. Lewis' *The Chronicles of Narnia* (1950–6) (Rabkin, 95). While modern adult fantasy owes an enormous debt to children's literature, the intentional association of the fantastic with childhood development has also been a factor in the genre's marginalization as a mainstream form.

The Victorian era was also a critical period for literature that reflected or responded to the burgeoning Industrial Revolution and an increasingly scientific understanding of the world. Robert Scholes describes George MacDonald's fantasy worlds as fully reflective of the era: "For MacDonald, a world is a world precisely because it has a system of laws: laws that harmonize with one another. This view is compatible, it should be noted, with both Victorian theology and positivistic science, which together formed the matrix from which the full-fledged modern genre of fantasy emerged" (12). Modern fantasy and science fiction thus emerged together as divergent but related responses to modern life (13). But where classic science fiction embraces the potential of science, fantasy responds by obliquely critiquing rationality and the underpinnings of the modern world.

As *film* genres, both science fiction and fantasy might be seen as expressions of the birth and evolution of cinema itself, and both genres can serve as barometers of technical innovation. If science fiction uses technology to tell stories about technology and science, we might say that fantasy harnesses cinema's ability to create illusions in order to tell stories about illusions themselves. Science fiction and fantasy are therefore to some extent "reflexive" genres. Special effects may not define the fantasy film (see *Harvey* and *Big*, for example), but poor effects can certainly detract from stories that depend upon them. In fact, the association of fantasy film with special effects begins with the birth of cinema itself. The French filmmaker Georges Méliès (1861–1938) is rightly credited with being the father of science-fiction and fantasy film. His famous short film

A Trip to the Moon (1902) is regarded as the first sci-fi film, and other one-reel shorts such as *Cinderella* (1899) established the fairy-tale tradition that would come to inform so many fantasy films. Méliès's work in theater and his background as a magician provided him with both the skills and the interest to create whimsical stories that employed clever effects and featured elaborate sets and costumes. Combining traditional theatrical effects with simple filmic techniques such as dissolves, stop-motion, fast and slow motion, and double exposures, Méliès made characters appear out of – or disappear into – thin air. He could easily turn one object into another, as in *Cinderella*, where stop-action turns a pumpkin into a stagecoach (Rickitt, 15).

Méliès is perennially contrasted with the Lumière brothers, who made short "slice-of-life" films such as the 1895 *Workers Leaving the Factory*, thus forever associating them with realism, or the recording of reality with little manipulation. Méliès, on the other hand, is associated with formalism, relying on tricks and illusions to manipulate reality or to create alternative realities. But this is not an entirely accurate distinction. For one, the Lumières also made narrative films that were clearly fictional vignettes. Furthermore, as Tom Gunning points out, *all* early films were seen as tricks and illusions, including realistic, slice-of-life films (4). In the early days of cinema, audiences marveled at the technology and "illusion" of reality as much as they would soon marvel at the elaborate fictional stories that define Hollywood films. Modern fantasies may employ effects in an effort to make us forget that we're looking at manipulated images, but today's viewers also take pleasure in the spectacle of modern movie-making and enjoy learning how illusions are created. This seeming paradox is one of the many intriguing dualities that inform our appreciation of fantasy film. "Unlike other films, science-fiction and fantasy films hover between being about the world their special effects imply . . . and about special effects and the wizardry of the movies themselves" (La Valley, 144). That movies themselves are a kind of wizardry provides a reflexive aspect to *The Wizard of Oz*, a film that illustrates complete immersion in a fantasy world while the wizard (in spite of himself) calls attention to the technology used to create fantasy and illusion.

As movie-making developed in the silent era, Méliès-style fantasies seemed increasingly quaint and American cinema turned to more "realistic" narratives (Worley, 23). One notable fantasy film of the silent era, however, was *The Thief of Bagdad* (1924), the first feature-length screen version of the Arabian Nights tale. Although a color version of *Thief* was remade with spectacular effects in 1940, the American Film Institute ranks the silent version ninth on their list of best fantasy films.

PLATE 3 *The Thief of Bagdad* (1924 Douglas Fairbanks Pictures): Silent film fantasy. (Courtesy of Photofest.)

Known for its beautiful photography, massive sets, and groundbreaking special effects, the movie tells the story of a thief (Douglas Fairbanks) who rescues a princess and also saves Baghdad from Mongol invasion. The story features many elements common to fantasy, including a genie, a flying carpet, and a central character transformed through his heroic magical journey (Plate 3). Fairbanks, who also co-wrote and produced the film, was said to have been inspired by the lavish sets of the meticulously crafted German Expressionist films of the era (Rickitt, 20).

Although German Expressionism was more influential on horror than fantasy *per se*, *Nosferatu* (1922), *The Cabinet of Dr Caligari* (1919), and others are relevant here for depicting full-fledged fantasy worlds through eerie *mise-en-scènes* designed to visually reflect their dark supernatural themes (often combined with Freudian or political subtexts). *Nosferatu*, the first feature-length vampire movie, used simple Méliès-style effects to endow the eponymous vampire with supernatural powers, superimposing his ghostly face above a coffin, and showing him disappear through closed doors, for example. This genuinely scary version of Bram Stoker's *Dracula* influenced Francis Ford Coppola's 1992 version. Fritz Lang's

Metropolis (1927) influenced later science-fiction films, including notable US movies like *Blade Runner* (1982). Even the design of *Star Wars* robot C-3PO owes a debt to this film. And in 1938, the comic-book superhero Superman would make his home in the fictional city of "Metropolis." Lang is also known for his adaptation of the epic German poem *Die Nibelungen* (1924), a two-part film featuring elements later found in *Rings*, *Harry Potter*, and other fantasies, including dwarves, a magic ring, a dragon, and an invisible cloak.

Hollywood was apparently reluctant to fully embrace the supernatural (as Rick Worland notes), either because it was thought that audiences might not buy into such stories or because German-style horror risked being too morbid for American audiences. Instead, supernatural movies in the twenties were more often comedic haunted-house stories. Many of these concluded that the haunting had actually been an illusion or a fraud (Worland, 52–3), a tradition more common to a strain of Gothic literature such as Ann Radcliffe's 1794 novel *The Mysteries of Udolpho* (Todorov, 41). But the next decade proved to be a golden era for US horror – a form much less dark than its German predecessors. *Dracula* and *Frankenstein* (both 1931) helped create a horror boom largely associated with Universal Studios. As with Mary Shelley's original 1818 novel, *Frankenstein* defies definitive classification. Many critics trace modern horror and sci-fi to this Gothic tale, but Rosemary Jackson and others track the Gothic strain back to Horace Walpole's *The Castle of Otranto*, published in 1764 (95). What truly distinguishes *Frankenstein* from previous fantastic tales is the combination of Gothic horror with the potentially dehumanizing effects of science and technology. In this seminal text, therefore, we can identify the parameters of a universe that spawns not just science fiction and modern fantasy, but horror as well, with each evincing different attitudes toward the modern world. So, while some include *Frankenstein* in the horror genre (Worland), and others lean toward science fiction (Kroeber, 19), most also acknowledge that the story is a hybrid – like Frankenstein's monster himself.

During the 1920s, science fiction and fantasy became popular in mass-marketed pulp fiction and magazines. *Amazing Stories* was considered to be science fiction and *Weird Tales* horror and fantasy, but there was considerable overlap. H.P. Lovecraft, for example, employed both sci-fi and fantasy elements in his horror stories. Such mixing influenced countless other authors, so that "by the middle thirties, you have a whole range of pulp writers who are now seriously interested in both modes" (Delany, 67). Along with romance and comic books, these stories were segregated from fiction that was marketed as bona fide "literature" in order to distance the latter from supposedly childish or lower quality fiction (66–8). By the 1930s and 1940s, comic-book heroes became so popular that many were adapted or serialized for the movies. (Lucas and Spielberg's 1981 hit *Raiders of the Lost Ark* is widely understood to be an homage to the serial adventures of this era.) But popularity did not eliminate the distinction between highbrow and lowbrow fiction, which would continue to plague science fiction and fantasy for several decades.

The advent of sound film in 1927 encouraged more realistic stories and acting styles, but it also opened the door to genres that thrived on witty dialogue (screwball comedies), music and dance (musicals), and special effects (fantasy and others). Indeed, special effects were increasingly needed to solve a variety of mundane problems endemic to the film-making process, problems that were exacerbated by the difficulties of adapting to synchronized sound and the growing preference to shoot on sets rather than on location (Brosnan, 47). Thus, in the 1930s, special-effects technicians were needed just to create the illusion of everyday reality. For example, while rear projection could be used to create a backdrop suggesting an alien planet, the same technique was equally necessary to create the illusion that a character on a soundstage was driving a car in traffic (Rickitt, 25). Fantasy and sci-fi thus benefited indirectly from technical innovations linked to sound and the trend toward filming on sets.

While satisfying the need to create the illusion of simple *reality*, innovative special effects could also serve as the basis for entire fantastical stories. *King Kong* (1933) is usually considered horror because of its scary super-sized simian, but is also considered fantasy or science fiction. The film has had a lasting impact on the popular imagination and is notable for its success in employing special effects to create fantastic creatures. (The American Film Institute rates it fourth on its top ten fantasy site.) As with many fantasy-themed films, its influences are varied, inspired in part by *The Lost World* (1925), based on the 1912 novel by Arthur Conan Doyle, and also by Edgar Rice Burroughs' novel *The Land That Time Forgot* (1918). Both *King Kong* and *The Lost World* featured prehistoric animals created by stop-motion photography. Willis O'Brien was behind the special-effects triumphs of both these movies and is widely hailed as one of the great pioneers of early special-effects animation techniques. Noël Carroll writes that monsters in horror stories are all about skepticism and the need for characters to come to grips with the reality of the phenom-enon. In as much as monsters "prompt a need for proof" (35), the special effects in *King Kong* and other monster movies are designed to display the creature in all its glory.

In 1937, Frank Capra's *Lost Horizon* relied on relatively few special effects to create a utopian fantasy, a strand of the genre that proposes idyllic societies that avoid the ills of the real world. In that film, inhabitants of the isolated mountain community Shangri-la appear to live for 200 years or more without aging. Although they seem to exist happily and harmoniously, there is some question as to whether the whole thing is a sham, a suspicion voiced by one of the visitors who arrives accidentally after a plane crash. The locals' agelessness is proven in the end, but it's never quite clear whether the phenomenon is a function of some undiscovered property of the mountain setting (science fiction) or whether something magical and truly inexplicable has occurred (fantasy).

In that same year, Disney pioneered the animated feature-length fantasy with *Snow White and the Seven Dwarfs*, one of the most popular movies ever made. Disney's impact on the film industry cannot be overstated. By focusing on meticulously crafted animation, it would come to dominate both animated and fantasy films for decades. As Jack Zipes argues, *Snow White* became the definitive animated fairy-tale film, altering the Grimms' popular version and setting the standard for all others to come (Zipes 1994, 84). Fairy-tale princes and princesses were ever after portrayed as lithe and beautiful, "prefiguring the Barbie and Ken dolls by a good twenty years" (2001, 84). Female characters became either pretty "ornaments" or evil and ugly villains, while male orphans and triumphant male "underdog" stories became a hallmark of the tales (1994, 89). Following the success of *Snow White*, Disney continued its success with more animated features, becoming a household name with classics like *Pinocchio* (1940) and *Peter Pan* (1953) (Plate 4), adapted from J.M. Barrie's 1904 stage play.

The story of *Peter Pan* has long been a favorite of Steven Spielberg's (recall the allusions in *E.T.*, cited in Ch. 1), and its title character has since become iconic of Spielberg films featuring male characters rejecting adult responsibilities in favor of fantastic adventures, as in *Close Encounters of the Third Kind* (1977). Alternately, it describes male viewers who revel in boyish adventure fantasies, such as *Raiders of the Lost Ark*. As with Mickey Mouse, the fairy Tinker Bell from *Peter Pan* has became one of Disney's signature figures, simultaneously conjuring up fantasy and irrevocably conflating it with Disney. But if most Disney movies are pure fantasy, the company's business practices have always been firmly rooted in reality. Long before the rest of the industry cottoned on, Disney mastered the art of "synergy" by creating a brand that extended far beyond the films themselves to theme parks, television shows, toys, souvenirs, and even

PLATE 4 *Peter Pan* (1953 Walt Disney): Fantasy and flying, Disney style. (Courtesy of Photofest.)

clothes. If you believe in Tinker Bell, go ahead and clap your hands – but then also hand over your wallet. You'll have to if you're going to pay for all the tie-in merchandise that Disney wants to sell.

The Disney phenomenon has spawned scores of scholarly books and articles, many of them negative. Most critics agree that the animated films are superbly crafted, but many accuse them of being sexist, racist, and at the very least blandly commercial. Furthermore, as a business, Disney has long had a questionable track record. (See Bell et al.; Davis; Giroux; Griffin; Wasko 2001; Zipes – all.) Blandness may have been the studio's undoing, and, after the ho-hum reception of *Sleeping Beauty* in 1959, Disney increasingly concentrated on live-action films, until the success of *The Little Mermaid* in 1989 led to a renewed cycle of animated fairy-tales.

Live-action fantasies have enjoyed a more mixed history than Disney's animation. Paramount, for example, hoped that its 1933 adaptation of *Alice in Wonderland* would share in some of the success garnered by *The Thief of Bagdad*. Unfortunately, audiences were not impressed. It seems viewers had paid to "see and not just hear" Cary Grant, W.C. Fields, and Gary Cooper, major stars rendered unidentifiable beneath elaborate costumes (Worley, 32). By contrast, the fairy-tale elements of *Babes in Toyland* (1934), a musical comedy starring Laurel and Hardy, prefigure both *Snow White* and *The Wizard of Oz* and draw on the same technology that "animated" *King Kong* a year earlier. Elements like the famous march of the (life-sized) wooden soldiers have led some critics, including Peter Nichols, to remark upon how affecting and even sometimes "scary" the fantasy was (181). Antedating the blockbuster *Shrek* (2001) by almost seventy years, *Babes* plays off a hodgepodge of fairy-tale characters like The Three Little Pigs, Red Riding Hood, and others to build its effective story-world. The combination of live-action fantasy with musical song and dance was touted a few years later when MGM released *The Wizard of Oz* (1939) as a "prestige film," demonstrating its state-of-the art special effects and high production values through musical fantasy. The strong affinity between musical and fantasy genres has had a much more robust tradition in Indian cinema, beginning with *Alam Ara* (1931) and *Indrasabha* (1932), and extending into the present with numerous hits including "masala" blockbusters (mixed genres) such as *Sholay* (1975) and *Pardes* (1997).

Another strand of fantasy that emerged in the 1930s and 1940s were stories in which ghosts appeared as full-fledged characters rather than the fleeting apparitions found in horror and folk tales (Waggoner, 11). Unlike spirits in the Gothic tradition, ghost characters in these films are featured in comedic or dramatic situations rather than horrific ones. Early comedic treatments of ghosts include a lighthearted British film, René Clair's *The Ghost Goes West* (1935), in which a Scottish ghost returns to redeem the honor of his clan and castle, and the somewhat similar US film *The Canterville Ghost* (1944), based on the novella by Oscar Wilde. Another notable comedy, *Topper* (1937), starred Cary Grant and Constance Bennett in a "screwball" ghost story. In both *Topper* and the British *Blithe Spirit* (1945), the ghosts' ability to move visible, solid objects while themselves remaining invisible becomes a source of horror or consternation for certain characters. But since the audience is in on the joke and the spirits are mischievous but not evil, the situation is played for laughs. By contrast, *The Invisible Man* (1933) explores the pernicious potential of invisibility when the power-hungry protagonist exploits his new abilities for personal gain. As we observe throughout the history of fantasy, invisibility can be used for good or evil depending on the generic context (Fowkes 1998). And as with magical spells, invisibility raises issues of power and control, a central element in much of fantasy and science fiction.

World War II dominated the country's (and Hollywood's) attention during much of the 1940s and so it's not surprising that ghost and angel films were common during this period. Peter Valenti retroactively coined the term "Film Blanc" to describe the optimistic nature of the period's films in contrast to later film noir (295). Some ghost and angel films, such as the British *A Matter of Life and Death* (1946), made explicit reference to the war, but many employed ghosts for romantic purposes, as in *The Ghost and Mrs Muir* (1947), now considered a classic. Such films provided reassurance that loved ones were not really lost forever and that those who had died in the war had done so for a higher cause.

The trend in supernatural stories of a dramatic or comedic bent would return to haunt US cinema in the 1980s and 1990s with films like *All of Me* (1984) and the sleeper hit *Ghost* (1990). A handful of these were remakes, including *The Preacher's Wife* (1996), a remake of *The Bishop's Wife* (1947), and *City of Angels* (1998), a remake of German filmmaker Wim Wenders' *Wings of Desire* (1987), the latter described by historian David A. Cook as a "magical masterpiece" (596). Many of these later films employed ghosts and angels as vehicles for dramatizing dilemmas of gender identity and romantic or domestic relationships. Invariably, ghosts and angels proved handy devices for stories of redemption, forgiveness, and second chances (Fowkes 1998, 2004).

In Europe filmmakers saw fantasy as a vehicle with which to disrupt the status quo through the manipulation of artistic conventions. Jean Cocteau, in contrast with Disney, crafted an adult, live-action fairy tale based on the eighteenth-century story *Beauty and the Beast* (1946). Disney is known for its mainstream conservative adaptations, but Cocteau conceived of filmmaking from an avant-garde perspective. Surrealists like Cocteau, Luis Buñuel, and others were interested in exploring the creative and subversive aspects of dreams and the unconscious. André Breton's 1924 "Manifesto of Surrealism" characterized the movement as a "badge of resistance to rational culture" (During, 30). Films made in this style often defy coherence, manipulating our sense of space, time, and causality. One of the earliest was Germany's *Ghosts before Breakfast* (1928), a short film by Hans Richter in which a variety of objects and body parts inexplicably fly about. Whereas in *Topper* a floating hat is a comedic device in a mainstream narrative (Plate 5), here a group of floating hats reappear randomly, becoming the only thread linking together an otherwise nonsensical sequence of objects, people, and events. While exhibiting some of the dream-like qualities of his more surrealistic films such as *Blood of a Poet* (1930) and *Orpheus* (1950), Cocteau's *Beauty and the Beast* is actually more mainstream – a lyrical fairy tale that has become an enduring classic. Its human candelabras and magical household objects became staples of later adaptations, including the 1991 Disney movie and the Broadway musical. On the other hand, Luis Buñuel's short surreal film *Un Chien Andalou* (1929) defies narrative coherence and still shocks

PLATE 5 *Topper* (1937 Hal Roach Studios): Invisible ghosts wreak comedic havoc. (Courtesy of Photofest.)

with its incongruous and occasionally disgusting images, including a scene in which an eye is sliced by a razor blade. Buñuel's feature-length *L'Âge d'Or* (co-written by Salvador Dali, 1930) provides a surreal critique of class and religion in a fragmented story involving a couple whose romantic union is repeatedly thwarted by the woman's restrictive family and a conservative society. Audiences found the erotic but often random imagery to be shocking and offensive. In one scene a woman sucks on the toes of a statue, while the most controversial moment showed Christ "emerging from a sadistic orgy," apparently provoking riots in the audience (Thompson and Bordwell, 164).

In the US, surrealism later infused *The 5,000 Fingers of Dr T.* (1953), a bizarre children's movie penned by Dr Seuss (Theodore Geisel) that explores the dread of childhood piano lessons as an extended dream sequence (Plate 6). As a mainstream effort, it was unsuccessful at the box office, but it now enjoys a certain cult status.

In the 1950s and 1960s, avant-garde and fantasy mixed worldwide with notable results. In Ingmar Bergman's *The Seventh Seal* (1957), for example, a knight challenges Death to a chess game, one of many fantasy-infused elements in the films of this celebrated Swedish auteur (Plate 7).

PLATE 6 *The 5,000 Fingers of Dr T.* (1953 Columbia): A surreal take on the dreaded piano lessons, courtesy of Dr Seuss. (Courtesy of Photofest.)

PLATE 7 *The Seventh Seal* (1958 Svensk Filmindustri): Ingmar Bergman's surreal allegory. (Courtesy of Photofest.)

In Japan, Kenji Mizoguchi issued the ghostly *Ugetsu Monogatari* (1953), and in Italy, Federico Fellini became celebrated for his dreamlike movies such as 8½ (1963). These and other innovative films play on both traditional elements of fantasy and the frisson of disjointedness and originality that their auteur directors pioneered. The impact of film-makers like Bergman and Fellini on filmmakers worldwide cannot be underestimated, despite the fact that many of these foreign masterpieces attracted much smaller audiences than most Hollywood movies. Two recent exceptions in the US include the moderately successful *Like Water for Chocolate* (1991) and *Pan's Labyrinth* (2006), the latter enjoying the fruits of an increased mainstream acceptance of fantasy, but both drawing on a tradition of magical realism. While long popular in Latin America, literary works like *One Hundred Years of Solitude* (1967) by Colombian writer Gabriel García Márquez have helped magical realism become a popular phenomenon in the US. As Thompson and Bordwell describe, magical realism combines realistic stories with elements of fantasy, myth, and folk tales and traditionally "sought to reflect the collective imagina-tion of colonized peoples, for whom everyday reality seemed only one step away from the supernatural" (614). Both *Like Water for Chocolate* and *Pan's Labyrinth* enjoyed success in the US, showing that aspects of experimental, avant-garde, and "art" movements can successfully pene-trate the US market when combined with more popular narrative conventions. While not widely known, many other filmmakers continue to be praised for their creative and experimental endeavors. In the 1980s, noted Czech artist Jan Svankmajer resurrected surrealistic tradition with his innovative twist on stop-motion and claymation techniques. His disturbing shorts such as *Dimensions of Dialogue* (1982) were followed by his live-action/animated film *Alice* (1988), a demented but critically acclaimed version of Lewis Carroll's story.

While international cinema saw much creativity in the 1950s (and beyond), that decade found the US gripped by the full-scale emergence of science fiction as a distinct film genre. The majority were sci-fi/horror mixtures, conveying a sentiment anathema to what fans originally considered the essence of science-fiction literature. Far from extolling the advantages of science and reason, these films routinely expressed the fear that an excess of rationality might itself be the problem. *Invasion of the Body Snatchers* (1956) was typical in expressing this anxiety. The strange behavior and sudden lack of emotion in the inhabitants of a small town are not the result of psychological stress or alienation, as the psychiatrist Dr Bennell first believes. Rather, the townspeople have been taken over by aliens who are physical duplicates of the originals but whose hyper-rationality and inability to feel emotions or love is precisely what makes them "alien" and scary. The rejection of science and rationality is why Rawlins argues that most sci-films are really fantasy masquerading as science fiction (160–74). Nevertheless, evil aliens and space exploration were all part of the 1950s sci-fi scenario in which the horrors of the atomic bomb combined with Cold War paranoia to stoke fears of the "Other." The iconography of the films is unmistakable with their rockets and spaceships, computers, robots, and scary aliens, thus helping to distinguish them from fantasy and Gothic horror.

While science and technology were a point of contention in science-fiction movies, they also contributed to the special-effects marvels that were used to create the films in the first place. The celebrated George Pal, for example, was instrumental in the effects created for classic science-fiction movies like *Destination Moon* (1950), "the seminal science fiction film" (Frank), *War of the Worlds* (1953), and the fantasy *tom thumb* (1958). But for a short time, the most fearful technology for Hollywood itself was television, putting pressure on movies to offer exciting visuals to lure viewers away from the small screen (Thompson and Bordwell, 301). This led to large-scale spectacles like those created by Ray Harryhausen, who had trained under Willis O'Brien. Harryhausen showcased his stop-motion animation and matte techniques in an *Arabian Nights* fantasy with *The 7th Voyage of Sinbad* (1958), the first in a handful of Sinbad movies and one that Harryhausen considered his best (Rickitt, 190) (Plate 8). This movie, like many released in the 1950s, acknowledge the burgeoning "youth" audience, as films were increasingly targeted specifically at *either* mature or youth sensibilities (King, 30).

Stanley Kubrick's enigmatic but breathtaking science-fiction opus *2001: A Space Odyssey* (1968) may have been a turning point for all types of fantastic cinema because of its high production values and serious philosophical approach to space travel. Until then, the 1960s had not been a great decade for fantasy, despite Disney's continuing contributions, including the mixed live-action/animation musical *Mary Poppins* (1964). But *2001* lent an aura of prestige to what had previously been seen as lightweight or lowbrow entertainment. In the Soviet Union, acclaimed filmmaker Andrei Tarkovsky answered Kubrick's film with the dream-like science-fiction film *Solaris* (1972). In the US, the 1970s marks a transitional period between some of the more iconoclastic films of the 1950s and 1960s and the eventual ascendance of adventure, sci-fi/horror, and fantasy that would follow in the 1980s and beyond. Thus, the early and mid-1970s were dominated by paranoia and pessimism, echoing the disillusionment of the Watergate scandals and the Vietnam War. But

PLATE 8 *The 7th Voyage of Sinbad* (1958 Morningside/Columbia): Harryhausen's stop-motion magic. (Courtesy of Photofest.)

by the end of the decade, a more optimistic vision emerged. Spielberg's *Close Encounters of the Third Kind* suggested that aliens were not to be feared but embraced, paving the way for the loveable and childlike alien in *E.T.: The Extra-terrestrial*.

Nobody had a bigger impact on the times than Spielberg and his sometime collaborator George Lucas, whose 1977 *Star Wars* combined science-fiction elements with mysticism and adventure, kick-starting a trend in blockbuster spectacles with a heavy fantasy slant. The confluence of a large youth audience and innovative special-effects technology – spurred in part by Lucas' Industrial Light and Magic – conspired with a number of factors to make fantasy films (of all varieties) more prevalent and more popular than ever before. Spielberg's *Jaws* (1975) is the prototype of the blockbuster movie, and Lucas' *Star Wars* (1977) became the model for franchises that created synergy, generating sequels and series with ancillary products such as DVDs, video games, toys, and souvenirs (Thompson 2007, 4). The merchandising franchises and synergy that Disney had long practiced increasingly became the preferred model throughout the 1980s as production costs rose and studios were acquired by multinational conglomerates. This model also proved to be a more reliable money generator than individual movies. Star power and story line were no longer enough. "A continuing series brought with it automatic name recognition once its characters and story gained wide currency. . . . Today the franchise is often the star" (Thompson 2007, 4–6). Popular series like *Twilight* are thus now the norm.

Another phenomenon of the 1970s was the counter-cultural Monty Python team, who introduced a comic medieval fantasy with *Monty Python and the Holy Grail* (1975), which was followed by a slew of largely unsuccessful "sword and sorcery" adventures with Arthurian themes and/or medieval settings. Films like *Dragonslayer*, *Excalibur*, *Clash of the Titans*, and *Conan the Barbarian* (all released in 1981) were set in ancient or medieval settings, providing an appropriate fit for stories of magic, heroism, and absolute good and evil. As Scholes argues, with the "mixture of pagan and Christian beliefs," the Middle Ages proves to be a popular setting for many fantasies (7). Variations included Terry Gilliam's *Time Bandits* (1981), which inverts *Narnia*'s wardrobe device by having a horse dramatically spring from a wardrobe into a little boy's bedroom, ushering in a time-travel adventure with a cast of comical but snarky dwarves (Plate 9). Originally known for creating innovative animation for Monty Python's television series, Gilliam later made his mark with a number of other fantasies such as Lewis Carroll's *Jabberwocky*

PLATE 9 *Time Bandits* (1981 HandMade Films): Terry Gilliam's snarky dwarves. (Courtesy of Photofest.)

PLATE 10 *The Dark Crystal* (1982 Jim Henson Productions/Universal): Jim Henson's muppets get serious. (Courtesy of Photofest.)

(1977), the brilliantly absurd and dystopic *Brazil* (1985), and the whimsical but emotionally charged Grail fantasy, *The Fisher King* (1991). Jim Henson provided a refreshing foray into fantasy that proved to be one of the few challenges to Disney's stranglehold on animated stories, building on his signature puppetry from the popular television shows *Sesame Street* (1969–81) and *The Muppet Show* (1976–81) to make whimsical movies such as *The Muppet Movie* (1979) and the more serious but notable *The Dark Crystal* (1982) (Plate 10). Despite a slew of mainstream contenders like *Willow* (1988), *Legend* (1985), and *Ladyhawke* (1985), the sword and sorcery angle fizzled after a number of box-office bombs. Several of these, like the ill-fated *Krull* (1983), were financial disasters, assuring that fantasy of the sword and sorcery variety would be considered box-office poison for years to come (Nichols, 163).

Escaping the brutish and formulaic sword and sorcery mode, Spielberg's *Raiders of the Lost Ark* proved to be one of the most popular adventure fantasies ever. Along with the phenomenal success of *E. T.*, the film helped usher in a different sort of big-budget fantasy for the whole family. Critics and scholars bemoaned the "juvenalization" of the movies, but Spielberg demonstrated that fantasy adventures were not exclusively for kids. Beginning in the 1980s, as budgets rose and the blockbuster model prevailed, it became critical to design movies that could satisfy a wide demographic. A film appealing only to mature tastes can't capture the large youth demographic essential for recouping costs. On the other hand, if a movie *only* appeals to youth, it probably won't be made unless it's relatively inexpensive (slasher films, for example). This is why PG-13 has emerged as the most desirable rating, signaling its appeal to all but the youngest viewers (Thompson 2007, 74).

In the 1970s, nostalgia for the pre-Vietnam and pre-Watergate world surfaced in an obsession with family and anxieties about its disintegration in horror films where house and home become contested sites of desire and fear (the 1979 *Amityville Horror*, for example). Just as a child becomes the vessel of evil in *The Exorcist* (1973), some films focused anxiety about domestic problems by displacing it onto an evil child, as in *The Omen* (1976). Whereas 1950s movies tended to combine horror with sci-fi in the figure of a monster from beyond, horror of this era suggests "that the horror is not merely among us, but rather part of us, caused by us" (Polan, 143). Vivian Sobchack argues that the traditional horror story is one in which characters struggle for and achieve "redemption through suffering and love" (1987, 35). By the 1980s, however, the family may not be a sanctuary from horror, but the very origin of it (R. Wood 2001).

Nostalgia for a supposed ideal nuclear family also surfaces in fantasy films of the era, exhibiting a desire to reconstitute the troubled family and ultimately restore it to its mythical place at the core of American life. Critics like Daniel Marcus have pointed to the explosion of films (e.g. *American Graffiti*, 1973) and television shows (e.g. *Happy Days*, 1974–84) that featured idealized notions of life in the 1950s, a time before the corruption, violence, and disillusionment that characterized the 1960s and 1970s. The wholesome nuclear family is seen as the source of material and emotional stability, providing the mirror image of horror's family.

The small town house of an earlier era is now the suburban *home* found in countless movies. Spielberg, for example, is known for stories featuring troubled suburban families who eventually recuperate a sense of home as an imaginary site (as epitomized in *E.T.* and *Close Encounters.*) The horror film *Poltergeist* (1982) (which Spielberg produced) puts the family in jeopardy but assures its togetherness at the end of the film. Ironically, the family must abandon their suburban dream home, and the movie ends with them safe in a motel. Spielberg thus removes the family from the physical house, but retains the sense of home as something relational that the family wins by having undergone and survived a horrific ordeal. Tim Burton's *Beetlejuice* (1988) humorously reverses the traditional haunted house trope by having ghosts effectively haunted by a dysfunctional (living) family that moves in after their death. But both families are joyously restored by the end. Thus horror and fantasy often address

PLATE 11 *Edward Scissorhands* (1990 Twentieth Century Fox): A classic Tim Burton live-action fantasy. (Courtesy of Photofest.)

similar ideas but provide different attitudes, different solutions, and different pleasures. Burton's considerable contribution to fantasy straddles fantasy and Gothic horror in films like *The Corpse Bride* (2005), featuring his signature stop-motion animation, and live-action films like *Batman* (1989) and *Edward Scissorhands* (1990) (Plate 11).

As digital technology became more sophisticated and more ubiquitous, animated and all kinds of fantasy began to dominate. Japanese animation (*anime*) would emerge as a global phenomenon, including Mamoru Oshii's *Ghost in the Shell* (1995), heavily influencing *The Matrix* (1999), while Hayao Miyazaki's *Princess Mononoke* (1997) and *Spirited Away* (2001) answered Disney's legacy with a distinctly Japanese flavor (Plate 12). Years earlier, Disney's *Mary Poppins* (1964) and *Bedknobs and Broomsticks* (1970) had combined live-action and animation to mixed success, but in 1988, Disney's groundbreaking *Who Framed Roger Rabbit* presaged a new type of sophistication in creating a hybrid live-action/ animated world. With computer-generated imagery (CGI) increasingly prevalent, and with the emergence of innovative studios like Pixar, the industry was finally ready to tackle fantasy on a grand scale. *Toy Story* (1995) was the first completely computer-generated film. Thompson notes that: "The holy grail of computer animation had long been the realistic depiction of human skin" (2007, 97). This would remain a problem until Peter Jackson formed a special-effects company, Weta,

PLATE 12 *Spirited Away* (2001 Studio Ghibli): Hayao Miyazaki's animated fantasy. (Courtesy of Photofest.)

specifically to solve problems in the creation of *Rings*. In 2004, Weta was given a special technical award for this feat. They also won another award for the "Massive" program, which allowed "mass duplication of human and animal figures that can be programmed to move independently" (2007, 97). The Massive program made possible the many battle scenes in the trilogy, where thousands of computer-generated soldiers appear to have autonomous and independent movement, thus replacing the need for expensive human extras.

Whereas *Toy Story* was overtly animation, and *Who Framed Roger Rabbit* made clear distinctions between its live-action and animated characters (even while collapsing the distinction at the level of story), new technology can efface the border between what we see as ordinary filmmaking and special effects, thus continuing to blur the line between our sense of reality and illusion in cinema. As Stephen Prince notes, digital effects were used to obliterate a cow in the Coen brothers' 2000 film, *O Brother, Where Art Thou?* (27). While we most likely understand that this bovine blow-up is a special effect, we might not realize that the cow was never really there at all, but completely digitally created. Furthermore, the filmmakers found themselves shooting what needed to look like the Dust Bowl in the lush environs of Mississippi. They again used digital effects, this time to create what *looks like* merely recording reality "on location" (28). So is this a special effect? Certainly. But the audience is probably unaware of it.

When discussions of fantasy film focus on the credibility of special effects, the emphasis tends to contribute to the misleading distinction between fantasy and more "realistic" genres (discussed in the previous chapter.) Focusing only on visual effects not only risks distracting us from other elements such as plot and theme, but also tends to shift attention from the fact that films have always relied on special effects. As noted, even basic sets and backdrops may require effects technology. Films that appear to be shot on location may actually have been shot on a soundstage or be the result of rear-screen projection, matte shots, or simple editing. For example, the gritty and supposedly "ultra-realistic" television show *N.Y.P.D. Blue* (1993–2005) routinely combined scenes shot in L.A. with brief exterior shots of New York City, thus creating the illusion that the action was taking place in New York. As Albert J. La Valley asks, is this type of practice "too common to be a *special* effect?" (143). If almost every cinematic manipulation is an effect, then (borrowing from Christian Metz) we risk seeing the whole of cinema as "a vast *trucage*" or trick (143). And this is precisely the point.

If we conflate fantasy film with special effects because such techniques create illusions, we perpetuate the false dichotomy that has historically worked against fantasy being taken seriously. (Conversely, we might ask whether we always *need* to take films seriously.) While all cinema is based on illusion, it is important to see how fantasy depends on a particular *type* of illusion. In other words, common cinematic effects may be differentiated from *special* effects. What makes them special? La Valley is correct when he writes that

> there must be a significant and important gap between the illusion of what we see on screen and what was used to produce it. Sets, even interplanetary and futuristic ones, are at the low threshold of this discrepancy; miniatures and glass shots are in the middle range; and optically printed shots combining things of many sizes as in *King Kong* or *Star Wars* are perhaps the most discrepant. (143)

With innovations in technology and a Disney-esque model of synergy and franchising, a beneficial climate exists for much fantasy, especially pre-existing print series that attract a pre-constituted fan base. Later chapters will explore the immensely popular *Harry Potter* films, *The Lord of the Rings* trilogy, *Spider-Man*, and the first film in *The Chronicles of Narnia* series. Disney's *Pirates of the Caribbean* (2003) is another notable fantasy success with its sequels and merchandising tie-ins. By 2006, the ten top grossing films worldwide were all fantasy or science fiction, except *Titanic* (1997). In the top twenty-five, "the only other nonfantasy, non-sci-fi film is *Forrest Gump* (at twenty one)" (Thompson 2007, 275).

So fantasy has finally hit the big time! But only time will tell if it remains a favored genre. As the film industry continues to outdo itself in creating multimillion-dollar spectacles, viewers are also more and more comfortable with small-screen technologies like laptops and cell phones. The repercussions of this for the fantasy film are not trivial. To the extent that the current spate of fantasy film is heavily involved in special effects, it thrives on big screens and big sound. An epic like *Rings* arguably loses much of its grandeur when viewed on a small screen. If more and more viewers choose to watch movies on small screens, this could conceivably create a divergence in the types of fantasy produced and consumed specifically for those venues. On the other hand, with virtual reality and Imax technologies, one can only "wonder" how our concept of fantasy will mutate. And, as video and computer games evolve, the interplay between movies and interactive modes of fantasy will grow and diversify. In the final analysis, while print literature has always been free to create impossible, imaginary worlds, the cinema has historically been limited by its own technical capabilities. With advances in digital and interactive technology, we may wish to reconsider the idea that fantasy represents the impossible and say instead that fantasy presents us with everything that is *possible*.

CHAPTER 3

A BRIEF CRITICAL OVERVIEW
Literary and Film Fantasy, Science Fiction and Horror

Literary Approaches to Fantasy

Most critical overviews of fantasy focus on print literature. With a few notable exceptions, such as Disney animated films, scholarly work on fantasy *film* has been limited, and most book-length studies concentrate on science fiction and/or horror while ignoring films that don't fit comfortably into either of those categories.

Some literary scholars break fantasy down into two opposing paradigms, what David Hartwell calls the "Lovecraftian" and "high fantasy" modes. In the former, named after the writer H.P. Lovecraft, fantastic occurrences intrude into the modern world (2). Lovecraft (1890–1937) is mostly associated with horror, although his tales were influential to the success of the pulp magazine *Weird Tales* (1923–54), which indirectly helped popularize all types of fantastic stories (Clute and Grant, 596, 1000). Lovecraft was influenced by Irish writer Lord Dunsany (1878–1957), who drew on myth and fairy tales and also created whole fantasy worlds with such works as *The King of Elfland's Daughter* (1924) and *The Gods of Pegana* (1905), thus inspiring countless other fantasy writers, including J.R.R. Tolkien (1892–1973), best associated with the other major strand of the genre, high fantasy. Rather than mixing everyday with the fantastic, high fantasy features self-contained realities, often in medieval settings, usually "pastoral, hierarchical, and politically conservative" (Hartwell, 2). Although Tolkien was not the first to invent a self-contained fantasy universe, he was "the first to create a sensible theory to explain and justify what he was doing" (Stableford, 142). That reflection has proved tremendously influential to later critics and fantasy writers of all persuasions.

A respected linguist and literary scholar, Tolkien spent a great deal of time thinking and writing about the nature of fantasy. In defense of what he calls "Faerie," Tolkien draws on his prodigious knowledge of language, mythology, and folklore, all of which contribute to the "cauldron of story" – a kind of metaphorical soup from which to draw ideas and inspiration. While Tolkien writes that fantasy actually defies definition, he does lay out some ground rules, distinguishing between the primary world of the reader and the secondary world that the author creates. This secondary "sub-creation" must be both self-contained and internally consistent. From a spiritual perspective, Tolkien sees this creative act to be an extension of God's creation, thus imbuing imagination and the act of sub-creation with a spiritual dimension (1966, 38–52).

According to Tolkien, fantasy is a rewarding experience in its own right, but also offers the benefits of *recovery*, *escape*, and *consolation* (75–87). By recovery, Tolkien means that good fantasy helps us rediscover the joy and wonder of our primary world through a process of de-familiarization, helping us to see our own world with fresh eyes and a new perspective. And just as recovery informs our experience of the real world, escape into fantasy is in no way a denial of reality but an affirmation of it. Further-more, fantasy does not oppose reason: "Fantasy is a natural human activity. It certainly does not destroy or even insult Reason; and it does not either blunt the appetite for, nor obscure the perception of, scientific verity. On the contrary. The keener and the clearer is the reason, the better fantasy will it make" (74).

Tolkien's understanding of consolation is linked to "the happy ending." Whereas tragedies end unhappily in *catastrophe*, Tolkien coins the term *eucatastrophe* to characterize a central feature of fantasy: "the good catas-trophe, the sudden joyous 'turn,' . . . a sudden and miraculous grace: never to be counted on to recur" (86). He concedes that truly good fantasies are hard to achieve, but emphasizes that the happy ending is not a cop-out or an expression of escapism in the sense of avoiding pain, or harsh reality. "It does not deny the existence of dyscatastrophe, of sorrow and failure: the possibility of these is necessary to the joy of deliverance" (86).

Although Tolkien's writing was influenced by his Christian background, he disdained didactic or allegorical fantasy, a criticism often leveled at C.S. Lewis (1898–1963), who was his friend and colleague at Oxford. Yet Lewis drew from the same "cauldron of story," and neither author believed that myth was to be equated with lies or "misunderstood history," a sentiment taken up by the contemporary fantasy writer Ursula K. Le Guin, who argues that fantasy "isn't factual, but it is true" (44). Here, Le Guin expresses a central tenet of the best fantasy: that our understanding of what is true is contingent on reality, but it is not synonymous with raw data. Quality fantasy helps us to process reality through "recovery" and, as with all fiction, through its ability to provide shape to our real-world experience.

Fantasy literature displaces religion by acknowledging modern cynicism and skepticism, according to scholars like Kath Filmer. She, Tolkien, and Lewis see fantasy as an almost-religious discourse where religious concerns are shifted to a literary field that draws on methods and "symbolic forms" which allow us to address spiritual and metaphysical issues. "Through symbol and metaphor, fantasy also creates and quests for meaning" (9). And, like Tolkien and Lewis, Filmer cites fantasy's ability to awaken and encourage *hope* as a central feature of the genre (2).

Others stress the importance of a fantasy world's completeness, a "reality" that the reader takes to be true (cf. Tolkien; Waggoner). For Tolkien, the validity of the fantasy must not be questioned or be a function of dreams or hallucinations (Tolkien 1966, 42). But saying that fantasy is presented as "true" does not imply that the reader is confused about the nature of fantasy and reality. As Tolkien says: "If men really could not distinguish between frogs and men, fairy-stories about frog-kings would not have arisen" (75). Waggoner also rejects the notion that escape is pernicious and instead focuses on the way that fantasy helps us rediscover reality (27).

In *The Game of the Impossible*, W.R. Irwin argues that fantasy fiction is a type of game between the reader and the text. Although he contends that: "To make nonfact appear as fact, is essential to fantasy" (9), the reader must possess the willingness to play along, a variation on Coleridge's "willing suspension of disbelief." Irwin stresses the need for internal logic and coherency in the story-world, but, unlike Tolkien, his insistence on awareness of the "game" being played puts him at odds with the assertion that the reader (or viewer) must be completely immersed in the fantasy world. It's a subtle point, but Tolkien believed that fantasy cannot be successful if one is actually conscious of suspending disbelief (1966, 60–1) One might argue that Tolkein's sort of ontological rupture is far deeper than the crass intrusion of one world into another, characteristic of the Love-craftian mode. In high fantasy it is our deepest (and *unconscious*) expectations of the world that are contradicted by an equally "true" but very different reality. The distinction between high fantasy and the Lovecraftian paradigm more suited to Irwin's perspective calls attention to the difference between *The Lord of the Rings*, which adheres to the former, and the *Harry Potter* and *Narnia* stories, which depend upon the reader/viewer responding to the disparities between the mundane and the fabulous.

Tzvetan Todorov's seminal work *The Fantastic* also considers the relationship between reader and text. Whereas Tolkien insists on the importance of accepting "fantastic" story elements at face value, Todorov gives the term a very specific meaning, focusing on the hesitation of both the reader and the characters when facing a supernatural or otherwise impossible occurrence. A key question concerns whether the phenomenon is external to the character(s) and therefore objectively real, or an internal phenomenon such as a dream or hallucination. The hesitation that characterizes Todorov's fantastic is generally not sustainable and gives way to either the *marvelous*, where the reader and/or characters accept the phenomenon, or the *uncanny*, in which the phenomenon proves to have a rational explanation. Todorov's notion of the marvelous is thus closer to what Tolkien and many others mean by fantasy (where mutually contradictory ontologies coexist), whereas the uncanny better characterizes science-fiction stories that justify and explain amazing events from a scientific framework (allowing only one system of reality to embrace everything that takes place). As Todorov acknowledges, however, many stories mix and blend these three modes.

The most expansive definition of literary fantasy argues that fantasy and mimesis (the imitation of reality) are diametrically opposed impulses that form the basis of *all* literature. Rather than trying to establish a separate fantasy genre, Kathryn Hume argues that a longstanding preference for and focus on mimesis has caused critics to denigrate and overlook the fantasy elements that pervade every type of literature. Realistic representations of the world are considered paramount, and so art that deviates from realism has traditionally been devalued. While scholars have invoked Plato's cave parable to explore the nature of cinematic illusion, Hume traces the disdain for fantasy directly to Plato, who distrusted poetry and all types of fantasy. Aristotle also ranked realism highly and claimed that all literature should be appraised according to how probable it seemed (Hume, 6). Hume explores a number of strands in the fantasy tradition, and concludes that fantasy is in no way less important than the mimetic perspective. The value of Hume's position lies in the acknowledgement that what we choose to call fantasy is a question of degree and not of kind. Just as fantasy, science fiction, or horror fall along a continuum, so do realist and fantasy elements.

Fantasy has the potential to challenge the status quo since it can explore what would otherwise be repressed, and so it is not surprising that psychological analyses of the genre are common. In *Fantasy: The Literature of Subversion*, Rosemary Jackson focuses on the many fantastic and Gothic texts that inform Todorov's work, seeing the fantastic as being particularly open to a psychological reading because of its connection to fantasy as a mental process. The notion that ghosts and monsters may be expressions of what we cannot or will not consciously acknowledge finds its way into much analysis of the horror genre (see, for example, Kawin; R. Wood). But while a psychoanalytic approach is clearly applicable to *all* fantasy, Jackson herself privileges only those she deems explicitly subversive both in content and in *form* (Kafka, Pynchon, etc.), and she rejects the type of fiction to which much modern fantasy owes its greatest debt, such as William Morris' *The Wood beyond the World* (1894), or George MacDonald's *Phantastes* (1858). While noting that works by Tolkien and Lewis share a similar impulse to the more subversive works, Jackson dismisses them because they supposedly "defuse potentially disturbing, anti-social drives and retreat from any profound confrontation with existential dis-ease" (9). For our purposes then, Jackson's purview is unnecessarily narrow and seems to suffer from the same blind spot (repression?) that so many critics of fantasy suffer from. Nevertheless, her discussion makes a compelling case for linking fantasy as a mental process to fantasy as imaginative, fictional subject matter.

Mikhail Bakhtin's notion of carnival is often called upon to help explain literature that challenges the status quo through satirical reversals and inversions. Although this Russian critic never applied his concept to fantasy, "carnivalesque" describes worlds temporarily and irreverently turned upside down, as in a fun-house mirror. The term fits nicely with many surreal fantasies, and classics like Lewis Carroll's *Alice* stories which explore logic and nonsense. Fantasies that feature circuses or carnivals may explicitly appeal to this aspect of the carnival setting.

Most popular definitions of fantasy include folk and fairy tales, from which many modern fantasies derive elements such as wizards and witches, fairies, ogres, talking beasts, and magic talismans. Jackson would reject traditional fairy tales as formulaic and passive, arguing that they "*discourage belief in the importance or effectiveness of action* for their narratives are 'closed.' Things 'happen', or are 'done' to protagonists, told to the reader, from a position of omniscience and authority, making the reader unquestioningly passive" (154). Eric S. Rabkin also relegates fairy tales to the margins of the genre precisely because their self-contained story-worlds violate Todorov's "fantastic" (38). As with Irwin, for Rabkin, characters and readers of true fantasy do not automatically accept the fantasy as "normal" but instead are aware that "the perspectives enforced by the ground rules of the narrative world must be diametrically contradicted" (8). By this definition, two quintessential fantasy texts are *Alice's Adventures in Wonderland* (1865) and *Through the Looking Glass and What Alice Found There* (1871). The fantastic is indicated in the latter by Alice saying wistfully to some flowers: "I *wish* you could talk!" Thus, when they *do* speak, Alice's astonishment "signals the fantastic" (4). The wish helps "plant" the ground rules that flowers don't usually talk, and her astonishment seals the deal. The ontological rupture of *Alice's Adventures in Wonderland* is physically signified by its protagonist's fall down a rabbit hole, a break between realities that has taken on its own life as an English-language idiom. Rabkin's formulation is useful in acknowledging that each work must set up its own rules. But because he relies heavily on a Todorov-style definition of "fantastic," he places fairy tales at the farthest end of the fantasy continuum since, as he says, in fairy tales we experience no astonishment in encountering a talking frog (35).

Bruno Bettelheim's psychoanalytic approach to fairy tales answers Jackson's rejection of them. In *The Uses of Enchantment*, child psychologist Bettelheim famously argues that even violent or scary fairy tales perform a positive function for children. Precisely *because* fairy tales are simple, unrealistic, and formulaic, children can safely confront and sub-consciously work through fears and anxieties that might be difficult to consciously acknowledge. From a Freudian perspective, one of the most prominent difficulties concerns the supposed Oedipal urge to kill one's father and marry one's mother. Although the Oedipal complex may seem farfetched (and rather convoluted in its application to female children), it can be understood in less "dramatic" terms as the child's fear and resentment of the powerful father threatening his bond with his mother. The boy must eventually separate himself from his dependency on – and desire for – the mother and must face up to his father. In doing so, the boy becomes more "man-like," thereby maturing and perpetuating the heterosexual family configuration. But the child must also repress this guilty "fantasy" of desiring the mother and harming the father, and so Bettelheim and others argue that the symbolic content of fairy tales helps children work through such conflicts on a subconscious level.

Although Freudians draw heavily on the Oedipal myth, the relation-ship between fairy tales, myths, and the unconscious is highly complex, particularly because each of these terms is defined differently by different scholars. (For concise overviews of the many competing theories of myth, see Segal, as well as Dickerson and O'Hara.) Just as Filmer argues regarding fantasy, noted scholar Mircea Eliade and others speculate that ancient sacred myths that explained the origins of existence, for example, were eventually replaced by folk and fairy tales as a secular means of "conveying religious experience" (Zipes 1994, 3). But while some take fairy tales as extensions of classical myths, Bettelheim makes a distinction, seeing myths as inherently pessimistic and tragic while fairy tales are optimistic and end happily. Furthermore, because the heroes of classical myth are *already* superior, a positive identification between the reader/listener and the protagonist is limited because "we can never live up to what the superego, as represented in myths by the gods, seems to require of us" (37). By contrast, fairy-tale heroes typically begin the tale as ordinary and humble and find success as the narrative develops. And so for Bettelheim, myths end up "hindering psychological growth, where fairy tales foster it" (Segal, 100).

Freud focused heavily on the unconscious as formed by the repression of Oedipal desires, but his colleague Carl Jung took off in a very different direction. Jung acknowledged that the individual unconscious is comprised of repressed and forgotten memories unique to the individual, but he also posited an inherited unconscious. This "collective unconscious" consists of universal and timeless archetypes such as the mother and father, the child, the shadow, and the trickster. The archetypes surface in our dreams and recur in myths and stories, thus resonating nicely with Vladimir Propp's study of fairy tales. In *The Morphology of the Folktale*, Propp identifies the striking similarities across a wide variety of Russian tales. Unlike Jung's psychological perspective, Propp would understand archetypal characters to be "functions" within various spheres of action. Thus, rather than seeing a child or princess as a psychologically motivated person or as an aspect of the psyche, here a character is defined solely by the function it fulfills within the narrative (although characters may fulfill more than one function).

Propp's analysis provides a rather limited framework for understanding the cultural significance of fairy tales. By contrast, Freudian and Jungian approaches are criticized for reading *too* much into simple stories. They also tend to elide cultural and historical differences and perpetuate sexist and patriarchal paradigms. Despite Freud's profound influence on modern life, Jung's views have found increased resonance in recent years, particularly in the creation and interpretation of popular texts. Brian Attebery, one of the most insightful scholars of fantasy, acknowledges the potential for Freudian analysis to illuminate horror, with its "suppressed secrets and disgust for bodily functions" (30), but considers a Jungian perspective to be better suited to the fantasy genre. While Freud focuses on early childhood development, Jung's theory is appealing in that it describes a lifelong process of growth and development. Jung's "individuation" describes a process in which a person matures, first by emerging as a conscious individual, but then ultimately by finding balance via a *reconnection with the unconscious* (Stein, 177). Attebery finds this to be consonant with fantasies as narratives of maturation and self-integration. "Whereas Freud looks to origins, Jung looks to ends: not where we came from but what we may grow into" (30). This may seem a contradictory way to characterize the many fantasies set in the past or in quasi-medieval settings, but it makes sense when we understand that the fictional past is only a rhetorical device, one of many that encourage the reader (or viewer) to engage with the text on a symbolic, not a realistic, level. For similar reasons, Karl Kroeber rejects a Freudian approach to fantasy and, like Attebery, disputes Jackson's argument that modern "romantic" fantasy is nostalgic. "To the contrary, it desires to improve a present situation that has become intolerable" (7).

Despite the many differences between Freudian and Jungian perspectives, most psychoanalytic critics would agree with Bettelheim that "myths and fairy tales speak to us in the language of symbols representing unconscious content" (36). For this reason, both Freudian and Jungian approaches find resonance in discussions of fantasies that see them as employing symbols from myths and fairy tales, but also those that see them as fulfilling psychological functions variously likened to those traditionally fulfilled by myths, fairy tales, and dreams.

One of the problems with psychoanalytic theory is that it risks ignoring the historical contexts in which fairy tales and other texts are created and consumed, a blind spot (a later problem of Oedipus) that is capably addressed by Jack Zipes, whose extensive work on the subject examines the evolution of folk and fairy tales from a social and historical perspective. Unlike Bettelheim, Zipes tends to be highly critical of the direction that fairy tales have taken. While long considered morality tales, first for adults and later almost exclusively for children, Zipes traces the increasingly conservative evolution of folk and fairy tales as they became literally "im-printed" on the popular imagination in their shift from oral to printed form. When Disney adapted these tales for film, the stories were sanitized and further altered to reflect a conservative worldview. and over time these became seen as the "official" versions. Zipes, like others, critiques the sexist and racist attitudes of these filmed versions and bemoans their imbrication in the unbridled capitalism of the Disney marketing machine (also see Ch. 9). If Bettelheim's famous work is entitled *The Uses of Enchantment,* Zipes' oeuvre might have been titled "The Uses of *Entrapment.*" In his view, one shared by many critics of Disney, the exigencies of the marketplace, combined with the mass-mediated nature of the stories, co-opt the original tales' meaning in the service of corporate interests.

Zipes' understanding of what might be called "modern myth" helps us to see the connection between traditional conception of ancient myths and the mythical nature of popular stories that circulate in the culture, including fairy-tale-inspired films. Zipes draws on Roland Barthes's explanation of myth, defined as "a collective representation that is socially determined and then inverted so as not to appear as a cultural artefact" (Zipes 1994, 6). In other words, fairy tales often achieve the status of myth by appearing to be eternal, expressing ideas and values that *seem* to have always been true. Such stories may seem "harmless, natural, eternal, ahistorical, therapeutic" (7), and yet, according to Barthes, myths come to function as "depoliticized speech" (Barthes, 143). This is important for Zipes' analysis of modern fairy tales because, as he says, "it was not the power of the gods that would help humankind. It was the rising bourgeoisie that spoke out in the name of all human beings while really speaking in its own interests, and these interests are the myths that pervade our lives today" (Zipes 1994, 4). Zipes' analysis of fairy tales thus has resonance for a number of fantasy films that draw on "mythical ideas" but which thereby lend themselves to ideological analyses that can uncover values and assumptions that we may have taken for granted.

Fantasy and Film

Zipes' work on fairy tales is invaluable for an understanding of fantasy film, but of course fantasy is not confined to fairy tales. In contrast to those like Irwin or Tolkien who attempt to circumscribe the boundaries of fantasy, a more open-ended approach can be found, for example, in *The Encyclopedia of Fantasy.* In this indispensable tome, John Clute and John Grant acknowledge the debt that modern fantasy owes to antiquity, but also explore the many tendrils of fantasy across genres, movements, and modern media – including film. Like Tolkien they note a number of the so-called "taproot texts" that contribute to the "cauldron of story," such as Apuleius, Bunyan, Cervantes, Chaucer, Dante, Malory, Rabelais, and Shakespeare, to name just a few (ix). But unlike Tolkien, their definition casts a wide net. They define fantasy as "a self-coherent narrative which, when set in our reality, tells a story which is impossible in the world as we perceive it; . . . when set in an otherworld or secondary world, that otherworld will be impossible, but stories set there will be possible *in the otherworld's terms*" (viii). Looser than the idea of ontological rupture, this definition can encompass all types of fantasy, and Clute and Grant's work provides a comprehensive look at many themes and motifs directly relevant to mainstream fantasy such as portals, wishes, dreams and myths, but also extends to an analysis of science fiction and horror.

It's no secret that in creating the science-fiction film *Star Wars*, George Lucas found inspiration in Joseph Campbell's work on myth, in particular *The Hero with a Thousand Faces*. Although diverging in a number of ways, Campbell's work draws heavily on Jung. Campbell's PBS television series with Bill Moyers, *The Power of Myth* (1988), helped to popularize a number of concepts that soon worked their way into films and film analysis. Campbell refers to the "monomyth" as the story in which a character adventures from home into a world of supernatural adventure, only to return home a hero, bestowing "boons" to the community (30). In addition to evoking archetypes, Campbell helped to popularize the idea that myths are a kind of collective dream. "Dream is the personalized myth, myth the depersonalized dream; both myth and dream are symbolic in the same general way of the dynamics of the psyche. But in the dream the forms are quirked by the peculiar troubles of the dream, whereas in myth the problems and solutions shown are directly valid for all mankind" (19). Screenwriting manuals such as Christopher Vogler's *The Writer's Journey* advised writers to put their protagonists on mythic "hero" journeys, and many filmmakers and critics made explicit references to movies as modern-day "myths" (Bordwell, 34). Whereas a Freudian analysis might point to the Oedipal conflict in Luke Skywalker's struggle with Darth Vader, a Jungian analysis might focus on the mythic aspects of the hero's self-realization. Rather than see everything as an internal, psychological phenomenon, as in a Freudian approach, Campbell's ideas began to inform fantasy films deploying archetypal characters and motifs that played out on a cosmic (rather than a personal) level (Bordwell, 34).

In her assessment of why strains of fantasy have recently overtaken realist impulses in literature, Hume argues that while realist fiction is concerned with observing the real world, the goal of "traditional literature was to present mythic patterns" (44). Arguing that realism is no longer satisfying in a world where meaning is increasingly contingent, Hume places us in a third stage where "we find a quest for ways of giving a sense of meaning" (44). Although complicated by the entire cinematic apparatus (which includes the technology of recording and the material conditions in which movies are produced and consumed), Hume's argument resonates with Jung and Campbell's approach to the importance of mythic content in our fictional films.

The conceptualization of fantasy as a psychological process also provides a critical connection between traditional psychoanalytic approaches to film, and films coded specifically as fantasy. Neo-Freudian theories, particularly those drawing on Jacques Lacan, have played a significant role in explaining the power of cinematic pleasure and illusion, thus linking fantasy as a mental process to the movies themselves. Regardless of content, movies provide fantasy scenarios that simulate dreaming for the viewer, a position popularized by noted film scholar Christian Metz and others. Although Campbell's dream/myth paradigm encourages us to see cinema as a collective and therapeutic dream, psychoanalytic film theory has been critical of this aspect of film, characterizing movie spectatorship as a regressive psychological process. But as Robert Stam writes: "The perennial comparison of film and dream points not only to film's potential for alienation but also to its central utopian thrust. Dreams are not merely regressive; they are vital to human well-being. They are, as the Surrealists emphasized, a sanctuary for desire, an intimation of the possible transcendence of dichotomies, the source of kinds of knowledge denied cerebral rationality" (167).

In *Formations of Fantasy*, Burgin, Donald, and Kaplan note that fantasy is almost always conceived as the opposite of reality, whether in a work of poetry or art (and thus intentional) or in the form of a hallucination (and therefore subconscious). "In this definition, fantasy is the *negative* of reality" (1). These opposites are characterized as being either internal and private, or external and public, recalling Todorov's conundrum concerning the origin of fantastic events – either internal and psychological, or external and, therefore, "real." But what is lacking is a way to understand the interaction *between* these two spheres. Here is where a psychoanalytic concept of fantasy enters, positing a space that links the two. According to Laplanche and Pontalis, fantasy is not the *object* but the setting of desire (26). The cinematic term *"mise-en-scène"* (used to describe the setting, the look of the film, or visual aspects within the frame) here provides a compelling analogy between dreams and film. "In fantasy the subject does not pursue the object or its sign: He appears caught up himself in the sequence of images" (26). Critically, the fantasizer has no fixed place or identification. He or she is "desubjectivized," and is 'in the very syntax of the sequence in question'" (26). As in dreams, then, in which the dreamer creates and thus effectively represents all the "characters," film viewers do not necessarily identify with only one character, but may find pleasure in the entire structure of the fantasy.

Film audiences take pleasure from fantastic situations as well as structures. The dreamy incapacity to express oneself or affect the environment has been used to good "effect" in some comedy ghost films where traditional qualities of the horror ghost shift from "fantastic" and paranoid to "marvelous" or comedic. Invisibility and incorporality may represent psychological "projections" of grieving loved ones, or dramatize the difficulty of the subject in maintaining a stable, but culturally mandated gender identity. Many such movies explore relations of gender, power, and powerlessness through the device of a hero's ghostly return. The revenant male is stuck in a role that strips away the simplest tools of power, utterance, and action, and is forced to develop more "feminine" techniques to solve his problem and move on. The audience enjoys the play of power reversal and vicariously joins the ghost on his quest for redemption and release. The ghost's plight, coupled with a reversed romantic trajectory (in which the goal is *giving up* a romantic attachment – "guy loses girl"), provides the viewer with a mix of pain and pleasure related to the self-inflicted discomfort we enjoy in thrilling and suspenseful literature. Devices of repetition and delay form both the content and the very structure of the fantasy, and join in other aspects of the ghost's plight to reflect the viewer's own powerless status as an "invisible" voyeur. The fantasy experience of the protagonist in these and similar films thus becomes one with the internal psychological experience of the viewer (Fowkes 1998).

Just as Jackson saw literature of the fantastic as being particularly well suited to a psychoanalytic reading, fantasy-themed films seem particularly amenable to analyses that can penetrate recurring symbolic ideas and images. Although both Freudian and Jungian theories risk naturalizing aspects of psychology and society that are at least partly cultural and historical, they nevertheless provide an opportunity to examine the relationship between individual and communal fantasies, and to speculate on the cultural significance of the themes and motifs that have taken hold of our collective imagination.

Fantasy, Science Fiction, and Horror

The critical literature on science fiction and horror is extensive and beyond the purview of this book. However, it is useful to revisit a few central ideas that can illuminate fantasy's close relation to those genres. As we have seen, the most profound connection lies in each genre's reaction to aspects of modernity. As Robert Scholes writes: "Given the positivistic matrix that dominated throughout nineteenth century England and America, continuing well into the twentieth century, works of fiction that sought to present alternate or secondary worlds were forced to align themselves according to the binary polarities offered by positivism: science or magic, extrapolation or escapism" (18). Drawing on anthropologist Bronislaw Malinowski, Vivian Sobchack writes that science, magic, and religion are three systems of thought that can be found in every society in some combination. One of the distinctions she draws between horror and science-fiction films is their attempt to deal with the unknown by appealing to some combination of these three systems. Horror resorts to religion or magic, while science fiction turns to science and technology to find a sense of security and control. "And, since they all deal with the unknown, where one fails to satisfy, another will step into the breach" (1987, 63). Although she doesn't include it in her discussion, fantasy's emphasis on magic and supernatural forces once again reflects the symbiotic relationship between the three genres.

A number of themes characterize the fantasy film, helping to distinguish it from its brethren, and as noted in the first chapter, each genre features its own iconography. Nevertheless, much overlap remains. The monster, for example, is one of a handful of motifs that may appear in all three genres, showing us "what we are not comfortable seeing but may need to look at anyway" (Kawin, 25). In horror or horror/science-fiction hybrids, monsters may represent the return of the repressed or the feared "Other" in disguised form. In most cases, the monster is killed or "exorcized," thus arousing but then allaying our anxieties. In fantasy, however, creatures that cause fear in horror or science fiction can be benevolent or even humorous and therefore represent not what we *fear*, but what we *desire*, an inversion spoofed brilliantly in *Monsters, Inc.* (2001), where the scary monsters that children fear turn out to be cuddly creatures who only use children's screams to help provide energy to fuel the monster realm.

Metamorphosis likewise appears in fantasy, science fiction, and horror. In science fiction, physical transformations may be caused intentionally by scientists, as in cyborgs, where critical discussions tend to draw heavily on Donna Haraway's work on the link between humanity, technology, and gender. When transformations are accidental, they tend to result in monstrous creations like Godzilla (hence sci-fi/horror). In pure horror, body transformations may be due to magic or other supernatural means, hence classic vampires, werewolves, and zombies. In fantasy, metamorphosis is more varied in cause and function and may also be the occasion for humor, satire, adventure, or the awakening of a new perspective for the character. In many cases, as in fairy tales, metamorphosis supports the general magical idea that "nothing is what it seems."

"Flights" of fancy, as in the fantasy *Peter Pan*, may operate on both the literal and metaphorical level, while in horror flight turns to fright as an expression of evil supernatural power (witches or vampire bats, for example). In science fiction, flying is merely an extension of real-world technology – spaceships, jet packs, etc. Nevertheless, the desire to fly and the freedom and power it affords links all three genres.

The overlap between genres is reflected in the approach taken by Joshua David Bellin, who takes an expansive view of film fantasy. Rather than bracketing off science fiction and horror, Bellin considers any film to belong to the fantasy genre if structured by a fantasy framework. He therefore considers a science-fiction film like *Jurassic Park* to belong to the same genre as *The Wizard of Oz*. Unlike other expansive approaches that celebrate fantasy (such as Hume's), Bellin concludes that even though fantasy films offer pleasurable experiences for the viewer, they routinely mask pernicious ideological messages, a mechanism integral to the very nature of the genre. In his condemnation of the "alienating" ideas underlying fantasy film, Bellin's view is thus reluctantly but categorically negative. The very nature of fantasy film works to erase its ideological project: "the longevity and vigor of the paradigm by which films strongly identified with otherworldliness, innocence, or spectacle are denied a historical genesis or function" (5). And therein lies their power, and hence their danger. Furthermore, Bellin notes the paradoxical but common love/hate response that so many bring to fantasy films, but argues that that the form cannot be separated from the content: "Quite the contrary, one should view the lovable fantasy and the hateful reality as interrelated and mutually sustaining" (7) Or, more specifically, "fantasy films function precisely to enable the paradox of *loving what one under other circumstances might recognize to be hateful*" (7). Examples include the racism that infuses the portrayal of King Kong, and the vilification of women (or femaleness) in *Jurassic Park* and *Alien* movies. Bellin's argument is detailed and convincing, quite rightly identifying the contradictory nature of the films in question. But he fails to note that "realistic" stories may be just as, if not *more*, pernicious. In writing about children's literature, C.S. Lewis writes: "I think what profess to be realistic stories for children are far more likely to deceive them. I never expected the real world to be like the fairy tales. I think that I did expect school to be like the school stories. The fantasies did not deceive me: the school stories did" (37). And as Brian Attebery so aptly remarks, "A realistic work is merely one that disguises the doubts built into its fictionality" (68). Bellin's thesis should thus be considered in light of the endless circularity of art (or entertainment) and reality. The one always reflects and informs the other. When we proceed, as Bellin does, from an assertion of the real world's many inequities, we are sure to find echoes of them throughout the universes of literature and film.

Gender is one of the "alienating" aspects of fantasy identified by Bellin that clearly links fantasy to science fiction and horror. Hollywood has a poor track record in this regard, and so it should come as no surprise that men or boys are the most frequent protagonists of fantasy film, while women are largely ignored (and almost always the victims in horror). *The Wizard of Oz* is a notable exception, as are a handful of others such as the *Alice* stories and *The Golden Compass* (which failed to achieve blockbuster success). The latter not only features a strong female protagonist but also takes on religion, rejecting *Narnia*'s Christian perspective. Sobchack (2003) notes the absence of both women and sexuality in most science-fiction films, whose focus is on traditional male pursuits: space conquest, science, technology and rationality. In science-fiction/horror hybrids, either women are hysterical victims to be rescued (or killed), or female-ness itself is seen as a source of something uncontrollable and dreadful, as in the sci-fi/horror *Aliens* (1986), where the tension between Ripley's femininity and her macho persona (established in *Alien*, 1979) is ultimately used in the service of her maternal instincts to save a little girl from a monstrous female alien – the "mother" of all cat fights.

Attebery acknowledges the absence of girls in classic coming-of-age fantasies, noting that modern fantasy's reliance on traditional storytelling themes can thus be both a strength and a weakness (87). But he notes the same failing in *realist* literature such as *Pride and Prejudice* or *Middlemarch*. "It is still the story of Cinderella, waiting for fulfillment with the right man. In a way, the realist marriage plot is worse than 'Cinderella,' for without the markers of fictionality – most notably magic –that are built into the fairy tale, we are encouraged to take these equally arbitrary story structures as reality" (92). If Attebery were writing about film, he might cite movies like *Pretty Woman* (1990) or *An Officer and a Gentleman* (1982). This argument doesn't get fantasy off the hook, but it does complicate critiques that seek to make fantasy *more* ideologically suspect than other forms of mainstream fiction film.

Neil Barron's encyclopedia *Fantasy and Horror* provides a comprehensive overview of horror and fantasy across a variety of platforms, including film. A number of fine anthologies explore mixtures of science fiction and fantasy, usually eclectic selections addressing literature and/or film. Two particularly useful ones are *Intersections* (edited by George E. Slusser and Eric S. Rabkin) and *Bridges to Fantasy* (edited by Slusser, Rabkin, and Robert Scholes). Both feature essays that debate elements distinguishing or connecting fantasy and science fiction (although the latter centers mostly on literature rather than film). *Shadows of the Magic Lamp* covers sci-fi, horror, and fantasy *film*, and is another splendid anthology by Slusser and Rabkin. While in *Bridges to Fantasy*, Jack P. Rawlins argues that most science-fiction films are really fantasy because of their emphasis on emotion (160–74), here Slusser and Rabkin argue the reverse, that even non-science-fiction fantasy films are effectively science fiction because of the technological basis of cinema, prompting us to rethink our notions of cinema as a primarily mimetic art. Indeed, film's capacity to record reality would seem to lend itself to a realist/mimetic purpose. Well-known theorist André Bazin saw the potential for realism to be the most important quality of cinema, distinguishing it from all other art forms. Slusser and Rabkin's point is a powerful one that turns most views of fantasy fiction upside down. Rather than seeing fantasy as a "mode" of storytelling that can then be broken down into sub-categories of fantasy, sci-fi, and horror, here science fiction becomes the umbrella category. Specifically in *Shadows of the Magic Lamp*, the authors see science fiction as the "form in relation to which other forms of fantasy film, and all film perhaps, shape and define themselves" (Slusser and Rabkin 1985, viii). The birth of cinema occurs simultaneously with many technologies that shaped the Industrial Revolution, the very ones that prompt the rise of science fiction itself, so that, in a way, science fiction provides the seminal foundation for the medium as a whole. Themes so often played out in science-fiction films resonate in related genres. "It is, for example, against science fiction's pretensions of collective rationalism that we understand the filmic horrors of personal and irrational alienation. Or in an opposite sense it is against science fiction's own nightside – its prediction of grim futures – that we chart the yearning for a nostalgic Arthurian past" (viii). The argument is cogent and compelling. On the other hand, it's more useful at the theoretical than at the day-to-day level of classifying films. Fans of science fiction would most likely be surprised and disappointed to encounter a so-called "science-fiction" movie about magic and fairies. It is imperative to see the profound relationship between science fiction, horror, and modern fantasy, but at the same time fantasy has certainly carved out a separate niche at the level of story, drawing on roots that long preceded the Industrial Revolution and the advent of science fiction. For that reason, it may be more useful to consider the fantastic (although not in Todorov's sense) as a mode that encompasses fantasy, science fiction, and horror.

Fantasy liberates our imagination from the constraints of the rational world with a consequential breaking of bonds. Mainstream fantasy often does this only to replace that liberation with its own version of constraint or control. Mainstream fantasy almost always binds fantastic qualities into a narrative which redeems the senselessness of the modern world by giving it shape and moral order. This is, in part, what Jackson and so many others find constraining and potentially harmful about modern fantasy, when it wastes the opportunity to explore discontinuities between two worlds by spending its energies on validating our own. To the extent that fantasy stresses its "fantastic" elements in Todorov's sense, it can liberate in the way that Jackson craves. But as it moves toward Todorov's "marvelous," its patness tends to circumscribe meaning. "Fantasy has always articulated a longing for imaginary unity. . . . In this sense it is inherently idealistic. It expresses a desire for an absolute, for an absolute signified, an absolute meaning" (Jackson, 179). But Tolkien (and many others) might disagree – not that a moral universe isn't central to his work, but that even while providing *consolation*, the best fantasy offers *transcendence* of the status quo, the prospect of something intangible beyond ourselves. Tolkien insisted that his works were not allegory and disputed the notion that fantasy imposes an absolute meaning on its audience. The reader (or viewer) has the freedom to take what he or she will from the text. Duck or rabbit, the picture flexes between two realities. Ambiguity, paradox, and contradiction are the very lifeblood of fantasy, inspiring the varied readings of movies like *Groundhog Day*, *The Wizard of Oz*, and other fantasy classics. The following chapters explore some of the best examples of the genre through some of these many lenses.

Additional Sources

Other fine scholars of literary fantasy (many cited in this book) include Lucy Armitt, Brian Stableford, Christine Brooke-Rose, C.N. Manlove, Richard Mathews, Peter Penzoldt, Stephen Prickett, Roger Schlobin, Robert Scholes, Tobin Siebers, Ann Swinfen, Marina Warner, and Gary K. Wolfe.

CHAPTER 4

THE WIZARD OF OZ (1939)
Over the Rainbow

The Wizard of Oz is one of the most famous and well-loved fantasies in cinematic history, and it provides a good introduction to some of the formal and thematic elements common to a large number of fantasy films. In some ways, *Wizard* is the quintessential fantasy film, drawing heavily from fairy tales, myths, and children's stories, while itself serving as a reference and influence for countless films to follow. The iconography is instantly recognizable (the Yellow Brick Road, the Tin Man, etc.), as is much of the dialogue, music, and lyrics. The phrase "over the rainbow" has become virtually synonymous with our notions of fantasy and longing – and, perhaps also, our collective longing *for* fantasy.

Intended as a prestige feature for MGM, *Wizard* succeeds admirably in delivering the high production values for which the studio was known. Even a number of loose ends and an occasional nonsensical bit of dialogue can't detract from the film's power and appeal. Some inconsistencies were, no doubt, a result of the many writers and numerous versions of the script. (For example, at one point the Witch inexplicably refers to an insect she's supposedly sent after Dorothy and friends, a reference to an earlier version of the script that didn't make the final cut.) But despite the fact that almost a dozen writers, four different directors, and dozens of others made important contributions to the final product, *Wizard* manages to deliver an unforgettable and singular cinematic vision. The movie owes some of its coherence to Associate Producer Arthur Freed, who would go on to change the nature of Hollywood musicals with the idea that they "blend song and dance with the plot so that all elements fit together" (Harmetz, 63). Besides the sheer charm of the lyrics and music (with Academy Awards for Best Musical Score and Best Song for "Over the Rainbow"), the musical numbers help knit the story together with the ongoing reprise of "We're Off to See the Wizard," coupled with Dorothy and friends' signature skipping walk. Many other musical motifs repeat throughout, such as the ominous musical sequence that announces the Wicked Witch, or the repeated tune and lyrics that link Dorothy to her Oz companions through their respective deficiencies ("a brain, a heart, a home, the noive!").

Repetitions and parallels structure the entire story, with Kansas neatly book-ending Dorothy's interlude in Oz, and parallels between Kansas and Oz providing intellectual, emotional, and visual symmetry. From her drab monochrome Kansas existence, Dorothy (Judy Garland) wishes to go "over the rainbow," and soon gets her wish when she awakens from a bump on the head sustained during the twister that strikes her aunt and uncle's farm. When Dorothy steps through the door of her house into Oz, she experiences an "ontological rupture" (see Ch. 1), an abrupt transition from her ordinary reality to a completely different but parallel fantasy world, one that immediately signals her heart's desire – at least from a visual perspective. Oz couldn't *be* more rainbow-colored, filled with bright flowers and the many bold hues of the Munchkins' whimsical costumes. Dorothy also gets the attention she craved in Kansas as she is hailed as a hero for killing the Wicked Witch of the East. It's not all happiness and rainbows, as we soon learn, but the symmetry continues with the appearance of the Wicked Witch of the West and Dorothy's encounter with her new friends on the Yellow Brick Road. Dorothy experiences Oz as simultaneously strange and familiar, an *uncanny* feeling that she has met these companions before, a sensation she mentions to the Scarecrow and the Tin Man shortly after meeting them. Freud used the term "uncanny" to describe a feeling of estrangement, a contradictory feeling of being simultaneously home/not home, a paradox at the heart of this film. And just as Dorothy finds her new friends in Oz strangely familiar, viewers can't help but enjoy a similar feeling, since the actors playing the Scarecrow (Ray Bolger), the Tin Man (Jack Haley), and the Cowardly Lion (Bert Lahr) have been previously introduced as farm hands in Kansas. Psychological affinities between the characters in Oz and

Kansas emerge in their dialogue, but also in the visual similarities reinforced through the farm hands' body language. While scolding Dorothy for not using her head, Hunk dips and whirls after hitting his thumb with a hammer, thus prefiguring the Scarecrow's wild and rubbery movements. Hickory suggests that he'll be honored someday with a statue, and strikes a frozen posture evoking the rusting Tin Man. And after rescuing Dorothy from the pig sty where she's fallen, Zeke practically swoons, hyperventilating and sweating with fear like the Cowardly Lion.

The Wizard of Oz himself is the counterpart of traveling magician Professor Marvel, both fraudulent "wizards" played by Frank Morgan. But the most striking Kansas character echoed in Oz is no doubt Miss Gulch as the Wicked Witch of the West (both played by Margaret Hamilton). As the villain of the piece, the Wicked Witch may be even more important than the title Wizard character because it is precisely her (and Miss Gulch's) menacing presence that drives the plot and gives the film its delicious edge. Along with the diminutive Toto, who provides another thread of repetition with his cheeky mischief and numerous escapes and returns, the Wicked Witch/Miss Gulch is the catalyst for the conflict in both Kansas and Oz. Miss Gulch's long dress and tall hat, her grinchy expression, and the menacing figure she cuts on her bicycle are all echoed in the Wicked Witch and her broomstick. The Witch's shrieking cackle, gnarled hands, unmistakable green-ness, and her pointed black hat – echoed by her pointy face and angular body – all assure her status as the canonical movie witch. In fairy tales and other fantasies, green skin often connotes something moldy, rotten, reptilian, or monstrous (The Grinch, The Hulk, Shrek). In this movie the angular green Witch contrasts sharply with Dorothy's pleasantly plump softness and glowing pink complexion. Glinda, the Good Witch of the North (Billie Burke), notes that only bad witches are ugly, a convention that spills over into other "fairy tales" such as the good and evil characters in most animated Disney films, including the landmark *Snow White and the Seven Dwarfs* (1937), to which *Wizard* was often compared (Harmetz, 21–2). Amazingly, the Wicked Witch enjoys only 12 minutes of screen time (Harmetz, 179), and yet she provides some of the most memorable scenes of the film, including her dramatic entrance and exit in Munchkinland amidst red smoke and flame, and the scene in which she and her broom swoop dramatically above the crowd at Emerald City before leaving the ominous skywritten message: "SURRENDER DOROTHY." The Witch's most memorable scene may be the climax of the film when Dorothy accidentally melts her with a bucket of water. Despite its *effect*iveness, this illusion was apparently one of the easiest to accomplish in a movie packed with complicated, innovative, and sometimes dangerous special effects. Hamilton had been badly burned while filming the pyrotechnic exits and entrances in Munchkinland, and yet the melting scene required only that she stand on a hydraulic elevator while her gown was attached to the floor. As the elevator was lowered, Hamilton descended, leaving only the gown, as dry ice vapors added to the illusion (Harmetz, 252). But the impact of the scene is undeniable. How surprising and satisfying to see an innocent splash of water reduce the hard, angular edges of the powerful Witch to a detumescent puff of cloth, all in a matter of seconds.

In addition to the Witch, *Wizard* features a number of other scary moments, including the extended tornado sequence, one of the most impressive effects. The tornado itself was actually a (not so small) "miniature," a 35-foot cone of wire and muslin that spun wildly as dust was circulated to help hide the fact that it was actually a hard surface. The twister was the most difficult and costly illusion of the film (Harmetz, 246–7), and it remains one of the most striking sequences – an example of an *illusion* that, ironically, lends realism to the "realistic" portion of the film.

Off in Oz, the nasty, grasping apple trees seem like Tolkien's Ents gone bad. But much more frightening are the monstrous flying monkeys. In close shots, each bluish face is characterized by a mouth frozen in a grotesque rictus (a gaping grin that contrasts with the grouchy frowns of the evil apple trees). The monkeys are even more impressive as a flying army, filling the sky like giant locusts before chasing and then scooping up Dorothy and Toto to imprison them in the Witch's castle – truly the stuff of nightmares.

Nightmares yes, and yet *Wizard* is a fantasy, and not a horror film. As with *Rings* and the *Potter* movies, scary threats provide the contexts in which to create emotionally charged situations that will challenge the main character(s) to rise to the occasion, eventually leading to a positive outcome. And as in *Potter*, scary moments are often relieved by a good dose of humor. The famous "lions, and tigers and bears" sequence shows Dorothy, the Scarecrow, and the Tin Man nervously anticipating the terrors that may be lurking in the woods. In folk and fairy tales, characters often enter scary woods to confront dangerous beasts before undergoing a positive transformation (Clute and Grant, 362). Here, the dangerous beast turns out to be a man-sized lion whose menacing growl precedes him off screen before he lunges dramatically at the trio. Genuinely frightening at first, he soon turns out to be nothing but a big pussy cat, and a hilarious one at that. He provokes pity from the ultra-sincere

Dorothy, but laughter from the audience as Bert Lahr goes on to steal scene after scene with his superbly campy, vaudevillian performance. (Garland was said to have cracked up on numerous occasions.)

Balancing the scary characters in the film, Dorothy's friendly companions and the Munchkins help endow Oz with its whimsical appeal. The tiny Munchkins provide a charming and humorous welcome to Oz, with the pink tutu-clad Lullaby League ballerinas, the tiny but thuggish Lollipop Guild, and the many silly but wonderfully clever lyrics by E.Y. (Yip) Harburg, such as the Coroner's report on the Wicked Witch of the East: "As Coroner I must aver, I *thoroughly* examined *her*. And *she's* not only merely *dead*, she's really most *sincerely* dead!"

The Munchkins (like dwarves in other fantasies) are just some of many classic fairy-tale elements featured in *Wizard*, including witches with brooms, wizards, crystal balls, talking beasts, etc. The fairy-tale elements and the allegorical nature of Frank L. Baum's original book have inspired a number of intriguing scholarly analyses. With the publication of *The Wonderful Wizard of Oz* in 1900, Baum (1856–1919) succeeded in his attempt to create a modern day fairy tale for children. Despite a checkered career and limited success with much of his other work, Baum's *Oz* books and the 1939 movie adaptation of *Wizard* have enjoyed enormous popular and critical attention. Some analysts of the film adaptation have focused on the allegorical nature of Kansas as a reflection of the Depression era or on the political or economic allusions suggested more strongly by Baum's original stories (Bellin; Dighe). A desiccated Kansas farm and a horrific tornado reflect not just the economic struggles facing the nation at the time of the film's release, but also the landscape ravaged by the devastating winds of the Dust Bowl. (Coincidentally, in 1939, another prominent film directed by *Wizard*'s Victor Fleming was *Gone with the Wind*. Whereas the wind in that title is largely metaphorical, Scarlett's desire to return home, in her case to Tara, is – like Dorothy's – quite explicit.) A number of critics also focus on elements germane to the fantasy genre, such as the Wizard's use of technology to create illusions (Bellin). The coming-of-age theme, the Wicked Witch, and the dream device also invite psychoanalytic readings, focusing on what Dorothy learns and seeing Oz as the product of her active subconscious. Some stress the positive nature of Dorothy's journey as she learns to trust herself, but her return home also suggests a more regressive reading. Ultimately, *Wizard* succeeds in maintaining the validity of a number of contradictory perspectives, an enduring hallmark of fantasy to "have it both ways."

Dorothy's journey to Oz can be read as a positive process which results in the reconciliation of conflicting desires – a necessary phase in order for her to mature and, presumably, take her normal place in society. Harvey Greenberg, for example, argues that Dorothy's journey represents the process whereby a child or adolescent confronts his or her conflicting impulses to remain part of the family (and therefore dependent) but also become autonomous and individual (and therefore independent). Paul Nathanson reads Dorothy's adventure from a Jungian perspective, as she "encounters a series of archetypes in the quest for maturity" (84). The Wicked Witch is Dorothy's "shadow," the aspects of Dorothy's personality that must be confronted and rejected, and the three male characters in Oz represent the "animus," the archetype of the opposite sex whose qualities Dorothy will need to assimilate (85–8). Daniel Dervin takes a Freudian perspective, focusing on Dorothy's struggle to acquire the witch's broom (a phallic symbol despite its domestic connotation), and then relinquish it to the surrogate father figure, the Wizard (Dervin cited in Nathanson, 65). From many psychoanalytic perspectives, the coming-of-age emphasis is an acknowledgement and celebration of the formative process that culminates in a person's individuation. Full of danger and contradiction for the child, the process is nevertheless a necessary and positive step in the progress toward adulthood. The tornado is merely an outward manifestation of Dorothy *Gale*'s rage at Miss Gulch and her subconscious anger at her aunt and uncle for ignoring her (Rushdie, 17). Glinda and the Wicked Witch thus represent Dorothy's conflicted feelings about her aunt. In fact, one powerful scene linking Auntie Em to the Witch occurs when Dorothy (imprisoned by the Witch) sees Auntie Em in the Witch's crystal ball and cries out to her, only to see Auntie Em replaced by the Witch taunting her with a caricature of her own plaintive cries. It's a horrific moment from Dorothy's perspective, underscoring her sense of entrapment, mocking her plight, and hinting at her conflicted feelings about Auntie Em. In any case, it is the inability or unwillingness of Dorothy's surrogate parents to protect her and Toto from the powerful Miss Gulch that prompts Dorothy to run away, a decision that prevents her from escaping the twister.

Some critics have stressed the regressive nature of Dorothy's return home, focusing on the circular rather than linear nature of the journey (e.g. Gordon). Dorothy returns from whence she came, and her adventures are trivialized as "just a dream" by the adults surrounding her. Indeed, the regressive nature of this return is of particular interest in light of the fact that the film features one of the few female protagonists of the genre (or any Hollywood film for that matter). From this perspective, the ending of the film reinforces Hollywood traditional insistence that a girl's dreams of independence should be tamed and that her capitulation should be happily and gratefully internalized, serving as evidence that what she has "always wanted" is in her own back yard. "Home" becomes not just a generic symbol for safety or regression, but a symbol of feminine domestication. In this sense, *Wizard* serves as one of many examples of a cultural insistence equating women with house and home, whereas men are associated with the larger, "more important" external world of work, exploration, and adventure. As Richard Selcer explains it:

> Historically, Europeans saw the home (or house) as a male preserve, summed up in the hoary maxim that "a man's house is his castle." Americans redefined the home in feminine terms, giving rise to the feminist baiting cliché, "A woman's place is the house." The idea of the woman in the home is a strong symbol in American culture, long expressed in the so called "cult of domesticity."

Can a movie of such endurance and popularity really be this contradictory? Can it be both a positive coming-of-age story *and* a regressive, sexist fantasy? Admittedly, both types of reading, as well as many other interpretations, have much to commend them. In fact the popularity and staying power of *Wizard* and other classic films may lie precisely in their myth-like ability to juggle conflicting ideas and impulses, thereby providing the possibility of various and sometimes opposite interpretations. This openness to diametrically opposed readings also points to a fundamental feature of many fantasy films. Just as fantasy trades on the contradiction between our sense of reality and unreality – it's real but it's not real – many fantasy movies implicitly engage in a contradictory impulse toward valuing both safety *and* adventure, past *and* future, dependence *and* independence.

While a young girl's return to house and home might be read as sexist, what do we make of Dorothy's uncle, who is unable to stand up to Miss Gulch? What about Professor Marvel and the Wizard (who appears in the film as a foppish, theatrical dandy), both of whom are exposed as powerless? Protagonists in myths and fairy tales often experience a lack of parental authority, a circumstance that forces them to face their fears and opens them up to their hopes and desires. This is one reason why so many of the main characters in fantasies are orphans – Dorothy, Harry Potter, Peter Parker (of *Spider-Man*), the children in *Narnia*, etc. As noted, while the male authority figures are weak or absent in *Wizard* (and in Oz rendered somewhat asexual by elaborate costumes), most of the female characters are incredibly powerful, including Dorothy and the Good

Witch Glinda (even while their costumes are clearly gendered female – a girlish gingham dress and pigtails in one case, and a glittery pink puff of ballroom gown in the other). Even before Dorothy fully realizes her own power, she exudes authority in a number of scenes, scolding the Cowardly Lion for attacking Toto, and even daring to chastise "the Great and Powerful Oz" for causing the Lion to faint with fear. This apparent gender reversal argues against a purely sexist interpretation of the movie.

Furthermore, Dorothy returns home only after wishing to *escape*, much like a *male* character in another well-known fantasy film, *It's a Wonderful Life* (1946). Here, the tension between George Bailey's desire to leave home and his capitulation to marriage and family creates the structure for the entire narrative and provides the film's emotionally charged ending. Throughout *Wonderful Life*, motifs of travel and adventure alternate with idealizations of house and home: *National Geographic* magazines, travel brochures, posters of Europe, etc., litter the *mise-en-scène*, contrasting with the staid and static image of the Building and Loan, whose mission is to provide houses (new ones, unlike the old "haunted" house that Mary and George eventually live in). In *Wizard*, Dorothy's house is not just the old home from which she desires escape but also becomes, ironically, the very *means* of escape as visual effects have it whirling dramatically through the air only to land on the Wicked Witch of the East. In doing so, the house becomes associated with the journey as much as the return. And as a mortal weapon, it also becomes the catalyst for angering the Wicked Witch of the West, thereby ensuring that Dorothy will face great danger and eventually become the hero of her own tale. The house in this film thus comprises the necessary contradiction at the heart of the conflict, at once the *home* of safety but also the embodiment of Dorothy's desire for autonomy and adventure.

While both *Wizard* and *Wonderful Life* ultimately celebrate the return home, neither can permanently shake the emotionally fraught and bittersweet tradeoff this entails. George (Jimmy Stewart) never does fulfill his wanderlust and Dorothy's quest turns out to have been "just a dream." Furthermore, as Salman Rushdie points out, the world to which Dorothy returns is an awfully austere and depressing place compared to the wondrous and colorful Oz (17). It is important to remember this, because we don't return to the film again and again to satisfy a longing for Kansas. We re-watch the film to return to the *process* which allows us to experience the contrast between Kansas and Oz, to embrace and then to relinquish Oz every time, in the bittersweet way that characterizes the final scene in the film.

Curiously, neither *Wizard* nor *Wonderful Life* resolves important problems or questions raised by its narrative. Although Dorothy has returned safely and happily home, the problem of Toto and Miss Gulch has not been resolved; and although George goes back to his timeline, greeted by a joyful scene of money brimming over the family table and friends and well-wishers crowding the house, nothing is mentioned of the villainous Mr Potter, who, having stolen $8000, would in most films receive his come-uppance at the end of the movie. Hollywood is known for tying up all the loose ends, and yet somehow here these unresolved issues seem inconsequential. Arguably, resuscitating these tensions would have seriously detracted from the emotional endings, resolutions that are reminiscent of Tolkien's idea of *eucatastrophe*, for the characters in both these movies are delivered from their adventures in a miraculous moment filled with joy, but also tinged with a sense of irrecoverable loss.

Wizard is iconic not just of fantasy film, but of Hollywood movies in general, because it illustrates our fascination with the cinematic experience as a ritual of narrative and spectacle, and as a vehicle for nostalgic connection with our past. The nostalgia stems from both the content of the film and its presence in our collective past. Anyone who grew up in the US has likely watched *Wizard* on television numerous times, as it was aired yearly beginning in 1956. As Aljean Harmetz has argued, it was the film's repetition on television that ensured its presence in the cultural imagination and helped spur the desire for its extended life through worldwide exposure on television, video, and DVD (22, 288). In this way, *Wizard* not only depicts a nostalgic journey away from and back home, it also invokes in its audience a sense of nostalgia for the imaginary home of our collective childhood as created through mediated stories and images (Bronfen, 65–93). In *Wizard*, we find the perfect expression of the fantasy film's tendency to combine nostalgic wish-fulfillment with an emphasis on childhood and a sense of home, whether real or metaphorical and cinematic.

It is interesting that the film is named after the Wizard and not the land of Oz itself. How can we reconcile our desire for illusion and for enjoying a fantasy film with the knowledge that the Wizard himself is a fraud? If the Wizard of Oz is a failed magician, his use of technology to create awe through visual illusion nevertheless recalls the connection between the technology of cinema and fantasy in general. Not only does Dorothy dream of Oz, but her initial introduction to fantasy images is through the frame of her open window, recalling the "dream screen of fantasy." It is here, while the twister hurls Dorothy's house through the air, that she first sees the Wicked Witch, as she morphs suddenly from Miss Gulch sailing by on her bicycle.

The cinema *is* fantasy, and one of this generation's wizards of cinematic fantasy and illusion is Steven Spielberg, who created *E.T.: The Extra-terrestrial* (1982), a film that self-consciously bears resemblance to *Wizard*. While in *E.T.*, the title alien (and not the child protagonist, Elliott, played by Henry Thomas) is the one who wishes to go home, his plight is linked to Elliott's, whose broken home evokes loss and rootlessness. Elliott's telepathic connection to E.T. underscores their kinship. Elliott not only empathizes with the alien but physically and emotionally experiences what E.T. feels and experiences. As with Dorothy, Elliott's fantasy interlude can be seen as a coming-of-age ritual. Dorothy's home is the harsh, Kansas countryside, but Elliott's is no less bleak. His blank, almost treeless suburban neighborhood, with its identical houses and pervasive banal materialism, exudes its own sense of barrenness and sterility. Like Dorothy, Elliott feels rejected by his elders, powerless and unloved. And just as Dorothy takes something away from her experience in Oz, Elliot also matures by the end of the film. Upon his departure at the end of the film, E.T. points to Elliott's heart, saying "I'll be right here." He implies not so much that "home is where the heart is," but that one's heart − metaphorically speaking − is where we experience our sense of home. Hence, there's no *place* like home (Bronfen, 73; Rushdie, 57), a lesson not lost on a child "alienated" by his actual home. The emphasis on deep emotions so clearly experienced by the characters in *Wonderful Life* and in *Wizard* (where, as Salman Rushdie points out, the characters cry an awful lot), here becomes more explicit in the dialogue of the film, where emotion and feelings become necessary for Elliott's maturation.

How fitting then that in *Wizard*, the Tin Man represents a contradiction lurking behind a fantasy tradition that responds to, but is suspicious of all that a Tin Man might represent. His silver and stiff metal body foreshadows countless cinematic (science-fiction) robots to come. His robotic flaw is that he is only a machine with no emotions, and therefore not fully human. But as with Dorothy, the Scarecrow, and the Cowardly Lion, the Tin Man already possesses what he supposedly lacks (a heart), thus embodying fantasy's own tendency to embody contradictions.

Science-fiction films like *Blade Runner* (1982) explore the same machine/human conundrum that the Tin Man provokes: Can a machine have emotions? Is a pile of tin capable of "human-ness?" Combined with the horrific moments in many science-fiction and fantasy films, such overlaps once again point to the common roots giving birth to modern fantasy, science fiction, and horror. After all, Baum's Tin Man is an imaginative by-product of the same Industrial Revolution that spawned so many science-fiction stories. *Blade Runner* was adapted from Philip K. Dick's novel *Do Androids Dream of Electric Sheep?* – a purely science-fiction question that dovetails with the Tin Man's questionable human status, but also returns us to the importance of dreams in fantastic stories of all kinds.

As framing devices, as inspirational daydreams, or as hallucinatory interludes, dreams (like Dorothy's) are an important element of many fantasy stories, including such classics as *Alice's Adventures in Wonderland*. But as suggested by Todorov's conundrum, they also raise an important question about the status of film as fantasy. Can a movie be considered a fantasy if it concludes that the fantasy experience is only a dream – an illusion? Although Tolkien would say no, a more expansive definition would require that we look at the individual film and the extent to which the dream interlude shapes or informs the overall narrative. The film must feature a significant ontological rupture, a departure from reality, and must downplay the interpretations that would lead us to experience the fantasy as only a dream or hallucination. Despite evidence that Dorothy has only dreamed Oz, the experience of the film as a whole undercuts the dream explanation. This is not just because of the time and attention devoted to Oz, but because of the relationship between the dreamscape and the overall narrative. Viewers most likely share in Dorothy's consternation upon awakening in Kansas: What do you mean it was just a dream? It seemed so real! (Plate 13.) We want to affirm the emotional experience of Oz just as much as Dorothy, even while rooting for her safe return. (Note that in Baum's original story Oz was no dream, but quite real.)

Much has been made of the transition from the sepia-toned black and white world of Kansas to the spectacular Technicolor of Oz, a transition that must have seemed all the more fantastic to audiences in 1939. While Technicolor had been employed in a number of films throughout the 1930s, David A. Cook describes *Wizard*'s use of color as "the most imaginative and sophisticated use of Technicolor yet" (219–20). The worlds of Kansas and Oz are clearly constructed as counterpoints to one another with the suggestion that black and white corresponds to "reality" and color connotes "fantasy" or something beyond day-to-day existence such as might be experienced in a dream. Interestingly, many people used to claim that humans are only capable of dreaming in black and white, not color. But a new finding shows that while in the 1940s, three-quarters of those surveyed claimed to dream in black and white, today, three-quarters say the opposite, that they dream in color. This reversal is

PLATE 13 *The Wizard of Oz* (1939 MGM): Was it really just a dream? (Courtesy of Photofest.)

attributed to a change in the number of people who grew up watching color rather than black and white television (O'Connor), another hint that our private dreams are intimately linked to our collective mediated experiences.

Likewise, *Wizard*'s musical sequences denote a utopian desire, a way of conveying emotion that goes beyond dialogue or plot and that links many movie musicals to the fantasy genre (Dyer). It may be "unrealistic" for people to suddenly burst into song and dance, but we accept this convention as part of the fantasy world of the integrated musical (pioneered by Freed). Although Dorothy's experience in Oz is permeated with song and dance, note that she bursts into spontaneous song even *before* she arrives in Oz – clearly not "realistic," if we are to argue that Kansas is supposed to be experienced as unfiltered reality. Oz and Kansas are not separate movies, or separate genres, but different sides of the same rainbow: they cannot exist without each other. Oz can't exist without Kansas because its existence depends upon Dorothy's desire to escape (expressed so achingly in song). Kansas in turn depends on Oz, because we can't love Dorothy's inhospitable Kansas enough to want to return home without the desire being created by the Oz adventure. This may help explain the emotional appeal of the film. Despite the bleak outlook of "reality" (Kansas), most viewers find themselves fervently wanting Dorothy to get home and share in her relief when she finally succeeds.

Even before the last scene, the film clearly hints that Oz is "only" a dream: Dorothy is hit on the head and falls unconscious onto her bed; she sees surreal, dream-like images float by her window (linking her dream to the cinema screen where fantasies unfold); Dorothy is the center of attention when she arrives in Oz and hailed as hero (a kind of wish-fulfillment dream); Dorothy's ruby red shoes are referred to as "slippers;" and, of course, she awakens in her bed upon her return from Oz. But Dorothy doesn't actually see Oz through the frame of the window. She first sees Oz through the doorway of her house, a portal through which she steps, allowing her to physically enter another world – Dorothy's ontological rupture. Furthermore, the distinction between dream and reality is a red herring. True, there are many indications that Oz is a dream-world. But it is not *just* a dream world. Or rather, its status as a dream in no way diminishes the real experience that Oz affords the spectator. For Oz is no more of a dream than Kansas – or, to put it another way, Kansas is just as much a fantasy as Oz. Both are cinematic constructions, designed in a symbiotic relation to create the fantasy of cinema.

CHAPTER 5

HARVEY (1950)
A Happy Hallucination?

Unlike *The Wizard of Oz*, *Harvey* eschews color and special effects to deliver a very different kind of fantasy film. Lighthearted but sophisticated in its humor and aimed at a more mature audience, *Harvey*, like *Wizard*, raises Todorov's classic conundrum regarding the epistemological and ontological status of a fantastic occurrence. Based on the 1946 Pulitzer Prize-winning play by Mary Coyle Chase, *Harvey* is the story of Elwood P. Dowd and his best friend Harvey, a six-foot (plus) invisible rabbit. As with *It's a Wonderful Life* (1946), *Harvey* is set in small-town USA and stars Jimmy Stewart. Stewart considered Elwood one of his favorite roles, one he would reprise on the Broadway stage in the 1970s. The invisible character and comedic sensibility link this film to a number of movies in the 1930s and 1940s – such as *Topper* (1937) and *Blithe Spirit* (1945) – that feature invisible ghosts or angels in humorous scenarios.

While *Wizard* suggests that Dorothy's experience in Oz has been just a dream, this interpretation is offered explicitly only at the end of the film. The very premise of *Harvey*, on the other hand, concerns the question of whether or not Elwood is delusional and experiencing a hallucination. The story revolves around Elwood's eccentric behavior and his sister Veta's attempt to have him committed to the local mental institution. She only decides to do so after Elwood interrupts a social event at which her daughter, Myrtle Mae (Victoria Horne), hopes to make social connections. When the guests are scared away by Elwood's attempt to introduce Harvey, Myrtle Mae becomes hysterical, believing that she has lost her chance to find a suitable husband. Thus ensues a charming comedy of errors in which both Elwood and Harvey avoid the straitjackets of reason and convention epitomized by the doctors. Far from being insane, it soon becomes clear that Elwood's ability to see Harvey actually makes him one of the sanest people in the film. In this respect *Harvey* belongs to a tradition of film comedy in which sanity and madness are temporarily inverted. For example, the allegedly "pixilated" Longfellow Deeds proves to be the sanest fellow in *Mr Deeds Goes to Town* (1936). *You Can't Take it With You* (1938), also starring Jimmy Stewart, features a family of likeable but highly eccentric (if not insane) characters. As in *Harvey*, these movies gently mock the pretensions and aspirations of the seemingly rational characters by celebrating the unconventional.

As Elwood's family and friends attempt to come to grips with his peculiar disposition, we infer that Harvey is a delusion resulting from Elwood's drinking. The link between drinking "spirits" and seeing spirits is often a source of humor in movies where a character attributes a ghost-sighting to excessive drinking (*Topper* and *Blithe Spirit*, for example). "Pink elephants" are a cliché of the drinker's hallucinations, but a large white rabbit isn't too far off the thematic track. Harvey may be a metaphor for Elwood's denial of reality, an interpretation encouraged by Veta, who implies that Elwood has become unhinged since their mother's death. Indeed, because he's invisible and inaudible to the audience, Harvey's presence is largely conveyed by a physical absence. It is primarily Elwood's reactions, his one-sided conversations, and his insistence on claiming space for his friend that limns Harvey's existence, further suggesting that his companion might not be real. But the film raises this possibility only to reject it, at least on the literal level. The physical space that Harvey occupies is only partly diegetic (occurring within the story-world), as characters unwittingly give Harvey leeway as Elwood maneuvers around them. But his presence is also extradiegetic, a function of camera framing that routinely leaves space for a character that we cannot perceive. And Harvey does, in fact, make his presence known to selected characters throughout the movie. In one instance, he plays a prank on the gruff sanitarium attendant, Mr Wilson (Jesse White), who has been asked to look up the definition of "pooka," Harvey's species of fantastical creature. Wilson reads aloud: "A fairy spirit in animal form. Always very large. The pooka appears here and there, now and then, to this and that one. A benign but mischievous creature. Very fond of rum-pots, crackpots . . . and how are you Mr Wilson?". . . . Mr Wilson does a double take: "How are you Mr Wilson?!!!" In scenes like this, Harvey uses his magical abilities to mischievously tease unsuspecting characters, thereby ratifying his existence for the viewer through the incredulous response he elicits. Elwood is certainly a "rum pot," but the allegation of insanity is belied both by Elwood's otherwise sane and civilized behavior and by several other clues that suggest Harvey has an actual material presence (see below). As we begin to understand that Veta *also* sees Harvey, and always has, we can reformulate the premise upon which the story rests. Rather than seeing Harvey as a "projection" of Elwood's psyche – his denial of reality – we can now see that Elwood's alleged insanity is actually a projection of *Veta's* denial. By the end of the film, not only are Elwood and Harvey vindicated, Veta also redeems herself when she chooses to acknowledge Harvey and validates Elwood's psychological reality.

Another bit of evidence that points to Harvey's actual existence is a hat that Dr Chumley (Cecil Kellaway) finds at the sanitarium he heads. In the film, hats are indicative of occupation, gender, or class. Elwood's hat is associated with his genteel, upper-class civility, and he makes a point of doffing it frequently upon meeting new people. The ridiculous over-the-top hats of Veta's friends gently mock both their gender and their pretentious class aspirations. Mr Wilson, the cab drivers, and others wear flat caps that connote both working-class status and in some cases their actual job (nurse, mailman, etc.). And finally, there's Harvey's hat. This is the anomalous residue of Harvey's person, the only material presence detectable by those who don't (or won't) see Harvey. The hat looks much like Elwood's and aligns Harvey with Elwood's genteel ways, but also japes at the convention with prominent holes cut to accommodate two very large rabbit ears. It is a simple, yet effective sight gag (Plate 14). Except for an occasional door magically opening and closing, the film avoids fancy special effects, due in part to the story's close adaptation of the original stage play. But it is also part of the charm of the story – the long stretches of time when we can imagine that Elwood is just talking to himself are punctuated by moments when Harvey decides to playfully intervene and make his presence known.

Another important, yet puzzling manifestation of Harvey is a huge painting of Elwood accompanied by a large white rabbit sporting a bow tie. When Dr Chumley questions Veta about it, Veta assumes he's referring to the painting of their dead mother that usually sits over the mantelpiece. She characterizes it as the pride of the house and goes on

PLATE 14 *Harvey* (1950 Universal): Pulling a rabbit out of a hat(?) (Courtesy of Photofest.)

to elucidate for Dr Chumley "the difference between a fine oil painting and a mechanical thing like a photograph. The photograph shows only the reality; a painting shows not only the reality but the dream behind it. It's our dreams that carry us on." Here, Veta unwittingly reveals her implicit understanding of Harvey's value and alludes to a key aspect of our enjoyment of fantasy film. Whether or not Harvey is "truly real" may not be the point, because he is "really true." As Ursula K. Le Guin writes:

> Fantasy is true, of course. It isn't factual, but it is true. Children know that. Adults know it too, and that is precisely why many of them are afraid of fantasy. They know its truth challenges, even threatens, all that is false, all that is phony, unnecessary, trivial in the life they have let themselves be forced into living. They are afraid of dragons, because they are afraid of living. (44)

Substitute rabbit for dragon and you have a fairly good assessment of Harvey's role in this film. Just as he has poked holes in his hat, Harvey's role is to poke holes in the conventions and pretensions that conceal the simple aspects of existence.

Harvey becomes the foil for characters like Dr Chumley's young assistant, Dr Sanderson (Charles Drake). Arrogant and locked into a narrow-minded conception of reality, Dr Sanderson also lacks an awareness of those around him. A psychiatrist should excel in relating to others, yet, in an ironic reversal, Sanderson repeatedly fails to really hear what others are saying or to notice the psychological and emotional reality before him (a fact which also permits numerous comic miscommunications). And he is alternately oblivious of or rude to his nurse, Miss Kelly (Peggy Dow), who clearly seeks his romantic attention. When Elwood first meets her, he turns to Dr Sanderson and remarks: "Isn't she lovely?" Miss Kelly seems surprised to be treated kindly for once: "Well thank you! Some people don't seem to think so." Elwood replies: "Well, some people are blind. That's very often brought to my attention." Harvey may be less like a pink elephant and more like the proverbial "white elephant" in the room – a representation of all the aspects of reality that we won't acknowledge because they don't fit our preconceptions or because we don't wish to face up to an emotional truth.

The preposterous and delightful notion of an enormous invisible rabbit should not distract us from the reason that Veta decides to commit Elwood. The cause of Myrtle Mae's panic is not just anxiety over attracting a husband, but stems from the fact that neither she nor her mother has financial or legal rights to the house. Elwood has inherited everything, a fact that annoys Myrtle Mae, who figures that if Elwood is committed, the house will effectively belong to Veta, and, by extension, to herself. Elwood's inheritance of the house haunts the movie's critique of the work ethic and gender economy of the era. As Elwood is the only male heir, the audience of the time expects him to inherit the house. But, atypically for a man of this era, Elwood doesn't work and seems completely uninterested in creating a family. His peculiarity therefore extends beyond his rabbit friend. "In the 1950s . . . there was a firm expectation . . . that required men to grow up, marry and support their wives. To do anything else was less than grown-up" (Ehrenreich, 11). Myrtle Mae, on the other hand, *must* get married because she doesn't own the house and, as a woman, she isn't *supposed* to work (an unspoken assumption of the film). Despite women's short-lived participation in the workforce during World War II, this post-war film portrays Myrtle Mae's only hope for happiness as marriage, a situation that the story fails to directly interrogate except through gently mocking her desperation. Yet Harvey disrupts the celebration of the small-town nuclear family as the culminating component of the American Dream, symbolized here by the house, just as in *It's a Wonderful Life*. Acquired through the hard work of the career husband and tended by the stay-at-home wife, the house emerges as the emotional and symbolic proof of success. The puritan work ethic, problematized but ultimately celebrated by Jimmy Stewart's character in *Wonderful Life*, is here casually rejected by Elwood.

Harvey does not, however, dispense with romance. Veta's machinations to secure a husband for Myrtle Mae are ridiculous precisely because they are so *unromantic*, simplistically centered on finding someone "respectable" from the right sort of family. But romance *per se* is upheld through the rapprochement between Dr Sanderson and Miss Kelly, which is made possible only from having met Elwood and Harvey. More importantly, instead of *preventing* romance for Myrtle Mae, Elwood's peculiar behavior and near incarceration at the sanitarium end up doing just the opposite when Myrtle Mae and Mr Wilson develop an instant infatuation. A hard-talking, cynical representative of the working class (who manhandles both Elwood and Veta at the sanitarium), Mr Wilson is an unexpected choice for a suitor, one who would certainly not be accepted by Veta's social circle. But unlike Veta and her pretentious friends, Harvey and Elwood have already set an example, for they make no distinction when it comes to class or occupation. Elwood befriends all kinds of people and treats each person as attentively and graciously as the next. He repeatedly invites strangers to dinner, from psychiatrists to ex-cons to cab drivers, all of whom express surprise and delight. And yet it is precisely such behavior that Veta sees as evidence of Elwood's insanity. As Veta reveals to Dr Sanderson, it is not so much Elwood's drinking that worries her, it's the implication of the kind of people she associates with a drinking establishment: "Don't you call it excess when a man never lets a day go by without stepping into some cheap tavern, bringing home a lot of riffraff, people you never heard of? If you don't call that excess, Doctor, I'm sure I don't know what excess is."

Despite the fact that Elwood enjoys inviting people home and the fact that Veta admits aloud that Harvey lives in the house with them, Elwood's sense of home proves to be less the actual house he inherits, and more the emotional home that Harvey makes possible. Hamid Naficy frames the issue of home in terms of belonging and dislocation, as seen so poignantly in *The Wizard of Oz*. But home is not just a place. It is also something that "can be carried in memory and by acts of imagination" (5–6). As Elwood explains, he and Harvey find happiness wherever they are, no matter whom they're with. By contrast, the sanitarium and the pseudo-scientific jargon of the psychiatrists do nothing to create a sense of connection or community, values linked to the small-town setting. In fact Elwood explains that when they first met, Harvey already knew his name.

But, he says, this didn't really surprise him because in a small town everyone knows your name. The irony is that Elwood is constantly encountering people he doesn't know in a world that seems to be rapidly growing more anonymous. At the same time, it remains largely segregated by class and occupation (not to mention race, another "invisible" aspect of the film). But Elwood and Harvey find themselves right at home in their *Cheers*-like bar, drinking and getting to know strangers at their home-away-from-home. Elwood explains this as they sit at the bar: "Soon the faces of all the other people turn toward mine and smile. They're saying: 'We don't know your name, Mister, but you're a very nice fellow.' Harvey and I warm ourselves in all these golden moments. We have entered as strangers – soon we have friends."

The psychiatrists in the film represent the opposite of Elwood's gracious openness and camaraderie. By medicalizing people's behavior, the psychiatrists alienate the characters from themselves and from others, ignoring the therapeutic qualities of empathy, sympathy, and simple friendship. The exaggerated rationality of scientists, doctors, and psychiatrists is often a trope of horror and science-fiction films, signaling a failure to acknowledge supernatural or extraterrestrial phenomena (a classic example occurs in *Invasion of the Body Snatchers*, 1956). In horror films, disbelief must be overcome, but the resulting confrontation with the irrational leads to an encounter with the characters' worst fears. In fantasy movies, it just as easily fulfills the characters' deepest wishes.

Harvey represents an antidote to narrow-mindedness, conformity, and the pressures of climbing the success ladder, giving permission to focus on the joy of day-to-day life. Harvey eventually works his magic on Dr Chumley, who realizes that Harvey has the power to provide spiritual and psychological respite. The daydream that Dr Chumley recounts to Elwood is strangely reminiscent of psychotherapy, featuring a woman who (like a therapist) speaks not at all, but provides the sympathetic understanding needed by the doctor. Harvey has the ability to stop time and to magically transport Dr Chumley to Akron, where he wishes to while away two weeks lying under a tree, drinking beer, and confessing his troubles. Chumley's fantasy reveals that his own approach to mental health is sorely lacking and may even create the very problems it seeks to cure. The name of the sanitarium, "Chumley's Rest," foreshadows his need for relaxation and provides an ironic commentary on the establishment's misguided methods. As in *The Chronicles of Narnia* (2005, 2008), Dr Chumley can actually experience this event and return without any time having elapsed. As Elwood explains: "Science has overcome time and space. Well, Harvey has overcome not only time and space, but any objections." Harvey once again proves a fine metaphor for our enjoyment of fantasy films that feature stories in which the usual rules are suspended – and willingly so.

The equation of success and sanity with "home" is evident through its alternatives: either the prison-like mental institution vilified in films like *One Flew over the Cukoo's Nest* (1975), or a lack of home altogether, as in *The Fisher King* (1991). In 1939 when The *Wizard of Oz* was released, homelessness was an all too real possibility for movie audiences who had suffered the twin agonies of the Great Depression and the Dust Bowl. But as the nation recovered and emerged into the post-war economic boom, the lingering fear of homelessness morphed into a *personal* rather than an economic or social problem. In *The Fisher King*, an English professor, Parry (Robin Williams), becomes homeless as a result of a mental collapse following the brutal murder of his wife. His tragic existence includes fantasy interludes in which he is hunted by a fearsome knight. Unlike Elwood, his fantasy world is a projection of his guilt and terror. His distress is played out alongside the unwillingness of New York radio DJ Jack (Jeff Bridges) to commit to his girlfriend, a rejection of the very type of emotional and domestic life that Parry has tragically lost. Their lives intersect when Jack learns that it was actually his own insensitive comments as a radio personality that caused the murder of Parry's wife. Thrown into despondency, Jack likewise ends up drunk and homeless. He tries to atone for his sin by acquiring what Parry believes to be the Holy Grail. Although the cup turns out to be a sports trophy, the quest itself, and the endeavor to help Parry, proves redemptive for Jack. As in *Harvey*, the allegedly insane character, Parry, exhibits a sense of romance and wonder that ends up teaching the "sane" character that he has been focusing on all the wrong things.

In another well-known fantasy, *Miracle on 34th Street* (1947), homelessness and insanity temporarily converge when Kris Kringle (Edmund Gwenn) becomes homeless after being fired from his job playing Santa Claus at Macy's department store. While clearly adored by the children who visit him, Kris ruffles feathers when he actually claims to *be* Santa Claus. Once made jobless and homeless, his alleged insanity becomes even more plausible to the skeptics. When he is befriended by the no-nonsense divorcee who originally hired him (Maureen O'Hara), he makes friends with her precocious and cynical young daughter Susan (Natalie Wood). But Kris is appalled to learn that Susan doesn't know any fairy tales and has no sense of imagination. And while other children might wish for a toy or a pair of skates, Susan's Christmas wish is for a "real" house instead of an apartment, and a "real" family instead of her fatherless one. But just as Parry and Elwood prove to be more sane than the so-called normal characters, Kris emerges as the epitome of healthy optimism and imagination. Not only is he cleared of charges of insanity and fraud, he also facilitates a romance between Susan's mother and her neighbor. Most importantly, Kris magically procures the very house that Susan had envisioned. Thanks to him, Susan's Christmas gift is the American Dream home, complete with a mother and a father. While not directly addressing his own homelessness, *Miracle* thus concludes by validating Kris's sanity while simultaneously linking it to the importance of house and home.

Harvey challenges a number of the central notions embedded in this American Dream. Working hard to attain a house to support a wife and family is what George Bailey first fears but eventually embraces in *It's a Wonderful Life*. By contrast, Elwood relinquishes wife and family, seems oblivious to the fact that he even owns a house, and prefers hanging around in bars to work or romance. This strange anti-hero is an apt hero for a fantasy film that seeks to question our values. But there is an interesting coincidence here, or perhaps it is no coincidence at all. What is the significance, if anything, of the fact that Elwood's friend is a rabbit?

From the Easter Bunny to bunny suits, bunny slippers, and children's stories such as *The Velveteen Rabbit*, *Peter Rabbit*, and *Goodnight Moon*, we usually think of rabbits as cute, defenseless, and childlike (as Kimya Dawson sings of her bunny suit: "when I wear it I look cute"). Tom Shippey even suggests that in naming the peaceful inhabitants of the Shire "Hobbits," Tolkien might have been suggesting a likeness to rabbits: "small, fluffy, harmless, irretrievably childish, never rising above the status of pet" (4). This is what makes the giant evil bunny in *Donnie Darko* (2001) ironic and so weirdly compelling, why the rabid rabbit in *Monty Python and the Holy Grail* (1975) is so unaccountably funny, and why boiling the bunny in *Fatal Attraction* (1987) is so abominable.

The rabbit may be fluffy and furry, but as a symbol it is slippery and rife with ambiguity. To begin with, Harvey is described as a pooka – a mischievous sprite. As such he could, it seems, take any form he wishes, but he chooses the rabbit, which has a long tradition in the world of fantasy, folk tale, and children's stories. In folk tales the *trickster* is typified in the Native and American folk tradition by Brer Rabbit, who gets the best of his adversaries through cunning and trickery. The rabbit is thus an apt choice as a vehicle for mocking those in power or those who feel superior, such as Veta's pretentious friends or the arrogant Dr Sanderson. Bugs Bunny, another famous rabbit, takes a cue from Brer Rabbit but is infinitely more campy, cheeky, and of course cartoony.

The rabbit as a figure of trickery is also associated with magic and illusion. It becomes synonymous with fantasy and with worlds that are not what they seem – after all, why else would magicians choose to pull rabbits and not puppies out of their hats? It is none other than the appearance of a white rabbit that begins Alice's adventures in Wonderland, a world in which Alice meets another lagomorph, the March Hare. The phrase "mad as a March Hare," referenced in the story, underscores the fine line between sanity and insanity in Wonderland and reminds us of the fine line between Elwood and the loony bin. *The Matrix* (1999) turns the motif of the White Rabbit inside out when Neo (Keanu Reeves) is first told to "follow the rabbit" and later swallows a pill and goes down the "rabbit hole." But rather than entering a fantasy world, he learns that his reality has been the illusion and that the real world is actually down the rabbit hole. The figure of rabbit as both trickster and site of illusion, meanwhile, is employed with much humor in the Energizer Bunny commercials. Here the appearance of the rabbit toy abruptly interrupts everything, signaling that what we have been watching is not the "real" commercial after all, but instead one for long-lasting batteries. (A wake-up to "reality" that parallels the effects of Neo's pill in *The Matrix*.)

As Clemens and Pettman write, rabbits are "ontologically unstable, virtual creatures" (60), a trait which even Madeleine of the children's book observes when a crack in the ceiling is described as having "a habit, of looking like a rabbit." And let's not forget the Easter Bunny, who, more than Santa Claus himself, typifies fantasy. Clemens and Pettman write that "the rabbit has proven itself to be a catalytic object for dialectical questions of presence and absence, as well as metaphysical explorations of madness, sanity, and those existential forms of psychic liminality which lie between these relative poles" (59). We should not be too surprised then that *Who Framed Roger Rabbit* features a cartoon rabbit in a film which complicates our sense of reality by mixing live-action and computer-animated characters in a way that collapses the distinction between the two. Not only do rabbits signal perceptual ambiguity as they emerge out of hats or disappear into thin air down a hole, they also therefore signal ambiguity of being and identity. And when a rabbit is conflated with the traditional pooka of folk tale – also variously spelled puca, or even Puck, as in Shakespeare (Breatnach, 105) – it reminds us that transformative identities and illusive appearances are a central aspect of fantasy.

While the rabbit is cute and cuddly, another association of rabbits is their propensity to . . . well . . . breed like rabbits, hence the fact that

Easter (rebirth) and eggs are combined with the rabbit in the myth of the Easter Bunny. But the same type of ambiguity that informs the rabbit as alternately (and often simultaneously) real or not real may also inform its ambiguous gender. For example, sexual ambiguity is very much a part of the Bugs Bunny character. Although Bugs is male, he spends an awful lot of time dressing up in women's clothing and being pursued by men. In true trickster style, he often surprises his male adversaries by planting upon them a big wet kiss before making his escape (Sandler, 166). And just as the Easter Bunny is the quintessential fantasy figure for children, the bunny suit is the quintessential signifier for dressing up in disguise. Indeed, the idea for Bugs Bunny may have occurred in *Porky's Hare Hunt*, a 1938 cartoon in which the animators had the idea of pitting Porky against a duck who disguises himself in a bunny suit (Sartin, 61). All this is to suggest that the rabbit is in some ways as quintessential a fantasy motif as fairies as wizards.

Curiously, it may have been the ambiguously gendered symbol that encouraged Hugh Hefner to employ the rabbit logo for his new magazine *Playboy* in 1953, only three years after *Harvey* was released. The *Playboy* rabbit was not the buxom female figure who came to be associated with the magazine's nude photos or the Bunnies of the Hefner mansion. No, the *Playboy* rabbit logo was the symbol for a new type of man, one who took guilt-free pleasure in leisure pursuits, which, as in the case of Harvey and Elwood, included copious consumption of cocktails. Elwood's rabbit habit may be denounced by some who characterize him as a disenchanted alcoholic (Hornstein, 8). But as in *Topper* and other ghost movies, alcohol is equated not just with "spirits" of the supernatural kind but also with the notion of leisure and camaraderie – letting go of everyday stresses and strictures.

Of course Elwood is far from being a playboy in the Hefner sense – in fact, for a Hollywood protagonist, his character is strangely uninterested in sex (or romance). Rabbits may be associated with fertility (hence the family pet's appearance and awful "disappearance" by watery grave in *Fatal Attraction*), yet *Playboy* focused heavily on only the sexual aspect of the rabbit's alleged fertility and friskiness. In doing so, however, it also rejected the rabbit's essential "productivity." Thus, if women are supposed to reproduce, men must be productive in the workplace to pay for it all. For Hefner, the rabbit comes to symbolize the liberation of the male from the stifling uniformity of working life, imposed in this era as an overwhelmingly male burden. After being disrupted during World War II, the rhetoric in favor of traditional gender roles resurfaces in the public discourse of the 1950s. Women are encouraged to stay at home, and men are supposed to go out and work at soul-killing jobs in order to pay for families and homes in the suburb.

If rabbits are silly, child-like, and playful, the playboy was perhaps the most obvious inkling of a new trend of men who wished to shun so-called "grown-up" commitments, later typified by the "child-man" director Steven Spielberg. (As described in Chs. 2 and 6, this type of man is said to cling to boyish pleasures instead of facing up to adult responsibilities.) For the ideal playboy, money is not an issue – for Elwood because he belongs to the upper class, where wealth is inherited, and for Hefner's model man because, without other obligations, he is able to spend his hard-earned cash on the type of boy toys that come to epitomize the bachelor life of James Bond: fine liquor, fast cars, expensive stereos, and other state-of-the-art electronic gizmos. Elwood may not be a direct precursor to James Bond or Hefner's playboy (both of whom were to make their entrance in 1953), but it is clear that in *Harvey* the gender roles embedded in the home/work dichotomy are implicitly interrogated in a spirit of light-hearted rebellion. While *Playboy* is criticized for its sexist objectification of women and its celebration of a hedonistic, consumerist lifestyle, the rabbit as symbol acknowledges that what is also at stake here is a notion of masculinity that rejects a traditional masculine role in favor of something less macho and less restrictive. The *Playboy* man is intended not to be a rugged cowboy hero, but above all to be fun and playful. In fact, the rabbit logo was, like Madeleine's ceiling rabbit, an image that had a *habit* of appearing or disappearing in pictures in the magazine, prompting readers to play a game of looking for it (Beggan and Allison, 343). The nature of the rabbit as not just cute and furry but also timid makes the rabbit a more feminine than masculine symbol. Beggan and Allison thus argue that the Playboy was meant to be "the integration, rather than polarization, of masculine and feminine representations," and the male playboy as rabbit became the symbolic vehicle by which to express this fusion (344).

In one sense, we might see *Harvey* as a supernatural "buddy movie" with all the homosocial attributes of such films. But Harvey is not just a male friend with whom to go drinking. Nor does the film ultimately promote the idea that Harvey is a projection of Elwood's psyche, although we can "see" him that way if we so choose. While Harvey is coded as male, his masculinity is undercut through his invisibility, his muteness (we don't hear him or see him), and the utter ridiculousness of his being a six-foot tall bunny. Harvey represents whimsical opposition to many of the values of the film's era, including those directly related to traditional masculinity, with its emphasis on work and success. While Dr Chumley tells Elwood that "we all have to face reality . . . sooner or later," Elwood simply rejects this. "Doctor, I wrestled with reality for forty years, and I am happy to state that I finally won out over it." With Harvey's help, Elwood manages to overcome the straitjacket of reason – and any objections.

CHAPTER 6

ALWAYS (1989)
Spielberg's Ghost from the Past

It may seem strange to devote a chapter to one of Spielberg's lesser known films, a fantasy that received mixed reviews and failed to make much of a splash at the box office. But *Always* is more interesting than it might seem, especially when considered as part of Spielberg's overall legacy. As both Lester Friedman and Nigel Morris argue, the film is meticulously constructed and features many of Spielberg's signature motifs. From its many intertextual references, to its skillful camera work and its play of light, *Always* epitomizes much of the director's work. And although it represents his first attempt at romance, the themes of male immaturity, separation, loneliness, and an obsession with flying link this film thematically to many other Spielberg films. Furthermore, *Always* permits a look at a distinct strand of the fantasy genre, namely romantic or melodramatic ghost stories. While ghosts may inspire fear in some movies, a film's overall *attitude* toward the supernatural is what distinguishes supernatural fantasy from horror (Kawin, 20). *Always* therefore follows in a tradition of film ghosts that are benign, benevolent, or even comic.

Just as *Harvey* presents a fantasy intended for adults, *Always* is clearly a "grown-up" film. With the release of the film, following as it did *The Color Purple* (1985) and *Empire of the Sun* (1987), many critics noted that Spielberg himself seemed to be growing up, relinquishing his obsession with children, "child-men," and childish action/adventure. More precisely, *Always* is one of several Spielberg films to address the director's obsession with the *difficulties* of growing up, since the protagonist, Pete, seems unable to establish a mature relationship with his girlfriend Dorinda. This immaturity is linked to Spielberg himself, who had recently failed to maintain his first marriage to Amy Irving prior to this film and who once admitted that he "doesn't like being an adult" (Taylor, 70). The prototype of Spielberg's child-man character, often said to be the director's surrogate, might be Roy Neary in *Close Encounters of the Third Kind*, a father and husband who exhibits a love of toy trains and *Peter Pan* while his children and wife just don't seem to "get it." (Countless critics refer to Spielberg as a kind of real-life Peter Pan.) The child-like awe that Roy exudes in the face of the similarly child-like aliens is by no means the defining trait of the main character in *Always*, although both characters are played with youthful intensity by Richard Dreyfuss. Rather this character's immaturity is linked to his boyish daredevil personality, his adolescent humor, and his inability to express emotions. Friedman writes that "Spielberg's male figures consistently grapple with their culturally constructed roles as sons, husband, boyfriends, and fathers" (22). While *Always* does feature some of Spielberg's signature adventure sequences, the action ultimately serves as the context for a more explicitly personal story.

In *Always*, Pete is a hotshot firefighting pilot who dies suddenly in the line of duty, leaving behind his girlfriend Dorinda (Holly Hunter). Dorinda had wanted Pete to become a flight instructor, relinquishing the danger of firefighting to settle down with her in domestic harmony. Like George in *It's a Wonderful Life*, Pete craves adventure and so vehemently resists. And although Dorinda begs him, Pete cannot even manage to tell Dorinda that he loves her. Moments after Pete finally accepts Dorinda's plan, he lets himself get sucked into one last mission. When he finally says the words "I love you," Dorinda fails to hear them over the roar of the plane's engine. Predictably, this is Pete's last flight, not because he retires, but because his plane explodes after its engine catches fire.

Spielberg's obsession with airplanes and flying (*1941, E.T., Close Encounters, Hook, Empire of the Sun, The Terminal*, etc.) here takes the form of a squadron of (mostly male) pilots who extinguish forest fires from aloft. While in many fantasy films flight is an expression of freedom and imagination (*à la* Peter Pan), here it also connotes Pete's flight from Dorinda and his inability to commit. When Pete dies and returns as a ghost, he is told by an angel, Hap (Audrey Hepburn), that he has been temporarily returned for a reason. He must help a young new firefighter take his place – in more ways than one. Not only must Pete help Ted (Brad Johnson) become a successful firefighter, he must also help release Dorinda from her grief so that she can become romantically involved with Ted and move on with her life.

Always is one of many movies in the late 1980s and 1990s that feature ghosts and/or angels in domestic or romantic relationships. While ghost movies can vary widely in plot and tone, a recent thread of ghost and angel movies features a male character (often the ghost itself) who has difficulty expressing emotions or romantic sentiments to his wife or girlfriend. *Kiss Me Goodbye* (1982), *Ghost* (1990), and *Truly, Madly, Deeply* (1990) are just a few of the many films that feature male ghosts in melodramatic and/or comic situations. In some cases, like *Ghost Dad* (1990) or *Field of Dreams* (1989), the emotionally distant male is an absent or otherwise unavailable father. Such films reveal a desire to work through difficulties of masculine identity within romantic or domestic settings where an obsession with work and/or emotional inexpressiveness become counterproductive (Fowkes 1998, 2004). *Always* was neither the first nor the last of such films, but it fits neatly into the moment. Spielberg has a knack for choosing stories that reflect the hopes and fears of his audience. As Friedman says of *Saving Private Ryan* (1998): "In Spielberg's case, one can never be sure if his work actually creates a cultural moment, if it acts as a focal point that brings together various strands of thought, if it shines a spotlight on already existing materials, or if it simply rides atop the waves of the social zeitgeist" (220).

Always was not, therefore, a new concept to many moviegoers, nor was it to Spielberg. In fact, it was a remake of *A Guy Named Joe* (1943), a film Spielberg had fallen in love with as a child. Directed by Victor Fleming (*The Wizard of Oz*) and starring Spencer Tracy and Irene Dunne, the original is set during World War II, where the title character is not a firefighter but a bomber pilot. While World War II is another obsession for Spielberg, the director elected to change the time and setting because he worried that audiences might not relate to that era or would dismiss the story as irrelevant to their lives (Friedman, 14). Spielberg had recently directed *Empire of the Sun*, a drama set during World War II, and perhaps his final decision was influenced by that film's failure at the box office. The irony, however, is that the change of era and venue is precisely what may have discouraged emotional investment for viewers. The risks that Pete takes (that so madden and sicken Dorinda) look egotistical rather than heroic. We never see the people on the ground whose lives are affected by the wildfires so it's difficult to root for Pete when he takes unnecessary chances. Likewise, the fear of losing a husband or lover, the subsequent grief, and the guilt associated with "moving on" would certainly have resonated more keenly with wartime viewers. The film shows an awareness of its own near-fatal flaw when Pete's friend Al (John Goodman) remarks that although their situation may seem reminiscent of World War II with its B-26 planes, Quonset huts, warm beer, etc., in reality: "There ain't no war here. . . . This is why they don't make movies called *Night Raid to Boise Idaho* or *Firemen Strike at Dawn*" (Friedman, 14). Ironically, titles apart, it seems that such films do get made. Of course, Spielberg would eventually return to World War II in *Schindler's List* (1993) and *Saving Private Ryan*, dramatic movies in which heroic sacrifice is central.

In *A Guy Named Joe*, Joe's lone wolf attitude is ultimately criticized for being counterproductive or downright dangerous during a war in which teamwork is of paramount importance. At the same time, however, his risk-taking is consistent with the traditional, rugged male hero as epitomized in Westerns and action films. But in *Always*, Pete's self-absorbed character is just one of many male movie characters of the 1980s and 1990s who struggle to reconcile their masculinity with changing gender roles. "What was perhaps a comfort to the widows of World War II evolves today as a fable for the sensitive male" (Kempley).

While Spielberg is often associated with special-effects-laden movies, *Always* saves its "special" effects for the firefighting scenes. Unlike many ghost movies, Pete's invisibility is treated quite simply as a matter of framing and editing (either including him or not as needed). For the most part, the viewer sees Pete, but understands that the other characters are unaware of him. In comedy ghost films like *Topper* and *Blithe Spirit* (the latter featuring the song "Always"), ghosts are invisible but have the ability to manipulate objects, thus causing fright for the characters but laughter for the audience. Those films tend to alternate between letting us see the ghosts and using special effects to simulate invisibility so we can experience what the characters see – objects apparently moving of their own volition. Unlike them, however, ghost-Pete does not have the ability to manipulate his environment. His inability to do so links him to contemporary spirits like Patrick Swayze's character in *Ghost*, who are relatively helpless and whose phantasmal existence is tortured precisely by their difficult attempts to communicate. These male characters' problems of communication as ghosts are manifestations of their previous inability to express themselves while alive (Fowkes 1998, 2004).

As with other film ghosts, Pete is not completely helpless or un-detectable to other characters. It's a convention of fictional ghosts to be heard but not seen, and sometimes only by certain people, as is the case with the medium Oda Mae Brown in *Ghost*. But in *Always*, Pete's only way of making himself known is when his voice becomes subconsciously detected by those around him. The fact that Pete's presence is only subliminal invites either a metaphoric or a psychoanalytic reading. On the one hand, Pete might be a product of Dorinda's mind, the result of her grief or her guilt for being attracted to Ted. When the newly dead Pete finds himself in a field getting a haircut – which Dorinda had previously suggested he needed – Dorinda's wishes and Pete's presence seem intimately connected. This interpretation is "undercut," however, since the film consistently privileges Pete's character over Dorinda's. As with many other melodramatic ghost films of the era, *Always* features a male ghost who emerges not as the haunting projection or hallucination of a grieving spouse or girlfriend, but as a protagonist in his own right. Many of these movies therefore focus less on the grieving survivor and more on the male ghost's quest to correct an injustice, express love, and move on.

Alternately, Pete might be seen as a metaphor for the subconscious in general. The angel, Hap, suggests as much when she says that everyone gains inspiration in the way that Ted will from Pete. Inspiration is literally breathed into us by someone who came before so that our ideas, talents, and inclinations only *seem* to have originated in our own minds. That Pete is able to get through to Dorinda most effectively when she is asleep further links ghosts with the subconscious and with dreams. At the end of another ghost film, *The Sixth Sense* (1999), Malcolm (Bruce Willis) succeeds in the same task when he tells his slumbering wife how much he loves her and she finally appears to acknowledge the message. Here, however, the same technique of communicating in no way implies that Malcolm's ghostliness is metaphoric or a projection of his wife's subconscious. In fact the entire film is constructed to make sure that the viewer, like Malcolm, is stunned to learn that that he is really a ghost (Fowkes 2004).

Another aspect of Pete's ability to make himself known subconsciously is the delight he initially takes in seeing people unwittingly follow his suggestions and commands. In the beginning, these moments of comic relief are extensions of Pete's need to feel in control and of his adolescent sense of humor, as when he tricks his friend Al into smearing grease on his face, thus reprising a joke he had played on Al while alive. But the joke is actually on Pete, since his ability to influence others is part of the cosmic plan for Ted to replace him. Even in this early scene we begin to see a conflation of Pete and Ted since Ted unwittingly supplies the oil and therefore would seem to be the source of the gag. As the film progresses,

PLATE 15 *Always* (1989 Amblin Entertainment): The ghost must give up the girl. (Courtesy of Photofest.)

Pete's attempt to control others begins to backfire. Dorinda becomes increasingly enamored of Ted, and this impulse is only reinforced as Ted begins to adopt Pete's habits, plucking at his eyebrow and whistling. Worse, the more Pete attempts to keep Ted from Dorinda, the more Ted ends up in her arms (Plate 15). When they encounter an old hobo who can hear Pete and who selectively repeats Pete's words out loud, Ted believe he's met some kind of oracle. Pete tries to use the hobo to give Ted advice on how to deal with another woman. But since Pete uses himself and Dorinda as an example, he keeps repeating Dorinda's name. And when Pete says things like: "After you're dead you can never go back to her" and "you can never turn around," the hobo only repeats the last few words. Ted is amazed that the hobo seems to know so much about his feelings for Dorinda and resolves right then and there to "turn around" and pursue her. Eventually, Pete stops trying to sabotage the competition and instead uses his abilities to pass on both his flying skills and his girlfriend to Ted.

Ironically, the very things Pete resisted while alive become his appointed tasks as a ghost: in one case he must effectively become a flight instructor for Ted, and in the other he must finally communicate his love for Dorinda. In *Ghost, Truly, Madly Deeply, Kiss Me Goodbye*, and even *The Sixth Sense*, male ghosts who had been unable to communicate their love all succeed in doing so only after becoming ghosts. The essence of most film ghosts, after all, is to haunt in order to communicate something to the living, and in these films the ghostly dilemma is intimately tied to a purported male deficiency in emotional expression (Fowkes 1998, 2004). One could argue that the device of the ghost is merely a handy vehicle for raising this issue only to evade the problem while appearing to resolve it. After all, the male characters are ultimately absolved from any true commitment or responsibility because . . . well . . . they're dead. Spielberg's next film, *Hook* (1991), makes explicit his longstanding obsession with *Peter Pan*, and would seem to show the director regressing. And yet, in all fairness, the film concludes with the father/husband actually relinquishing his childhood memories for the sake of his adult commitments. Friedman argues that even Indiana Jones eventually gives up his rugged individualism. By the last film in the series Jones has become more, rather than less, dependent on those around him: " . . . the more Indiana Jones learns to interact emotionally with others, the less he fulfills the traditional role of the conventional action hero, the man who is usually as alone at the end of the movie as he was when it began" (78). Furthermore, the tongue-in-cheek approach to Indie also undermines a reading of these films as celebrating the traditional hero. Far from reveling only in childish pleasures, one can find evidence that much of Spielberg's oeuvre is an attempt to work through a modern male dilemma: men are exhorted to be rugged individuals but they are simultaneously supposed to commit to wives and families – two diametrically opposed and incompatible impulses also faced by George in *It's a Wonderful Life* (R. Wood 2003).

But while *The Last Crusade* (1989) may end with its hero giving up some of his "indie-pendence," *Always* finds Pete in exactly the opposite position. Although Pete has subconsciously bonded with Dorinda, the conclusion of *Always* rings hollow because the film itself never relinquishes the notion that "it's all about Pete." The lone wolf attitude that the film ostensibly rejects is reaffirmed at the end as Pete, like the classic Western hero, rides (walks) off into the sunset. The smarmy expression and the patronizing "that's my girl . . . and that's my boy" remark undercuts the notion of sacrifice and selflessness that were called for in both the original and this update.

Caryn James argues that an aspect of *Ghost* that distinguishes it positively from *Always* is the way in which it addresses the viewer's cynicism. James praises *Ghost* for featuring characters who are obviously skeptical about the possibility of ghosts, in particular the bogus spiritual medium Oda Mae Brown, played with relish by Whoopi Goldberg. When we first meet her, she *knows* there's no such thing as a ghost because she makes her living fooling people into thinking otherwise. Although the viewer can see and hear Sam (Patrick Swayze), Oda Mae can only hear him, leading her to suspect that she must be crazy – "hearing voices." So when she finally acknowledges Sam's presence, the viewer has the opportunity to work through the skeptical responses that would necessarily precede the acceptance of ghosts in the real world. James writes that "belief in the afterlife is the dirty little secret lurking in these new films." According to James, today's cynical audiences require this process and *Always* apparently deprives them of it. This is not strictly true, however, since none of the other characters in *Always* is asked to grapple with the existence of ghosts (as Pete never manifests himself visually or aurally). Furthermore, James makes the mistake of conflating the viewer's belief in film ghosts with real ghosts, a common problem among those who criticize fantasy.

Asking viewers if they believe in film ghosts is as nonsensical as asking if they believe in protagonists. While some people may believe in the reality of ghosts outside the film world, *Always* does not pretend to address that question for the viewer. Some movies, like *The Blair Witch Project* (1999), try to make the viewer believe in the possibility of something scary and ghostly outside of the film by employing codes of cinematic realism and purporting to be documentary in nature. This intentionally conflates the codes of realism and horror in a way that may or may not strain credibility. But as a fiction film, *Always* does nothing of the kind and doesn't purport to. It need only adhere to the rules it creates for itself within its own story-world. James therefore falls victim to a kind of category error – attributing a property or characteristic to an object which it could not possibly have (namely reality). As with many fantasy films, *Always* operates at the level of Todorov's "marvelous" – the viewer is asked to accept the presence of ghosts, and the film does not encourage us to question it. We "believe" in Pete as a ghost in the same way we "believe" in Hobbits and Orcs in *The Lord of the Rings*. Indeed, this is a hallmark of fantasy. By definition, its subject matter presents what is *not* possible in the real world.

But there's another layer here that relates to Pete's abilities as a ghost. In *Giving up the Ghost*, I argued that many screen ghosts are like film viewers, and vice versa, functioning as "invisible guests" who are able to watch the action unfold but are unable to affect the outcome of events. But Nigel Morris makes a fascinating observation that also links Pete's voyeurism to the rest of Spielberg's work: "The typical Spielberg identification-figure is a spectator, often also a surrogate director" (7). In Spielberg films we often experience the wonder and awe of a phenomenon through the awe-struck faces of a character like Roy

Neary as he witnesses the alien spacecraft. In *Always*, even before death, Pete watches Dorinda dance from a stairway above, suggesting that he is not so much a part of the scene as an observer of it. And as Morris argues, Pete not only observes others, his telepathic powers also allow him to "direct" them, coaxing the characters to "perform" to his specifications. Morris cites many such instances. As a ghost, Pete advises Ted that he is "overdoing" it (referring to his conversation with a girl in the bar), and on numerous occasions Pete sits in the backseat of a car or airplane giving directions to either Ted or Dorinda. (Apparently Spielberg even engaged in this sort of "backseat directing" in certain scenes in his 1971 movie, *Duel* [168].) And the film is loaded with characters looking through or being seen through "screens, window and lenses" (166).

This is just one of the many self-referential aspects of a film that is infused with intertextuality. Another example is the way that Dorinda and Pete relate to one another, an aspect of the film that was criticized by many reviewers. One critic was alienated by the dialogue, writing that this is "a world in which nothing feels right. Here in the late 1980s, guys call their gals 'funny face' and get called 'you big lug' in return; fliers have 'moxie' until that moment when 'their number is up'" (Benson). This language may be a holdover from dialogue in the original movie (Morris, 162), a strange oversight considering that Spielberg updated the movie to the present day. Caryn James opines that: "We never believe in the passion between Ms Hunter and Mr Dreyfuss, for the jokey, friendly banter that suggested so much between Tracy and Dunne seems cold and hollow when dropped into the present. Without this metaphorical passion, 'Always' really does seem to be about ghosts."

Of course, the film really *is* about ghosts in a number of ways, including the fact that it's a remake. Just as ghosts return to try to "get it right," remakes – and many supernatural movies *are* remakes (*Meet Joe Black*, 1998, *The Preacher's Wife*, 1996, *Scrooged*, 1988, etc.) – allow the filmmaker to try to get something right about the past by recreating it in the present (Fowkes 1998). In making *Always*, Spielberg was paying homage to an era that he loved and to a movie that inspired and moved him. To date, Spielberg had banked much of his career on a nostalgic revisioning of TV shows and films from his childhood. *Raiders of the Lost Ark* was inspired by adventure serials of the 1930s and 1940s and *E.T.* owes a thematic and emotional debt to *The Wizard of Oz*. But *Always* is a strange hybrid of Indiana Jones-style flippancy and *E.T.*-style emotion. Roger Ebert (1989) writes that a lot of the dialogue "sounds 'written' instead of 'spoken' – as if these guys learned to talk by studying old pulp magazines." Ebert has unknowingly nailed it. It's obvious that Dorinda and Pete know full well that they've got quotation marks around everything they say when they're sparring with one another. It's clear from much of their interaction that the two routinely speak from a kind of script as a way to mask their true feelings. This is Pete's technique for distancing Dorinda, and Dorinda throws it back at him. She craves emotional connection, but since she can't have it she joins him in his – and Spielberg's – homage to the language of a 1940s movie. It is indeed belabored, but the characters evidently know this as they frequently laugh at themselves and each other in the most ridiculously fake and exaggerated way. "They just about bust a gasket, they work so hard" (Kempley).

The sense of play-acting also speaks to Dorinda's femininity. She's a spunky tomboy who flies planes but she is thrilled when Pete gives her a girly-dress because of the way that "he sees" her in it. Dorinda displays both masculine and feminine characteristics but neither stereotype quite fits. She seems to be acting out a charade when she tries to be tough with Pete (and as tough *as* Pete when she flies) and she goes to great length to pretend that she has slaved all day in the kitchen to make Ted a home-cooked meal. But as Kempley says, she *does* just about bust a gasket she works so hard. Both Pete and Dorinda are caught in a play/movie in which they must deal with traditional gender roles because that's the only "script" available. And that's the script Spielberg knows. As Judith Butler argues, gender is not an inherent quality. Gender is always a performance (1990, 25).

Always is the film that "confirms Spielberg as a director's director," according to Morris (175). And, as a remake, the film is, in effect, a movie about a movie. Despite his obsession with World War II, Spielberg's movies are not tributes to the past – they are tributes to *mediated* versions of the past. They are ghosts of ghosts. He was once quoted as saying: "The play's the thing. . . . In every movie I have made, the movie is the star" (Taylor, 39). Or perhaps we should say, Spielberg's love of movies is the star. And part of Spielberg's love of movies is his search for a sense of home.

From *The Sugarland Express* to *E.T.* to *Saving Private Ryan* and *Schindler's List*, many Spielberg films dramatize his obsession with finding or going home. *Always* might appear to be an exception. Taylor, however, argues that *Always* is "a ghost story where 'home' is life itself" (44). This is true of many ghost films, particularly when ghosts return to help the living. Yet we have seen that the movie is less about the living characters, Dorinda and Ted, and more about Pete fulfilling his mission through death. The end of *Always* makes it clear that, as Spielberg's surrogate, Pete is still the hero of the story. True, his heroism is marked by sacrifice and selflessness, but he's not about to give up getting credit for the assignment. And when he says "that's my girl . . . and that's my boy," it's as if Pete is channeling Spielberg in directing the final moments of *his* (Spielberg's) mission – completing this movie after so many years of having wanted to do so.

Pete walks off to some sort of "heaven," but in *Close Encounters* and *E.T.*, Neary and E.T. both find "home" in outer space. This once again underscores the connection between home and emotion discussed in previous chapters. The home to which we long to return is a fantasy – not so much a physical place as a psychological one – an emotional home. The homes (often suburban) in Spielberg's films are not nostalgic sites of comfort – far from it. For Spielberg, home and family are both the source of longing but also the cause of profound disappointment. As a collective ideal, home risks being a constant reminder of what is lacking. Pete cannot return to an earthly home with Dorinda, but he also cannot ascend to his heavenly home until he fulfills his cosmic duty. Of course for pilots during World War II and those awaiting their return, the issue of going home would have been a central preoccupation. Here, that emotionally charged notion is "extinguished" by updating the plot and altering it to replace war pilots with firefighters. But, just as *Close Encounters* features Richard Dreyfuss as a man who rejects his family and ends up beyond the sky, *Always* features Dreyfuss rejecting his would-be family (Dorinda) only to be effectively rejected himself by dying and ending up in heaven. Therefore, for Spielberg (whose home life was troubled by a distant and ultimately deserting father), home must be found somewhere else. For both the viewer and for Spielberg, home is sometimes best found at the movies – the ideal medium of fantasy.

CHAPTER 7

GROUNDHOG DAY (1993)
No Time Like the Present

"A thousand people freezing their butts off waiting to worship a rat. . . . This is one time where television really fails to capture the excitement of a large squirrel predicting the weather." These are the words of the obnoxious and egotistical weatherman Phil Connors (played by Bill Murray) whose day inexplicably starts repeating itself over and over again when he goes on assignment to cover a Groundhog Day celebration in the small town of Punxsutawney, PA. Ironically, this is one time when a movie *succeeds* at capturing the excitement of a "rat" *failing* to predict the weather.

Each morning Phil wakes up in Punxsutawney to find that everything that has happened in the past twenty-four hours has been magically erased and he is forced to re-live February 2 all over again. *Groundhog Day* is neither science fiction nor a traditional time-travel movie, but its manipulation of time links it to other movies where the subversion of time provides the main character with another chance to solve a problem and get things "right" (*The Terminator*, 1984, *12 Monkeys*, 1995, *Run, Lola, Run*, 1998, etc.). Movies like *The Terminator* and *Back to the Future* (1985) are predicated on the notion that a character can change outcomes in the present by going back in time to change past actions. But what if the character were stuck in a time loop that provided *unlimited* "do-overs"? This is the premise of *Groundhog Day*, a funny, brilliantly executed film that has become something of an (oc)cult classic. As with Pete in *Always* (who effectively subverts time by returning from death), Phil at first fails to grasp the nature of his predicament and therefore spends much of the movie unwittingly delaying the resolution by making all the "wrong" choices. Upon discovering that there are no lasting consequences to his actions, he becomes a kind of perverse, reverse superhero, using his extraordinary power to take advantage of others. One of his many exploits involves trying to have sex with women, including his lovely colleague, Rita (Andie MacDowell). Eventually, Phil makes a transition away from exploitation, saving people from accidents and death and developing his own talents and skills. Only when he begins thinking of other people and stops trying to manipulate them does he break the spell, ending the time loop and winning Rita's heart.

Phil's predicament plays out as a series of scene repetitions, with most "new" days beginning with a close-up of numbers flipping from 5:59 to 6:00 on the clock radio in Phil's hotel room. As they do so, the radio activates and we hear Sonny and Cher singing "I Got You Babe." The camera then typically pans over to Phil being awoken by the song and realizing that he is still stuck in the same day. The clock radio sequence provides Phil's ontological rupture, and its repetition in the movie helps convey the sheer monotony and absurdity of Phil's situation. At first, Phil reacts with understandable disbelief when events repeat exactly as the day before, at one point asking Rita to slap him "awake" (in true groundhog fashion, fore-"shadowing" her many cold responses and the repeated slaps she will later inflict on him). He even goes to a doctor and a psychiatrist, raising Todorov's question as to whether or not the phenomenon is all in his head. This explanation is soon rejected though, as the clueless doctor (played by director Harold Ramis) recommends him to a nervous psychiatrist (David Pasquesi) who is so ludicrously out of his league that he finishes their unproductive session by asking Phil to return for more sessions: "How's tomorrow for you?" As Thompson notes, these short, humorous scenes function to undercut the authority of the doctors, thus helping to cement the reality of the time loop (1999, 139).

In the beginning Phil repeats his *own* actions each day, heading over to cover the festival, and repeatedly plunging into a slushy puddle as the insurance salesman Ned Ryerson (Stephen Tobolowsky) guffaws in the background. But as he comes to grips with the reality of the repetitions, we see a variety of new scenes caused by Phil's own activities – the only things *not* stuck on replay – and he soon experiments by interacting with the rest of the town. Realizing that no consequences are lasting, Phil takes

PLATE 16 *Groundhog Day* (1993 Columbia): Time closes in. (Courtesy of Photofest.)

advantage of his situation by engaging in unhealthy, guilty pleasures. Rita looks on in disgust as Phil smokes, guzzles coffee from a large carafe, and stuffs his face with treats from a table groaning with fatty and sugary food. In one scene Rita asks him if he's ready to leave town, but he replies that he'd rather just linger in the café. The clocks in the background are a constant reminder that for Phil there's no such thing as wasting time (Plate 16). Later Phil will attempt to literally "kill" time by smashing the nefarious clock radio to bits. On his final attempt, it lies in a mangled heap on the hotel floor, its discombobulated speaker continuing to taunt him with a static-ridden, fizzling version of "I Got You Babe." Of course he awakens the next day, the clock radio intact, Sonny and Cher in fine form.

The diner proves to be a fertile environment for Phil as he learns how to exploit his repeating day. It's here that he first meets a young woman named Nancy (Marita Garaghty) and realizes just how easy it is to seduce her. It's a simple process of gathering personal information and then the next day tricking her into thinking they were old friends in high school. Phil's exploitive and cynical attitude contrasts sharply with the friendly small-town setting and the Groundhog Day ritual that he treats with such contempt. Phil's Bed and Breakfast recalls the *mise-en-scène* in *It's a Wonderful Life* and countless other movies where Victorian houses with cozy antique furniture and white picket fences exude nostalgia for family and community. The town square where the Groundhog festival takes place features a quaint gazebo, and the town's main street still supports a homey diner and a traditional movie theatre (no modern mulitplexes here). Rita is charmed by the townspeople who stay up all night dancing merrily to polka music, but Phil predictably dismisses them all as "hicks." While Phil derides the town's quaintness, Rita expresses an affinity for it, signaling that if Phil wants to seduce *her*, he'll have to learn to appreciate the pleasures and values that it represents.

Although we're meant to reject his cynicism, the movie helps us to identify with Phil's perspective so that we can root for him to escape the time loop. Perhaps the groundhog ceremony is a bit *too* cute, too staged, with the town officials sporting old-fashioned top hats as they mug for the cameras. Maybe this is all just a small town's desperate bid for tourists and TV exposure. As Ryan Gilbey argues, Murray's performance and his extra-textual persona are critical to the film's success: ". . . we enter into a conspiratorial relation with Murray: he's on 'our' side, the side of subdued lunacy and transgression, against 'them', the squares, the stiffs, the stupidos" (28).

And then there's Ned. He's such a hideous and hilarious character that we empathize with Phil and share his revulsion each time Ned appears. His spastic, lurching assault on Phil is echoed by his caricatured speech – "I sure as *heckfire* remember you!" Ned exudes "hick" in the worst sense of the word. "Bing!" The unwelcome anonymity encroaching on Elwood's town in *Harvey* doesn't seem so bad if it means being able to avoid the Neds of the world. But by the end of the film, Phil has taken a distinctly George Bailey-like turn, embracing the small town he had tried to escape and, like George, literally "bailing" people out of all kinds of problems. Phil even helps Ned by buying every insurance policy he has to offer.

But Phil has broken with the inevitabilities of ordinary reality, and insurance is the last thing he needs. Ned Ryerson's job as an insurance salesman depends on the statistical (im)probability of accidents or death, an ironic juxtaposition to Phil's repetitive existence, which, on the most fundamental level, defies statistics. The clock, a common household appliance that generally measures the passage of time and signals the inevitability of growth, aging, and death, is now used to illustrate the *violation* of this inevitability. Phil can't die (or get hurt in any definitive sense) but is nevertheless doomed to unavoidable indignities like being eternally accosted by a salesman whose services are ludicrously irrelevant.

The concept of statistical probabilities is introduced at the beginning of the film through Phil's weather forecasts. The pure improbability of a blizzard is driven home like the snow once Phil predicts virtually no chance of bad weather and a 100% chance that he'll be leaving town the next day. But it's no accident that Phil is a TV weatherman. The role motivates his presence in Punxsutawney and provides a thematic connection to seasonal time and to weather-inflicted magic (weather being a common component of ontological ruptures in films such as *The Wizard of Oz*, *Big*, *Narnia*, and much of Gothic horror). The weatherman's banal existence (and his repeated obligation to cover the Groundhog Day ritual) alludes to cyclical, seasonal time and to Phil's empty and monotonous life. He's stuck in a rut, suffering until the spring "thaw" brings warmth – exactly what will need to happen to Phil's hardened heart.

The probabilities that causes will lead to effects is the mainstay of both the weatherman's forecast and the insurance salesman's actuarial tables. And they form the internal logic of mainstream films whose narratives are constructed in cause-and-effect sequences. But for Phil, all that is shot to hell. Sort of. Just as Phil arrogantly errs in his assessment of probabilities about the weather, he likewise fails miserably to increase the probability that Rita will want to have sex with him. As he had done so successfully with Nancy, Phil probes Rita's likes and dislikes and the next day pretends that these are "coincidentally" his own preferences – that his favorite drink is sweet vermouth, that he knows French poetry, and that he always toasts to world peace. At first, he believes he's making progress as Rita appears to be enthralled by their affinity for one another. This contrived inevitability rings hollow, however, as we are allowed to watch it play out from the inside. A series of quick cuts shows a number of missteps and then corrections that lead to only incremental success with Rita over the course of many days. When Rita first reveals that she studied French poetry in college Phil rudely blurts out "What a waste of time!" Although he tries to salvage it, the moment is blown and Rita turns noticeably cold. Luckily, he has plenty of time to figure out how to respond appropriately. He subsequently proceeds to "waste" his time by learning French poetry so he can then recite it to the very surprised and impressed Rita.

The so-called "coincidences" that Phil manufactures would be signs for the audience of traditional romantic comedies that these two characters are "soul mates," literally "made for" each other. But here the coincidences are exposed as the machinations born of stereotypical gender roles. A cynical man like Phil supposedly endures the drudgery of a date (dinner, polite conversation, etc.) with the sole expectation that the evening will culminate in sex. The woman, on the other hand, is expected to be interested in deep conversation and a long-term relationship. This trope is nicely captured in the cult fantasy *Bedazzled* (1967), in which the sweet nebbish Stanley Moon (Dudley Moore) wants nothing more than to bed his coworker Margaret, who barely notices him. (*Groundhog* director Harold Ramis also directed a disastrous remake of this film in 2000.) After a suicide attempt, Moon finds himself in a Faustian bargain with the Devil (Peter Cook), who gives him seven wishes, all of which involve scenarios in which Moon tries desperately but fails miserably to win Margaret. At one point, the Devil gives Moon the classic advice that Phil seems to be following throughout much of *Groundhog Day*: "If you can stay up and listen with a fair degree of attention to whatever garbage, no matter how stupid it is, that they're coming out with 'til ten minutes past four in the morning . . . you're in." Well, never take the Devil's advice. Like Phil, Stanley makes numerous attempt to "get it right," but he experiences his own sort of time loop as he is perpetually set back to square one when "loop"-holes in his hastily devised wishes are exploited by the Devil. Likewise, Phil finds himself endlessly repeating the courtship process but can never reach his goal. If superficial encounters and one-night stands are his usual approach to women, then Phil is doomed to end up alone (again) each day anyway, so that dating as a vehicle for sex is revealed as its own kind of Groundhog Day purgatory. To be released, Phil will have to change his actions and attitudes to accommodate the more romantic and long-term type of relationship favored by Rita.

Groundhog Day follows a trend of popular romantic comedies in the 1980s, dubbed "the new romance" by Neal and Krutnik (70). As in *Always*, Phil must trade some of his stereotypical masculinity for traits more compatible with modern romance and a more feminized (or feminist) version of manhood (Thompson 1999, 136–42). Gilbey describes Rita's preferences in a mate as qualities of the era's "New Man": "He's kind, sensitive, gentle" (60). Instead of just pretending, Phil finally *does* become a "New Man," learning French, learning to play the piano, and adopting the playful, more caring personality associated with Rita. Phil's initials even recall the "politically correct" notion that Phil "must exchange outdated (and non-PC) patriarchal and chauvinistic traditions for a new openness if he is to emerge from the past (and become PC)" (Gilbey 60). Predictably, Phil and Rita clash humorously before the collapse of the conflict so that the movie fulfills the "guy gets girl" convention of romantic comedy.

But *Groundhog Day* treads a fine line between comedy for the audience and the sense of despair that Phil increasingly experiences. After indulging himself in a variety of earthly yet unfulfilling delights but failing, nonetheless, to win Rita, Phil grows so desperate that he repeatedly attempts violent suicide. He flings himself in a visually elegant, slow-motion arc off a building, and despondently drops a live toaster (with toast) into his bath, his death indicated only by the lights flickering in the hotel's dining room. In the most dramatic scene, he tries to kill both himself and the groundhog by driving off a cliff. The scene echoes that of many other movies as the car sails through the air before smashing to the ground far below. Rita and the cameraman, Larry (Chris Elliott), watch from above, stunned and concerned – but not so stunned and concerned that Larry fails to get the entire episode on tape (a funny but cynical moment in a movie critiquing cynicism). Soon after, the car explodes in a ball of flame. No one could survive that – except Phil. We actually witness his pale white body, dead in the morgue. But the film then cuts back to that infernal, eternal clock again, and Phil is magically restored. Phil's ashen face begins to register his fatigue and despair, his hair becoming frizzy and unkempt, his slumping posture signaling defeat. Despite his own inability to die, Phil is unable to save the life of a homeless man (Les Podwell) whom he had previously ignored. Phil tries to help the old man, taking him to the hospital, feeding him, and even giving him mouth-to-mouth resuscitation. But the old man is too far gone. Trapped in Phil's hell, he must die again and again each day.

Even though Phil pulls himself back from the brink of despair and begins to embody small-town values with his friendliness and willingness to help, the film continues to avoid sappiness, in part through a number of humorous moments that gently undercut Rita's romantic vision of the town. Despite its quaintness, many of Punxsutawney's inhabitants exhibit less than stellar qualities, from the dissolute drunkards at the bowling alley to the piano teacher who kicks her student out the door in favor of a rich stranger offering a thousand dollars for lessons. And, as with the bittersweet ending of *Wonderful Life*, a hint of ambivalence surfaces at the end of the movie. After the romantic coupling of Phil and Rita breaks the time loop, the two emerge from the Bed and Breakfast with all the giddiness of new lovers. Phil indicates his change of heart, saying: "Let's live here!" alluding to marriage, and finally embracing the town he had spent the entire movie trying to escape. But Phil then qualifies this happy ending by quipping, "We'll rent to start," thus suggesting the "probability" that his union with Rita may fail. While most happy endings suggest a "timeless" solution ("and they lived happily ever after"), Phil's desire to rent connotes something more temporary – a stark contrast to the potent symbol of home ownership as the culmination of romantic and familial stability. The song that ends the movie reinforces this ambivalence with the repeated lyrics, "almost like being in love."

The film also avoids seeming too pat by depriving the viewer of any obvious motivation for Phil's repeating day, a point of contention during the pre-production phases of the film. Would audiences accept Phil's predicament without an explanation? The studio initially insisted on providing one, much to screenwriter Danny Rubin's dismay. In one version of the script the time loop was attributed to a gypsy curse and in another, penned by director Ramis, a scientist pontificates about black holes and singularities causing time to fold back on itself (Gilbey, 18–19). By leaving this aspect of the story intentionally vague as Rubin wanted, the film contradicts the conventional wisdom that audiences need to have everything spelled out for them. Instead of being confused by a lack of motivation, most viewers and critics applaud this aspect of the film (Gilbey, 11; Kauffmann). The ambiguity helps to account for the variety of interpretations the movie has inspired, characterizing it as an expression of everything from Buddhism, Christianity, and Judaism to Existentialism and even Wicca. Some read the groundhog as a metaphor for Jesus, a symbol of rebirth and redemption, while "Hindus and Buddhists see versions of reincarnation" (Goldberg). A Jungian interpretation might note that Phil reconnects with his more feminine side (his "anima") through Rita, or highlight the connection between Phil and the groundhog since both he and the groundhog (also named Phil) are forced to confront their "shadows." In Jungian theory, the *shadow* represents repressed, socially unacceptable aspects of one's personality. In contrast, the *persona* is the public "face" that "forms the psycho-social identity of the individual," a mask that hearkens back to the ancient roots of theater (Stein, 109). In most people the persona dominates, assuring that we "act" appropriately in a variety of social contexts. In some people, however, the shadow dominates and personal power is the singular goal (107). How fitting that Phil's persona is so damaged as to be relegated to his stints in front of the camera. His inability to "perform" in real life is accentuated in one scene when Rita seems skeptical about his romantic patter and he responds: "I'm just trying to talk like normal people talk. Isn't this how they talk?" The many slaps that he endures as Rita repeatedly rebuffs him (depicted in a rapid montage) show Phil finally and repeatedly "facing up" to his reprehensible nature.

The lack of explanation for the time loop adds to a sense of Phil being in a purgatory of his own making, as his previously established character flaws become hellishly magnified in Punxsutawney. If Phil had once believed himself superior to others, he soon becomes god-like and seemingly omniscient as he impresses Rita with his knowledge of the townspeople and of future events. And if Phil had previously fancied that the world revolved around him, his narcissism now becomes the inescapable fabric of his reality. Each day really *does* focus solely on him and on how his activities and decisions affect others. Phil is like Sisyphus in the ancient Greek myth, doomed to roll an enormous rock up a hill only to have it roll back down. His entire existence is occupied by that repeated act, suggesting the pointlessness and absurdity of life. In Punxsutawney, Phil's rock is one hell of a snowball. The time loop exaggerates his general stagnation and uncovers the fact (famously explored by Camus) that Sisyphus' attitude is the prison that constrains him. Gilbey notes the many scenes that visually allude to prison through the suggestion of prison bars: Phil is often tightly framed in front of venetian blinds (in the diner, at the doctor's office). Gilbey even describes the striped wallpaper at the hotel as "candy-coloured prison bars" (35). And of course Phil actually lands himself in jail at one point by going on a joy ride that ends with him (in classic Bill Murray attitude) ordering fast food from the officers who approach the car window. "Too early for flapjacks?" he deadpans when the police don't respond to his joke. Cut to a brief but effective shot of the jail door slamming shut in Phil's face with a resounding, metallic thud. He'll be out of jail the next day, by definition, but he will escape his existential prison only when he stops trying to outwit the system and simply learns to invest every moment with awareness and meaning.

Besides the lack of explanation for the time loop, another bit of mystery lies in a lack of motivation for Phil to repeat the good deeds he ends up doing. If everything reverts to the status quo the next day no matter what Phil does, why bother? One answer is that he's trying to create the perfect day he wishes he had been condemned to in the first place (lobsters, pina coladas, love-making), and/or because he's "practicing" to be the kind of guy that Rita would love (Thompson 1999, 139–46). Or perhaps Phil will be "saved only after he performs mitzvahs (good deeds in the Jewish tradition) and is returned to earth, not heaven, to perform more" (Goldberg). Or, maybe Phil is such a jerk that the time loop is his opportunity to work off his bad karma. This is a kind of "Hollywood karma" in which protagonists learn from and then atone from their mistakes, as Murray's character does at the end of *Scrooged* (1988), a loose remake of Dickens' *A Christmas Carol*. Depending upon one's definition, however, karma may have less to do with direct cause and effect and more to do with how a person's choices inform who they are. "People are 'punished' or 'rewarded' not for what they have done but for what they have become, and what we intentionally do is what makes us what we are. . . . Happiness is not the reward for virtue; happiness is virtue itself. . . . When your mind changes, the world changes" (Loy and Goodhew, 36–7). While some have criticized *Groundhog Day* for unfairly trapping the other "innocent" characters in Phil's personal hell (e.g. Simon), this perspective illuminates the connection between Phil's attitudes and actions and the world in which he finds himself.

Whatever your religious or philosophical bent, *Groundhog Day* also inspires reflection upon filmmaking itself, providing yet another much-loved aspect of the film and one that links time to cinema itself. Not only do narratives depend upon the linear progression of cause and effect, but the filmic process physically demonstrates the passage of time as the film stock moves through the projector (or did until the advent of digital cinematography). Thus Mary Ann Doane describes cinema as "*the exemplar of temporal irreversibility*" (27). But instead of presenting a reversal of time as if playing a record backwards or running the film in reverse (as occurs via a universal TV remote in *Click*, 2006), *Groundhog Day* skips back in time like a record needle skipping back to the same place on a scratched vinyl record, the concrete cyclical time of a technology gone by. Phil is living a broken record of his own life, not so much in the groove, but in a rut, and his task is to figure out what will cause the needle of time to finally move forward. While *Groundhog Day* does not completely subvert the "arrow of irreversibility" (as Doane puts it), it does exploit time's relationship to narrative cinema when Phil attempts to manipulate his environment, effectively varying "causes" to achieve different "effects." But the ability to watch a film over and over again implies a different and somewhat paradoxical phenomenon. Most movie plots are described in the present tense, an implicit acknowledge-ment that events recur and unfold as if in the present each time we watch the film. In that sense, *all* movie characters are effectively stuck in a repeating storyline, an observation which forms the basis of Woody Allen's reflexive fantasy, *The Purple Rose of Cairo* (1985), in which a movie character played by Jeff Daniels tires of his repetitive existence on screen and steps out of the movie and into the audience.

The reflexive qualities of *Groundhog Day* are legion, including Rita's playback of Phil's videotaped weathercast, which Thompson locates as the point where Phil truly begins his seduction of Rita (1999, 142). The simple prop of a broken pencil clinches the reality of the time loop for Phil and obliquely alludes to the "erasure" of effects each day. But it also alludes (perhaps coincidentally) to the many rewrites the film underwent as Rubin and Ramis also attempted to "get it right." And Phil's predicament bears similarities to the actual process of filmmaking. In repeating the same "scenes" every day, Phil seems to be acting in a movie where scenes are typically shot over and over until the director feels that s/he has gotten it right. In the repeated scenes of Phil heading to the Groundhog Day ceremony, he caroms in Rube Goldberg-fashion off of characters who travel on fixed trajectories. In one scene, when Phil pushes Ned away, Ned rebounds like a spring, continuing on his original trajectory in accosting Phil. By the end of the movie, Phil illustrates the connection between motion and time by circumventing these pre-ordained trajectories – arriving on "the scene" early to catch a boy falling from a tree, for example.

The Truman Show (1998) makes a similar reflexive maneuver as the actors hired to create the televised town travel in pre-ordained vectors, repeated over and over again as if they were shooting a movie – or a TV show in this case. The Truman Show is thus a kind of variation of Groundhog Day. Rather than being the target of an insurance salesman, Truman is himself one, once again providing ironic commentary on a world where no insurance is necessary because all probabilities have (supposedly) been accounted for. Truman exists not so much in a time loop as in a space loop bounded by a giant spherical dome. All roads lead back to the town, and ferry tickets are by necessity all roundtrip. And instead of trying to manipulate others as Phil does, Truman (the one "true" man in the movie) is the naïve one being manipulated. But in their highly constricted worlds, both characters are ultimately the only ones with "free will," able to change the course of events while all the other characters appear to be on autopilot. And while Truman may be an unwitting actor in a TV show, Phil actually begins to emerge as the director of his own show, in one scene audibly "orchestrating" the predictable events: "A gust of wind. A dog barks. Cue the truck" (Corliss; Gilbey, 57).

Groundhog Day also recalls a number of television shows. In traditional episodic series, little if any causality links individual episodes. The premises of TV series like Gilligan's Island (1964–7) and the British cult classic The Prisoner (1967–8) depend upon the idea of endless repetition until the series can conclude. Each episode provides a new chance for the characters to escape from their respective islands and each episode ends as they fail to fulfill this goal, thereby prolonging the series. There may occasionally be some continuity between episodes, but this is not a necessary condition as it is in soaps and serial dramas. The characters seem to have selective amnesia, rarely referring to past events. Here what counts is the continuity brought to the series by the viewer. And by the same token, it is the viewer's memory of Phil's ongoing attempts to change the repeating patterns that make the film work. While at first Phil merely wants to have sex with Rita, he eventually falls in love and wants her to fall in love with him – a tall order when you realize that as far as Rita is concerned, he only has one day to convince her that he's not the jerk he was "yesterday." But because the viewer has seen it all unfold in screen time, Rita's change of heart is experienced as the culmination of a long process.

Another interesting aspect of *Groundhog Day* relates to the fact that most mainstream films tend to feature a character with a central goal that drives the entire narrative. *Groundhog Day* complicates this process. At the beginning of the film, Phil's goal is to land a job at a major television network. His assignment to cover the groundhog ceremony is clearly the type of story that Phil expects to pawn off on others when he gets his big break. That initial goal is soon replaced with Phil's attempt to figure out why his day is repeating. According to Thompson, once he resigns himself to the fact that there is no explanation, and therefore no easy solution, Phil risks being left without a goal, thus disrupting the usual cause-and-effect, goal-oriented formula upon which mainstream movies depend. Phil can eat pie all day long, rob a bank, and even make the ultimate irreversible choice to kill himself because his choices "cause" no "result" (1999, 140). But since Phil cannot affect anything *except* what happens in a single day, once he figures out what his goal is (to bed Rita), each day becomes jam-packed with choices and effects. Phil's reset button is pushed each day, giving him another chance to change his destiny, an analogy more explicitly alluded to in films like *Run, Lola, Run*. "A film that is seemingly free of effects thus becomes a panegyric to linear causality" (Thompson 1999, 140). But this is not "truth or conse-quences" but "truth *and* consequences."

In order to overcome the "ontological rupture" that disrupts causality beyond a single day, Phil must see beyond his immediate goals to a larger truth. And he is able to make this mental journey because his memory and the viewer's is the thread of causality that links each day's events. In the end, it is the repetition of cause and effect within each day that transforms what Phil has originally desired and that provides him with his real goal – not just to make Rita love him but to learn how to live and how to love. By "doing," Phil actually changes his "being." And so, ironically, although his initial goal is to manipulate *others*, Phil ends up changing *himself*. In the process he changes the world of his own making and reinstates the arrow of irreversibility. Until the next time we watch the film . . .

CHAPTER 8

BIG (1988)
Body and Soul/"Hearts and Souls"

"Oh grow up!" – an all too common criticism of fantasy film. But, as with all wishes, the words betray themselves. In *Big* a little boy wants to grow up too soon and, through the ministrations of magic, the genre replies to its critics with a charming riposte. Twelve-year-old Josh's wish is granted and he awakens the next morning to find his body magically transformed into that of an adult. Like Phil in *Groundhog Day*, Josh rises from bed to experience a fantasy interlude requiring no special effects. Fading to and from black simulates the process of sleeping and waking, as the young Josh (David Moscow) miraculously awakens in the body of a grown man (Tom Hanks). Fearing he will be late for school, the adult-sized Josh desperately attempts to force himself into a pair of child-sized jeans. Hanks is hilarious as he cavorts frantically about the room, eventually plunging off camera with a thud as his adult-sized legs fail to fit into the diminutive trousers. While Josh's body is outwardly replaced with that of a grown man, however, he carries within him a playful spirit that challenges the cynicism of adulthood and ultimately celebrates childhood itself.

Like Dorothy in *Wizard*, Josh's wish precipitates an adventure that almost immediately evokes nostalgia. When Josh's mother (Mercedes Ruehl) fails to recognize him, it recalls the moment in *It's a Wonderful Life* when George Bailey's mother doesn't know her own son, one of a series of encounters that finally compels George to return back home. In *Big*, by contrast, the mother's rejection is an opening complication that *expels* Josh from his home, assuring that he cannot return until his wish to become little again is granted.

As with so many protagonists in fantasy film, Josh (Tom Hanks) is effectively orphaned. Without parents or a home, Josh makes his way to his own Emerald City, here the Big Apple, where, like Dorothy, he learns that much of the apparent wisdom and authority of adults is illusory. Against all odds, Josh finds a job at a toy company, a surrogate father in his new boss, Mr MacMillan (Robert Loggia), and a mother replacement/ girlfriend in coworker Susan (Elizabeth Perkins).

Big plays off of the ghost film convention that the body is only a shell. The audience knows that Josh is really a child, but those around him are misled by his body's outward appearance, which signifies a host of everyday associations, from employee and coworker to potential love interest. Yet to the audience and his best friend, Billy (Jared Rushton), Josh is a doubled presence. Josh is both boy *and* man, a physical representation of the infamous "Peter Pan syndrome" discussed in earlier chapters. Outwardly, he's "grown," but emotionally, he hasn't "grown up." The disjuncture is humorously conveyed through a number of scenes in which Hanks' tall adult body dwarfs that of his best friend as they pal around and engage in childish pleasures. We can imagine that other characters might temporarily mistake Josh as an older brother or father to Billy. But Josh's actions and Hanks' brilliant performance as a child/man successfully undercut the impression of adulthood that his large body signifies. Josh exudes childish delight but also exhibits the type of single-minded absorption that characterizes kids engaged in imaginative pursuits. The image of a grown man gleefully blowing silly string out of his nose or seeming to take quite seriously a physical tussle with a large inflatable dinosaur are just some of the many humorous and memorable scenes that help convince us that Josh is really just a kid. And Hanks' body language is unmistakably boyish as he repeatedly fidgets with an abundance of boyish energy and pokes and punches Billy in typical adolescent rough-housing. Later in the film he finds himself embarrassed by Susan's desire to discuss their relationship. He resorts to feebly and childishly punching her when he is unable to respond to her questions. Susan: "How do you feel about all this?" Josh: "How do I feel about what?" Susan: "How do you feel about me? Josh snorts: "What is *that* supposed to mean?" Josh is so immature and inexperienced that he doesn't even "get" the question. As in movies such as *Teen Wolf* (1985), the transformation of Josh's body can be read metaphorically as the frightening change that occurs during adolescence when the body appears to be adult but the mind and emotions are still not fully mature.

Josh's inability to understand the adult world, and the adults' tendency to (mis)read his childlike views as mordantly refreshing commentary, recall a number of recent films such as *Being There* (1979), *Dumb and Dumber* (1994) and *Bill & Ted's Excellent Adventure* (1989). In these movies, doubled meanings make for funny situations. When Josh interviews for a job, he is asked about his schooling, which he innocently identifies as "George Washington." The interviewer responds knowingly, "Oh G.W. My brother-in-law got his doctorate there. Did you pledge?" Josh replies: "Yes. Every morning," playing on the dual meaning of pledging a college fraternity and reciting the pledge of allegiance in elementary school. Needless to say, Josh gets the job. Another double-coded scene takes place in Josh's apartment, in which he has installed not a "double bed," but separate bunk beds. To Josh's apparent surprise, Susan admits that she wants to spend the night with him. Josh: "You mean sleep over?" Susan: "Well, yeah!" Josh: "Well, okay. . . . But I get to be on top!" Doubled meanings and Josh's naïveté in the face of a complicated adult world resonate in one of Hanks' later movies, *Forrest Gump* (1994), where (for example) the clueless title character is naïve enough to believe that the "coons" being kept out of the local school in Alabama are actually raccoons, which, he explains, his own Mama would have just chased off the porch with a broom. Innocent misunderstandings of the adult world also inform a series of child/adult body-switching movies (like *Vice Versa* of the same year and *Freaky Friday*, 1976 and 2003). One of the funniest scenes in *Big* trades on the unsophisticated eating habits of a child compared to the cosmopolitan food tastes of rich adults. At the company party, Josh encounters unknown delicacies, gagging visibly on caviar, his black-coated tongue hanging out unceremoniously as he sputters in disgust. And he quite earnestly attempts to nosh on each kernel of a miniature baby corn, carefully rotating the tiny cob as he meticulously nibbles each row.

Josh's "big" male body is both a positive and negative signifier. At the very outset it invades the domestic space of his home and makes his mother scream for help as she sees what appears to be a strange man in her living room. Her fear (and the humor of the scene) only increases as Josh desperately attempts to prove his identity by pulling his jeans down to show her his birthmark. Not only does his own mother mistake him for some type of sexual pervert, but when Billy first encounters the adult Josh at school, he automatically assumes that this adult stranger is trying to kidnap or molest him. Outside of domestic or grade school contexts, however, Josh's adult male body is welcomed, signifying privilege and competency. Although at first undercut by his hilariously inappropriate clothes choices (including the rhinestone-studded white tux he wears to the company party), he soon finds himself showered with all the bells and whistles of a successful executive, complete with enormous office and a salary that permits him to live in a spectacular and spacious loft. The successful city life portrayed in so many movies of the 1980s is an ambivalent aspiration. In *Wall Street* (1987) and *Working Girl* (1988), for example, it evokes not only success but also *excess* and greed. Likewise, *Big* uses the device of the child in a man's body to showcase glamor and success while simultaneously exposing the shallow and petty attitudes of the corporate world.

Josh's simplicity effortlessly critiques the corporate world without recourse to the reformed cynicism of Phil in *Groundhog Day* or the plot devices of *Harvey* and *E.T.* His essential "playfulness" emerges in ironic contrast to the attitude of his coworkers, who jostle to get ahead of each other but whose market research reveals little insight into how kids actually play with toys. When Mr MacMillan asks him about the results of a marketing report Josh blurts out, "What's a marketing report?" which MacMillan takes to be a rhetorical question connoting insight instead of ignorance. Josh repeatedly but unintentionally helps to endear himself to the boss, assuring his success at the company, while his befuddled coworker Paul (John Heard) seethes with jealousy. Josh's lack of ego and ambition reflect the joy of childhood idleness, where toys and games are nostalgically positioned as the antithesis of ambition, work, and chores. Whereas the work/leisure dichotomy is a fragile concept in *Harvey*, linked as it is to alcohol and an invisible rabbit, here that same tension plays out in a more mainstream arena. We don't all have the "leisure" to avoid work (as Elwood does) and we don't all have a sympathetic (invisible) companion with which to while away the hours. But adults were all kids once – kids who played with toys. Although Josh has to "work" to make his way in the big city, his work is actually play. Thus the work/leisure dichotomy in *Big* is temporarily collapsed and a playful attitude becomes both the antidote to cynicism *and* the path to corporate success.

Josh's loft apartment is filled with toys, and although Susan at first recoils from the setting, she quickly accepts it. After all, these are the trophies of a man with enough money to buy nostalgic objects as expensive signifiers of success. To the audience, though, it's still funny. A rich guy might have a pinball machine, a large-screen TV, and a basketball hoop, but here they're not embellishments – they are the substance of his entire apartment. For Josh, not only is work the same as play but public and private space collapses as Josh does his "work" at home. *Big* opens with Josh playing a computer game in his bedroom, nagged by his mother to finish his chores and take out the garbage, establishing the work/play dichotomy precisely in order to collapse it as Josh's play soon *does* become his daily chore. (The idea is spoofed in *Galaxy Quest*, 1999, when a mother becomes exasperated when her nerdy gamer son won't stop playing his computer game to take out the garbage. Little does she know that he's not playing a game *about* saving the world, he is *actually* saving the world, a reversal of the scenario in *War Games*, 1983, in which a teenager's computer game almost *destroys* the world.)

Josh's metamorphosis funnels him squarely from upper-middle-class, white suburbia into a projected adult life in white corporate culture – a world whose only worries are related to consumption, status, and sex. In this world Josh *sells* kids toys so he himself can *buy* toys like jukeboxes, inflatable dinosaurs, and basketball hoops. And so naturally, Josh finds himself in a toy *store*. The commodification of toys, taken to its logical conclusion in the animated *Toy Story* movies, which Hanks voiced, is the antithesis of childlike joy. In *Miracle on 34th Street*, toys are a vehicle for Macy's department store's profit-making machine, representing the cynical commercialization of Christmas that Kris Kringle must counteract by re-imbuing toys and Christmas with the values of wonder and imagination. In *Big*, however, FAO Schwarz serves not as a symbol of corporate mentality to be overcome, but as the magical locus of the film – a place where play is invited and where Josh models spontaneous play for his boss. (Compare this to the sterility of Toys R Us with its warehouse design, parodied in the *Toy Story* movies, in which stories about toys are equally stories about stores.) At FAO Schwarz, a piano keyboard magically becomes "big," transforming a musical instrument into a toy and turning a toy into a marketing device to appeal to kids and adults alike (both within the film and for the viewers). The dreaded music lessons so often endured by children at their parents' behest, as in *The 5,000 Fingers of Dr T.* (Plate 6), here erupt as a fantasy musical number (Plate 17). As in the musical genre, the sequence exudes utopian promise, reconciling two opposites: piano playing as a chore of repetition and drudgery, "everyday after school," and piano "playing" as an expression of fun and creativity. Josh's exuberant dancing recalls a pre-adolescent boy who can't sit still for piano lessons, but instead uses his entire body to perform what he's learned. The full-body public performance of "Hearts

PLATE 17 *Big* (1988 Gracie Films/Twentieth Century Fox): The dreaded piano lessons redeemed. (Courtesy of Photofest.)

and Souls" and "Chopsticks" becomes a moment of childhood rebellion writ large and, as enthusiastically rendered by Josh and MacMillan, becomes an expression of childhood nostalgically and enthusiastically shared across generations.

Josh's lack of self-consciousness in cavorting around the toy store (ironic because it is precisely his embarrassment about seeming childish that prompts his original wish) is now subject to an adult's selective memory of the wonders of childhood, including piano lessons. By combining child and adult, Josh essentially ratifies both – the reality of the child's world and the appropriateness of an adult's nostalgia for it. Just as the body of Tom Hanks becomes the locus of the boy/man syndrome, it is the body that expresses the playfulness that the movie calls for. From the gross-out snot humor to trampoline antics and full-body piano playing, the grown man's body is transformed into a joyful manifestation of boyhood enacted through successful interactions with commodities. The consumption of toys is confirmed as child-like but not child-ish. It is charming, not immature – an expression of imagination, not acquisitiveness.

That the fantasy genre has often been dismissed as childish or as being the sole purview of children is the ironic outcome of our having split children off into a separate category to begin with. The notion of childhood as a separate state is relatively recent. In pre-modern and medieval contexts (the latter featured in many fantasies), no clear division was made between child and adult, and the binary distinction between work and play did not break down into adult/work and kids/play (Kline, 96–7). But once children were seen as *other* than adult, they were then subject either to dismissal (because not serious or important), or to adult nostalgia (because their "otherness" made childhood seem lost and irrecoverable).

Although Josh succeeds in the adult world, the movie periodically reminds us of the trope of the helpless child in need of protection by showing the hysterical mother and the contrast between safe suburbia and the dangerous "big" city, dramatized by a few nights' adventures in a seedy hotel (unfortunately coded as dangerous in part through negative ethnic stereotypes). As in *Home Alone* (1990), where a child also becomes "effectively" orphaned, the abandoned child scenario in *Big* provokes initial anxiety but soon gives way to adventure and the opportunity for fun. Both films make negligible the father's role, leaving the mother as the nostalgic focus of reunion. In both films, the male child uses toys to succeed in an adult world – in *Home Alone* to fight off hostile intruders and in *Big* to survive in a hostile corporate world. The stock figure of the precocious kid in *Home Alone* and so many other movies derives much of its humor from the idea that kids are "supposed to be" helpless and naïve. But *Big* again allows us to have it both ways. Josh is naïve and scared when he first arrives in the corporate world (thereby affirming the innocence of childhood) but later proves ingenious there.

Despite his success in the workplace, Josh ultimately rejects life in the big city to return to his childhood. He rejects not only the adult world but also an adult's idea of toys. Josh's coworker Paul proposes a toy robot that transforms itself into a building. Whereas in *Wonderful Life*, George's aspirations include building skyscrapers when he grows up, Josh intuitively appreciates their inappropriateness as playthings for kids: once the robot has been transformed into a building, it doesn't "do" anything. Unlike the house/home to which Josh must return, tall buildings represent the adult realm that Josh resists. Like this "toy," Josh has been instantly metamorphosized into something big that imperils the flexibility of a child at play. The building is an empty status symbol, synonymous not with play, but with work. As a corporate icon, the skyscraper is the ultimate phallic symbol and is rejected by Josh, who is not yet ready to become a man.

In many ways, Josh really does get his wish, despite the fact that his bigness is only physical. His supposedly childish and idle computer gaming is ratified by the adult world when his own toy design improves upon the company's best concept (as in *Galaxy Quest*, dramatizing the hope that one's personal obsessions will be validated by others). And Josh does acquire a girlfriend, satisfying his original wish, which was prompted by his desire to impress a girl by braving a carnival ride. But ultimately, Josh repudiates his "premature matriculation" into the adult world through his realization that he is not ready to have a relationship with Susan. While temporarily enthralled with his own bigness and success, he ultimately longs to return home.

Josh's desire to impress a girl is an ironic foreshadowing of the adult world he forsakes, precisely because his motivation for wanting to ride the rollercoaster is pure bluster. When he finally *does* go on a rollercoaster with Susan it is not to *impress* her but to experience the sheer joy of the ride. But in this second visit to a carnival, the childlike joy of riding a rollercoaster gives way to a serious adult dance with Susan, thus marking a second turning point for Josh, simultaneously consummating his wish and reinforcing his desire to reverse it. The amusement park is the perfect illustration of Bakhtin's notion of carnival, a world in which norms are inverted: young becomes old, old becomes young, and social norms are transgressed. In this second encounter at the carnival, old and young meet halfway in a romantic, nearly sexual, and seemingly taboo union. (Similarly, in the 1971 cult classic *Harold and Maude*, an elderly woman and a young man break with age conventions by making love after attending a carnival.)

Just as Josh had originally wanted to prove something by riding the rollercoaster, Paul wants to prove his superiority to Josh by playing a competitive game. Here *Big* acknowledges the slippery connection between games as play and games as competitive rituals to prove manhood. When Paul cheats in their handball game, Josh appeals to his sense of fairness and attempts to prevent Paul from playing further by withholding the ball. This results in a physical scuffle in which Josh gets beaten up, the only way Paul can "win." The scene and its aftermath, in which Josh is soothed by Susan, implies that if Paul is a model for the successful male, then Josh is clearly not ready for manhood. At the same time, Paul's "appalling" behavior shows us that we don't want Josh to be ready for this world. The testosterone-imbued corporate world is a different kind of game altogether, and Josh is out of his league.

In fact, Josh is everything Susan's former boyfriend and coworker Paul is not. He isn't competitive or cynical, he's not macho, and he's not take-control. Throughout the movie, Josh and Paul provide exaggerated contrasts in masculinity, and neither character ultimately changes, despite the fact that in Josh we have yet another variation of the era's "new man."

If Phil in *Groundhog Day* redeems himself in part by adopting the more traditional feminine qualities associated with Rita, here the masculine ideal is transformed through the prism of childhood. The opportunity to model a more appealing type of masculinity arises when Josh and Susan attend a dinner party as a couple. When the male host won't help his kid with his homework, Josh jumps up and offers to help, dramatizing the romantic partner as an ideal husband and engaged father. But for the romance between Josh and Susan to work, it seems that Susan is the one who must undergo the real metamorphosis of the film.

When Susan first encounters Josh, she sees another opportunity for an office romance with the company's latest rising star. Paul alludes to this opportunistic cliché with some bitterness. They seem more like rivals than lovers, vying for the attention of the boss and using their romantic alliance to cement their own success. After the scuffle on the handball court, Josh complains to Susan that Paul shouldn't have punched him. Susan explains that Paul feels threatened because Josh has pulled ahead in the corporation by eschewing all the "usual" conniving tactics: "You're not playing his game," she says, to which Josh replies "I tried to play his game. He beat me up." Here, Josh refers literally to the handball game, not grasping the metaphorical nature of Susan's comment. Instead of fighting back and becoming more like Paul, Josh ends up being mothered by Susan, who tends his wounds and helps to reinstate him as an injured child on the playground, rather than a competitor in a macho sporting event. At the same time, the scene repositions Susan as a nurturer, escaping the limits of her role as competitive executive.

Near the end of the film, Josh's inability to commit to Susan again raises the specter of the stereotypical, immature male. He tries to explain to her that he's really a child, but Susan's heard it all before. He's "not ready to make commitment . . . not ready to accept responsibility." Once again, the humor here depends on the doubled meaning. Josh can't commit – not because he's childish but because he actually *is* a child, reminding us of the lovely joke earlier in the movie when Paul asks Susan why she prefers Josh and she replies emphatically: "He's a *grownup!*"

Despite the fact that Susan is portrayed as a successful career woman, the recovery of her maternal instincts emerges as the "real" transformation in a film whose main character is transformed only on the surface. The film employs traditional gender stereotypes to celebrate boyishness as a desirable aspect of masculinity, but does little to interrogate what this means for femininity. In *Big* (as in life), boys must display their disdain (or shame) if caught in the vicinity of a girl's toy, as Josh illustrates when Billy catches sight of a female doll in his office. And most of the toys featured in the film are coded explicitly as appealing to boys. Besides the scorned doll, the only other reference to girls playing with toys is the comment that girls would never play with bug-transformers unless the bugs were cute "lady"-bugs. For the heterosexual romance to work, Josh must be child-like but not girl-like. Thus the film insists upon "boy"-ish toys, and the physical exuberance associated with boys at play.

In this respect, *Big* is one of many '80s Oedipal comedies (as characterized by Marsha Kinder) in which the son replaces the father and sleeps with his mother surrogate. But the Oedipal conflict is blurred by the temporary nature of the situation: "Such transgression is possible only because the boy doesn't actually replace his own father; he merely wears his father's clothes. The site of Oedipal transgression is displaced from the family to business" (6). Ironically, the fantasy device of allowing child and man to become conflated ultimately serves not so much to erase the distinction between childhood and adulthood as to reinforce that very rift. Josh's success as an adult, followed by his choice to return to childhood, expresses a longstanding tension between the desire for kids to mature (or be precocious) and the accompanying fear that kids may be growing up too fast, becoming "pre-maturely adult" (Buckingham, 35).

Big collapses the work/play dichotomy through toys, and the child/ adult dichotomy through the body of Josh. But by returning Josh to his childhood home, the film ultimately re-inscribes childhood as a separate, sacred time to be celebrated. Paradoxically, then, the movie argues for a more playful, less cynical adult world (complete with the consumption of toys for all ages), but it does so through reinvesting these values squarely and nostalgically in childhood. Creating and maintaining that distinction is the ultimate "work" of *Big*.

CHAPTER 9

SHREK (2001)
Like an Onion

Once upon a time there was a man who would be king. His name was Walt. He lived in the magic kingdom of Disney and ruled the world of animation with his fairy-tale stories lovingly marketed as wholesome family fare. The kingdom thrived until Walt died and his empire seemed to lose its bearings, at which point the Disney corporation looked into its magic mirror and realized it was no longer the fairest in the land. (Of course, many critics would charge that Disney had been anything but "fair" in its business operations – but that's a tale for another day.) By the 1960s, Disney's old-fashioned stories failed to work their magic in a cynical world. But happily, fairy tales always end well. Beginning in the 1980s, Disney aggressively updated both its stories and its business model, innovating with a mixture of computer animation and live action in pioneering films like *Tron* (1982) and *Who Framed Roger Rabbit* (1988). Ten years later it teamed up with rival Pixar to make the blockbuster *Toy Story* (1995). *Toy Story* was the first of a new generation of 3-D computer-generated stories that provided family fare appealing to children but also layered with adult jokes and clever intertextual references that older viewers appreciated.

Shrek, produced by Disney rival Dreamworks, continues in this tradition, cementing a trend in sophisticated, funny entertainment, rife

PLATE 18 *Shrek* (2001 Dreamworks): Beauty and the beast(s) – not your usual suspect(s). (Courtesy of Photofest.)

with *double entendres* and multiple levels of meaning reminiscent of cheeky television programs like *The Simpsons* (1989–) (Plate 18). In *Shrek* the title character nicely captures this self-reference when he describes himself as a complex character with many layers – "like an onion." Although it won the very first Oscar for an Animated Feature with its superb 3-D animation, *Shrek* is also known for putting a new spin on some old fairy-tale conventions. The movie riffs on all kinds of recognizable characters such as The Gingerbread Man, who responds to threats of torture with the taunt: "Eat me!" Much of the humor throughout the film derives from imagining fairy-tale elements in contemporary settings. The Three Blind Mice wander around with dark glasses and canes, and The Magic Mirror reflects bad television with a send-up of *The Dating Game* – Snow White may *live* with seven other men but "she's not easy!"

As a spoof of fairy tales, *Shrek* does more than just make a lot of jokes, it also exposes the underlying gender codes that form the very structure of the tales. While including scores of references to fairy tales and pop culture, the whole point of *Shrek* is to invert the traditions embedded in Disney versions of *Sleeping Beauty*, *Snow White*, *Cinderella*, and *Beauty and the Beast*. Adapted from William Steig's 1990 book *Shrek*, the movie also follows in a tradition of comedic films and stories of the last few decades such as William Goldman's splendid *The Princess Bride* (1987). British writer Angela Carter wrote many revisionist tales, including the collection *The Bloody Chamber and Other Stories* (1979), which features two rewrites of *Beauty and the Beast*. As in *Shrek*, one of these, "The Tiger's Bride," ends with the revelation that the heroine, Beauty, is really a tiger and thus just as beastly as the Beast. None of Carter's critically acclaimed works have enjoyed much big-screen success (with the possible exception of her werewolf tales, adapted by Neil Jordan in 1984 as the fantasy/horror film *The Company of Wolves*). Nevertheless, Hollywood has found a taste for funny fairy tales, producing two successful *Shrek* sequels (2004, 2007), as well as a host of other revisionist takes on the form – some animated (*Hoodwinked*, 2005), some live-action (*Stardust*, 2007), and some a mixture of the two (*Enchanted*, 2007).

Fairy tales and the oral folk tales from which they sprang once served a positive, communal function. Noted scholar Jack Zipes has written extensively about fairy tales, both old and new, explaining their longevity and tracing their evolution from oral folk traditions to print literature and ultimately to film. Zipes finds fault with most modern fairy tales, especially Disney's. In fact Zipes' book *Why Fairy Tales Stick* might just as well be entitled "Why Fairy Tales *Stink*." In contrast to Bruno Bettelheim's defense of the form in his analysis of children and fairy tales, Zipes and many others criticize most contemporary versions, accusing them of being more about technical skills and marketing than about imagination and wonder. Worse, many of Disney's classics are considered to be sexist and racist, a troubling observation indeed given Disney's dominance as a purveyor of family entertainment around the world. For example, racial stereotypes appear in a number of animated films, such as the black, jive-talking crows in *Dumbo* (1941), but also in the more recent *Aladdin* (1992), where the Middle Eastern merchant Jafar is characterized as savage, and in *The Lion King* (1994), where the "demented and dangerous" hyenas are coded black (Byrne and McQuillan, 100). Male characters are privileged as active and effectual heroes, as in *Snow White* (1937), while "good" female characters such as Snow White, Cinderella, and Ariel in *The Little Mermaid* (1989) are defined by their virginal beauty and passivity (Zipes 1994, 87–91). Overt sexuality is dangerous in females and is often characterized by jealousy of younger women (Bell, 107–24). Bad females are also likely to be ugly, as in *Sleeping Beauty* (1959), where Maleficent's green skin and pointy chin recall the Wicked Witch of the West. Against this backdrop, many critics applaud *Shrek* for its challenge to the forms that have bound Disney to antiquated social mores.

Shrek begins deconstructing fairy-tale conventions from its very first moments, as a storybook opens to the phrase: "Once upon a time." These are the magic words that for fairy tales serve as the equivalent of doors, wardrobes, or rabbit holes, beckoning us into another world. Storybooks as introduction or framing device are used in many other fairy-tale films, including *Sleeping Beauty* and *The Princess Bride*. In *Shrek*, the stylized storybook offers illustrations of turreted castles and dragons while a voice recounts the story of a princess who must be rescued from her tower by a brave knight. Once the knight has slain the dragon he'll then release the princess from her curse by giving her love's first kiss. They will then live happily ever after. "Like that's ever gonna happen," scoffs the narrator. As a hand rips the page out of the book we pull back to meet Shrek, an ogre who uses the happy ending for his own end(s) – as toilet paper. The raucous Smashmouth "All Star" anthem then erupts as the opening credits feature a humorous montage of the joyfully disgusting life of an ogre.

Shrek has no intention of rescuing any princesses. He's a contented bachelor who wants nothing more than to be left alone (and to occasionally scare the bejeebers out of those idiots with the pitchforks). But as with all reluctant movie heroes, Shrek soon finds himself on a mission to fulfill the romantic knightly quest. It seems that the puny Lord Farquaad wishes to marry the lovely Princess Fiona, but is too cowardly to rescue her himself. Effectively blackmailed by Farquaad's ethnic cleansing, which sends fairy-tale characters to seek refuge at Shrek's idyllic stinkhole, Shrek is forced to take on the task and so finds himself thrust into the hero's role. The film features many irreverent and unflattering references to Disney and Disneyland associated with Farquaad and his kingdom Duloc, including a parody of Disney's song "It's a Small World" that stops just short of being truly "cheeky," continuing the potty humor from the opening sequence ("Please keep off the *grass*, Shine your shoes, wipe your . . . *face*."). Duloc is unmistakably modeled on Disneyland itself, with its turreted castle, and its meticulously clean and orderly streets. As with Disneyland, too, Duloc requires that visitors queue up in a zigzagged rope line before passing through a turnstile.

As Shrek faces his new task, he becomes the incongruous hero of the very fairy-tale story he has previously rejected. Drawing on Vladimir Propp, Zipes explains that in fairy tales the main character is "*as-signed* a task, and the task is a *sign*. That is, his or her character will be stereotyped and marked by the task that is his or her sign" (2006, 49). *Shrek* acknowledges these assignments but subverts them to create an unusual "assignation" – an unconventional love affair. As an ogre, Shrek's assignment is to be ugly, evil, and scary, and he largely fulfills this mission with his super-sized, green body, bulbous nose, and protruding ears. True, Shrek appreciates the grosser things in life, demonstrated early on as he is seen making dining room candles from his own ear wax and eating a variety of disgusting food. But in fairy tales, appearances can deceive. Underneath all those smelly layers, he's actually a nice guy. He understands that at least part of his "ogre-ness" is just a role he is playing and he has to remind the stunned villagers of *their* role: "This is the part where you run away."

As a princess, Fiona's as-sign-ment is to await love's first kiss, but she, too, knows she is playing a prescribed role. Locked in the requisite tower, Fiona resembles many other Disney princesses, with her pretty pert face, tiny waist, pale skin, and flowing gown. Pretending to be asleep in true Sleeping Beauty style, complete with a hastily arranged bouquet of flowers clutched to her chest, Fiona composes herself to await the promised event. In his uncomfortable new role as hero, Shrek arrives in his not-so-shiny armor and, much to Fiona's disappointment, fails to deliver the kiss or act in a courtly way. Fiona expresses indignation that Shrek's not following the script properly: "What are you doing?" "But this isn't right!" Apparently, somebody didn't get the memo – or else they flushed it.

The fairy-tale formula is further derailed when Shrek removes his armor and Fiona learns that her prince charming is actually a big ugly ogre. But the ogre as love interest is not a particularly revisionist aspect of the film. A beautiful woman and a monstrous male are paired in *Beauty and the Beast* as well as numerous other folk and fairy tales (Warner). In *Beauty and the Beast*, Belle's love eventually redeems the Beast, turning him back into the handsome prince he once was. But in *Shrek*, Fiona is cursed to turn into an ogre every night when the sun goes down. Breaking with convention, it is not just Shrek, but the princess, who is the beast in this tale. Furthermore, although Fiona appears at first to follow her assignment as a sheltered and helpless love object, she soon proves that this is all a charade. She is actually a skilled fighter, a good hunter, and a good sport: the "sign" of the princess is a sham.

Providing a narrative delay and extending our last handhold on convention, Fiona's insistence on nocturnal privacy reads like a romantic device in situation comedy. The clash of this couple, like that in classic romantic and screwball comedies, arises because the hero and lady come from opposite worlds (upper vs lower class) and/or because their personalities seem to be diametrically opposed. Reminiscent of the characters in *It Happened One Night* (1934), Fiona is introduced as the spoiled rich girl while Shrek is the not-so-sophisticated lower-class guy. These tensions assure that they spend time sparring with one another rather than falling too quickly into one another's arms. When Fiona demands that they stop for the night and find shelter in a cave, it recalls the familiar opposition between pampered female and rugged, no-frills male. But the give and take becomes ever more flirtatious as the characters gradually prove their worth and demonstrate their compatibility with one another. Shrek is not the "monster" she first thought, and Fiona is not the helpless female he supposed. He turns out to be a good cook (barbecue, naturally), and Fiona is not spoiled or prissy as Shrek assumed she'd be. When their mutual admiration finally turns into love, we're saved from schmaltz with parodies of the clichéd romance montage by way of ogre-inflected humor. They romp in verdant fields, of course, but they sweetly gift each other with candy floss made out of bug-filled spider webs and animal balloons made out of snakes and frogs.

Fairy tales and screwball comedies also share a love of false appearances. In the latter, characters frequently disguise their identities or engage in some type of masquerade, including adopting fake accents (McDonald, 24). Although Fiona still looks like a princess, she gradually drops her affected way of speaking. In the beginning of the film when she believes that Shrek is a valiant knight, she says: "I would'st look upon the face of my rescuer." Later, when accosted by Robin Hood, she snarls: "Look pal, I don't know who you think you are!"

As with most screwball or romantic comedies, the developing romance is initially thwarted by a false identity and by the misunderstandings that arise from it. When Fiona reveals to Donkey that she turns into an ogre every night, she despairs that she is too ugly to be loved: " . . . who could ever love a beast so hideous and ugly? 'Princess' and 'ugly' don't go together." Shrek overhears and believes she is referring to him and that she could never love him. If Shrek thinks that a princess could never love an ugly man, he certainly doesn't understand fairy-tale conventions (from The Frog Prince to Beauty and the Beast, overcoming superficial appearance has been a hallmark of the princess persona). Fiona, on the other hand, is correct. An ugly princess is an oxymoron in the fairy-tale world.

The title of Beauty and the Beast illustrates the functional and defining conflation of femininity with appearance since "Beauty" is not just a description, but the character's actual name ("Belle" in the French and Disney versions). In traditional fairy tales such as Cinderella and Sleeping Beauty, the princess must be passive, obedient, and hard working but, above all, beautiful. Ugly women are evil by definition, as illustrated by

Cinderella's stepmother and sisters, the evil stepmother in *Snow White*, and Maleficent in *Sleeping Beauty*. Zipes explains that in the earliest versions of fairy tales, when a female character was described as "beautiful," physical details were rarely provided. Rather, beautiful simply meant that the character was well mannered and compliant. When mass-mediated versions of the stories provided visual representations of the characters, however, a certain body type became associated with beauty (Zipes 1994, 75 and 2004). Disney in particular has played an enormous role in shaping our idea of what a woman should look like and has helped to perpetuate the idea that all girls should aspire to be princess-like: a woman should be youthful and slim but not athletic, more childlike than womanly, and always graceful and gracious. She should have smooth "alabaster" skin, and long flowing hair, echoed by a long flowing dress. She won't be allowed much talking, but mellifluous singing is permitted and even encouraged (soft rock, OK – heavy metal, not so much).

The importance of beauty to femininity is underscored in *Snow White* when the evil stepmother becomes jealous of the heroine and wishes to harm her simply because she is younger and more beautiful, a classic narrative drawn from ancient sources like Apuleius' *Cupid and Psyche*, where the goddess Venus is jealous of a mortal woman's beauty. This pernicious ideology is replayed in the live-action *Stardust* (2007), where Lamia (Michelle Pfeiffer) attempts to kill a young woman Yvaine (Claire Danes) in order to become young and beautiful again.

The cult of the beautiful and helpless princess is not confined to the big screen but has permeated US culture for years. In her 1981 book *The Cinderella Complex*, Colette Dowling argues that girls are socialized to be dependent and passive, waiting for a man to come along and define their existence. And Jennifer Waelti-Walters sees fairy tales that perpetuate these ideas as providing "the first steps in the maintenance of misogynous sex-role stereotyped patriarchy" (quoted in Kelley). Ramin Setoodeh and Jennie Yabroff have written about Disney's Princess line of clothes, accessories, and housewares. In 2000, this $4 billion business was originally aimed at children but now also targets grown women. Wedding gowns designed by Disney are designed to resemble those of its princesses, like Belle's dress in *Beauty and the Beast*. Disney's *Enchanted* tries to update the princess role by poking fun at the saccharine-sweet qualities of its traditional princesses and by having Giselle (Amy Adams) shed these when she accidentally leaves the animated and enters the "real" world. But the film belies its notionally revisionist mission by linking her transformation to a shopping spree during which she modernizes her real-world feminine image by buying new clothes. Oh the magic of credit cards.

Ogre-ness is equated with masculinity in *Shrek* just as beastliness is in *Beauty and the Beast*. But the latter tale is not just about looking beyond the superficiality of appearances. The eighteenth-century versions of the story center on the female's need to accept an arranged marriage. The Beast is not just an enchanted aberration, he is the physical manifestation of the sexual brute that informs the masculine ideal. The young woman must learn to love the beastly husband to whom she has been given in marriage by her father. In learning to love the beast, the story is a vehicle for "redeeming the brute in the man" (Warner, 297). One only has to compare the beastly but loveable Shrek to Lord Farquaad to see how the latter is designed to be an emasculated and therefore unacceptable model for Fiona. His simpering voice, his short stature, and his pampered, prissy lifestyle are all counterpoised to essential qualities of the "real" man in the story, who happens to be big, dirty, smelly, and emotionally unaware. Now that's a man! In *Shrek 2*, the Fairy Godmother's son, Prince Charming, serves the same purpose as Farquaad – he has long blond hair, takes way too much pleasure in his own appearance, and even wears glittery lip gloss – the "kiss" of death for his relationship with Fiona.

So while *Shrek* inverts many fairy-tale conventions, it doesn't neces-sarily subvert cultural norms. Fiona becomes more like Shrek, but Shrek doesn't change much, a point Fiona brings up in *Shrek 2* when Shrek attempts to defend his boorish behavior by reminding her that he's an ogre and "that's not about change." This seems consistent with the real world, where it is (finally) acceptable for women to be like men, but is still taboo for men to exhibit qualities associated with women. When they do, they must have an alibi (as in *Always*, *Big*, and *Spider-Man*) or they will be ridiculed like Farquaad and Prince Charming for being "inadequate," or slotted into a homosexual niche. Shrek is not a subversive character in this regard. He is merely as-signed the traditional role of masculinity. Furthermore, while it may seem that the film promotes the message that appearance isn't important, it's hard to buy the conceit that Fiona is so scary ugly when she's in her ogre mode. Besides a little green tinge, she looks much like an ordinary, comfortably plump woman. What's wrong with that? Just as Belle and the audience love the Beast as much *because* of his beastliness as in spite of it, it never really was about what Shrek looked like. The assignment for beauty is all Fiona's. And if you happen to look like Fiona, what you get is an ogre.

Fiona's assignment to be beautiful is inverted, but Donkey's "ass"-signment, literally to be an ass, is not surprising. The donkey, a traditional character in folk tales, serves as a fool who also exposes the foolishness of other characters. "The animal most closely associated with merriment and folly is the ass; but paradoxically, donkeys are also the beasts most endowed with powers of divination and wisdom in fairy and folklore" (Warner, 136). A rich tradition stretches back through Shakespeare's Bottom, pursued by a powerful female, Titania, in *A Midsummer Night's Dream* (just as Donkey is wooed by an intimidating she-dragon), and before that to the man-turned-donkey in Apuleius' *The Golden Ass* (also called *The Metamorphoses*, second century CE), and featuring within it the tale of *Cupid and Psyche* (Warner, 145).

Although Donkey is the source (and the "butt") of many of jokes, he also expresses a kind of folk wisdom (mostly pop psychology) that reflects the subtext of the movie. Shrek may be an ogre by birth, but he's not really much of a monster. He's a lot more like one of those TV sitcom guys, a clueless, sometimes gruff teddy bear who needs to lose a few pounds (*The Honeymooners, King of Queens, Roseanne*, etc.). He's not known for his refined manners – he eats disgusting food, burps, and scratches himself, and seems oblivious to emotional and personal hygiene. He's not romantic, but he's basically a nice guy. Donkey's role is to pierce through all those layers of masculinity (ogre-ness) to help Shrek integrate better with other people, including women.

Eddie Murphy's hilarious Donkey is a highlight of the film, and his voice is immediately recognizable. Familiar voices are part of the pleasure for adult audiences of animated films, particularly when the stars' on-screen and off-screen personas permeate the animated character, as in *Aladdin*, where Robin Williams' improvisational humor infuses the Genie with his own comic genius. *Shrek*'s all-star cast is plainly advertised during the "All Star"-themed opening – we know we're going to be spending time with Mike Meyers, Eddie Murphy, Cameron Diaz, and John Lithgow. (Note, by contrast, that Disney often gave minimal if any credit to voice actors, preferring instead to feature his own name prominently.)

It's not easy being green. Just ask Kermit, the Wicked Witch of the West, the Hulk, the Green Goblin, and others whose greenness signals not All Stars but "out-casts." But what about being black? The use of Eddie Murphy's voice for Shrek's donkey side-kick is reminiscent of many live-action buddy movies in which a white male star (in this case Mike Myers) is paired with a black partner, as in *Lethal Weapon* (1987) or *Die Hard* (1988). But the role of Donkey risks being implicitly racist as Murphy's exaggerated jive lingo recalls the "Jim Crows" in *Dumbo* and creates a comic but subservient and parasitic character. Although Donkey makes a funny sidekick for Shrek, his role is partly funny because it subverts the convention that the prince will arrive on a stately white horse. Donkey is not stately – he's short, stocky, and rather ungainly. And he sure as heck ain't white, further underscoring the contrast in racial terms.

Mulan (1998) exemplifies a more modern style of Disney film and has been rightly praised for revising gender stereotypes. But *Mulan* also features a character very similar to Donkey and also voiced by Eddie Murphy. Karen Durbin describes the dragon Mushu as "something of a flimflam artist and – a staple of Disney's contemporary animated features – an ethnic joker who supplies the hero with a comic foil. . . . In this case the ethnicity [is] . . . very black, very street and very motor mouth." But as Angela Aleiss notes, while Disney has begun to include a more ethnically diverse mix of characters into its animated stories (in *The Lion King*, the hyena is voiced by Whoopi Goldberg, etc.), an exploration of the black experience has been sorely lacking. Yes, Eddie Murphy supplies a black voice, but the characters are not themselves black, reflecting the more or less "snow white" tradition established by Disney. (One notable exception is Jethro, voiced by Danny Glover in Dreamwork's *The Prince of Egypt*, 1998.) After saving Fiona from the dragon, Shrek goes to help Donkey, explaining, "Well, I have to save my ass." While Donkey is necessarily the "butt" of the Shrek's jokes, the performance is reminiscent of the Stepin Fetchit stereotype as Donkey bobs and weaves his way through the movie, avoiding hard work and sucking up to Shrek. And he is never given a real name, just Donkey. While Fiona's plump, non-white body is a source of pleasure and pride at the end of *Shrek*, in *Norbit* (2007) Murphy plays a woman with a (very) plump, non-white body which is nothing but a source of derision. This time the woman is black, not green, and the entire movie is an endless series of fat jokes made at the expense of women. "She is mean because she is fat. She is fat because she's mean" (Pols). It's not easy being green, but try being fat and black. Well, as in fairy tales we should know that appearances are never what they seem.

As a so-called "revisionist" fairy tale, perhaps *Shrek* is not what *it* seems. After peeling back some of the layers, we find that it's not quite as progressive as it appears. Just like Shrek himself, *Shrek* the movie is like an onion. It doesn't stink – in fact it's quite loveable on many levels. But its many layers of comedy and its engagement with racial and gender stereotypes flavor a rich stew of ideas for both critics and viewers alike.

CHAPTER 10

SPIDER-MAN (2002)
The Karmic Web

Heroes with superhuman powers have been with us since the most ancient of myths and the oldest chimerical imaginings. Comic-book character Billy Batson invokes the name of the wizard who taught him to transform himself into Captain Marvel by saying the magic word "Shazam!" – a word that forms an acronym for the legendary characters from whom he derives his superhero strength: Solomon, Hercules, Atlas, Zeus, Achilles, and Mercury. And as with many mythical figures, heroes like Spider-Man claim their power by breaching the ontological divide between human and animal to become superhuman. The birth and development of comic books draws from this deep well but also represents a distinct and uniquely modern subgenre of fantasy and the formulation of a new kind of hero. With mythical roots and a modern context, an important aspect of the comic-book superhero genre is its tie to science fiction, which surfaced in reaction to the Industrial Age and became widely popular with young audiences in pulp magazines and comic books in the 1930s. Many comic-book superheroes are "super" precisely because of scientific or quasi-scientific origin stories. Superman comes from an alien planet, Captain America derives his special abilities from the effects of an experimental serum, and the X-Men's diverse superpowers are the result of genetic mutations. And Spider-Man is no exception. Peter Parker's abilities stem from a genetically engineered spider that bites him on a high-school field trip. So does that make *Spider-Man* a science-fiction film? After all, Peter is gifted at science in both the movie and the original comic and his nemesis, Norman Osborn (aka the Green Goblin), goes insane after taking an experimental formula to create a super-soldier.

Although this reminds us again that fantasy movies often draw from more than one generic tradition, the recent *Spider-Man* movies lean heavily toward fantasy. In the *Spider-Man* films the science-fiction elements serve mostly as a pretext for a predominantly fantasy scenario. First and foremost, Peter's scientific acumen signifies his profound nerdiness, a pivotal aspect of his character that overshadows any scientific skills he displays. We might compare Peter's transformation to that of Tony Stark in *Iron Man* (2008). In that film (whose science-fiction elements turn increasingly more fantasy as the story progresses), Stark (Robert Downey Jr) employs his scientific genius to build a robotic, superhuman suit. A substantial portion of the opening act of the movie is devoted to this process and to the special effects associated with the technology. And in the original *Spider-Man* comic book, Peter designs a *mechanical* device that allows him to shoot webbing from his wrists. But in *Spider-Man*, the movie, Peter Parker (Tobey Maguire) goes to bed with a spider bite and wakes up to find himself inexplicably transformed (more like Josh in *Big* than Tony Stark in *Iron Man*). Just as in *Star Wars* Luke Skywalker's light saber owes as much to magic as to science, Peter's ability to spin webs, climb walls, and leap from building to building is more a magical gift he must learn to harness than a scientific or technological achievement. The purely fantasy quality of Peter's new persona is further reinforced when he initially attempts to "force" his web-slinging capabilities. Instead of appealing to scientific or physical principles, he spouts lines from (other) comic books, including Captain Marvel's magic word "Shazam!" And like Luke, Peter succeeds *not* when he understands the physical process, but when he stops over-thinking the technique. Throughout the movie, Peter/Spider-Man appears to call on a special inner reserve which causes the spider webbing to emanate magically and directly from his wrists (Plate 19).

Peter does apply some skill to his new persona when he creates his Spider-Man suit, but the endeavor is as much artistic as it is technical. Although he makes his own costume, the emphasis is not on Peter stitching together or "building" the suit (as in *Iron Man*), but on *designing* it. Lest we fear that being a costume designer is not masculine enough for a male superhero, Peter is shown *drawing* versions of Spider-Man's

PLATE 19 *Spider-Man* (2002 Columbia): Spider-Man's web – a "force" to be reckoned with. (Courtesy of Photofest.)

persona as if he were, himself, a comic-book artist. Thus, his superhero identity is not just an extension of his physical nature, it is also a product of his imaginative faculties. Furthermore, the necessity of creating a special costumed identity is the direct result of Peter's fantasy of owning a car in order to win the affections of his neighbor and classmate, Mary Jane Watson (Kirsten Dunst). His method of fulfilling this psychological fantasy is . . . pure fantasy! He intends to compete in a professional wrestling match, a highly theatrical activity involving masks and costumes in the service of a male empowerment scenario. Costumes and masks are traditionally associated with theater and carnivals where citizens disguise themselves in revelry and debauchery, temporarily reversing the rules of society (a phenomenon, as noted above, investigated by scholars like Bakhtin). Peter's bright-red costume is nothing if not theatrical and carnivalesque, with its stylized web pattern covering him *almost* from head to toe, but leaving a lovely lycra-clad leg gap that creates the requisite superhero "go-go" boots (*à la* Superman and Batman).

Of course, professional wrestling is a kind of carnival version of the sports world. Unlike legitimate sports competitions, where rules are meant to be followed, in professional wrestling the "rules" are repeatedly broken and "more than not, the bad guy wins. Referees are powerless to prevent the villain's humiliation and degradation of the helpless victim" (J.W. Campbell). This sets the "stage" for the fantasy world of the superhero film, where exaggerated good and evil will compete through outlandish spectacle and hyper-athletic stunts. But it also establishes the context for the emergence of superheroes in general by mirroring the inherent injustice of the real world and the ineffectiveness of authority in the face of evil. This is precisely the type of world that Spider-Man will have to contend with and is the very reason that superheroes are necessary. For, as Lawrence and Jewett argue, it is the job of the superhero to step in where traditional authority has proved ineffective (7–8).

The wrestling arena epitomizes an ultra-male, ultra-macho world. If milquetoast Peter Parker can win here, then he is indeed a superhero and a "real" man worthy of Mary Jane's attention. But it becomes clear from the outset that the game is fixed. Professional wrestling "masquerades as a competitive sport, but it is not. The results are pre-determined and the participants adopt personalities and characters that may well not be their own, but the result of the imaginations of script writers" (Pratten). And this "script" includes a constant violation of its own purported rules, as Peter soon learns when he finds himself unexpectedly locked in a cage with no way to escape his formidable opponent. Luckily, Peter has superhuman powers, providing an unexpected turn of events for the spectators. While at first they taunt Peter, the crowd ends up cheering him, signaling his spectacular triumph and ratifying his new identity in the underdog-turned-hero script that will dominate the rest of the film.

Just as wrestling is carnivalesque in its excessive spectacle and its lack of sportsmanlike conduct, Peter's advantage is that he himself is now part of the carnival and subsequently turns expectations upside down. He is the complete opposite of his solid, sweaty, and brutish opponent, Bone Saw (played by wrestling champion Randy "Macho Man" Savage). Spider-Man's mysterious full-body costume, his slender build, and his acrobatic skills recall a circus performer, and they give Peter a unique advantage as he turns the prison/cage into a virtual spider web, perfectly suited to his unique abilities to fling his entire body dramatically from one end of the cage to another. It's as if a circus acrobat challenged the strong man to a trapeze competition. No contest – Spider-Man excels in "flying," a persistent trope of fantasy.

That Peter has expected this match to be a legitimate sports competition further establishes him as a nerd and a rube within the movie's logic. But the desire to compete in this arena handily motivates his desire for a theatrical costume in a story set in a quasi-realistic, present-day New York (unlike the fictional cities of Batman's Gotham or Superman's

Metropolis). And his triumph occurs in the context of wrestling's dialectic of suffering and retribution. As Roland Barthes argues, the injustice and rule-breaking of wrestling is integral to the sense of justice enjoyed by the audience when roles reverse and "pay back" is delivered (22). The professional wrestling phenomenon creates a parallel to the experience of the film itself. By letting the outsider/underdog win, even in an arena where everything is scripted, the movie establishes the ground of its own illusion. The flamboyant artifice of the costumes and exaggerated action is pure spectacle, an extension of the body's "total signifying function" in the drama, like the special effects designed to titillate and thrill in disaster and science-fiction films.

Peter, however, is not triumphant. The rules shift yet again as he learns that he will not receive the full amount of prize money due to a technicality in the wording of the challenge. (Ironically, the chronically late Peter wins the match *before* the time limit is up, establishing one of the many qualities that will define Spider-Man as Peter's opposite.) When he protests, the wrestling promoter's comment once again links the lawlessness of the wrestling arena to the world outside the ring: "I missed the part where that's my problem." But what comes around goes around. Right after robbing Peter of his rightful winnings, the promoter (Larry Goodman) is himself robbed. Peter now succumbs to this "pay back" mentality, snidely throwing the man's words back at him and allowing the robber (Michael Papajohn) to escape. In doing so, Peter unwittingly contributes to an environment in which Spider-Man's skills will be required – a world where everybody cheats and nobody cares. And so . . . what comes around *keeps* going around. As a result of his bad attitude, Peter's Uncle Ben (Cliff Robertson) is murdered by the very same robber.

The wrestling episode, followed by the robbery and his uncle's death, is an important sequence because it addresses Spider-Man's motivation and answers a question relevant to all superheroes: If a superhero can have anything he wants, "why does he spend nearly all his time taking care of others?" (Morris and Morris, 6). Whereas *The Lord of the Rings* questions the desire for power, a related but opposite question regards its potential for good. *Spider-Man* asks and answers this question early on. Peter had hoped to exploit his powers to win money to buy a car and impress Mary Jane. But he is wracked by guilt and haunted by his uncle's words: "With great power comes great responsibility." Even in the face of rampant injustice and indifference, the film suggests a kind of invisible but karmic "web" connecting each person's actions to everybody else's. Peter now has a compelling reason for doing the right thing and he then assumes the burden of his powers. (This "karmic web" recalls the cause-and-effect thematic in *Groundhog Day*, echoed physically by the characters' pre-set movements throughout the town, where altering any given character's trajectory – whether physical or metaphorical – has the potential to change everything.)

Spider-Man's motivation for shouldering his responsibility for his powers is important because, unlike Batman and Superman's endorsement by the authorities (Wright, 184), he operates on his own, making him the object of suspicion. When J. Jonah Jameson (J.K. Simmons), the editor of *The Daily Bugle*, accuses Spider-Man of being a vigilante, he's not just exploiting the phenomenon to sell papers. He also exposes the shadow potential of all superheroes (Lawrence and Jewett, 40). Do we really want citizens, especially *masked* citizens, taking the law into their own hands? Visions of the Ku Klux Klan come to mind. (In fact, *The Watchmen*, 2009, a dark and violent movie, explicitly characterizes its superheroes as "vigilantes.") Since no one knows who Spider-Man really is, his actions are open to criticism and his motives to suspicion. But, by providing the audience with a solid psychological motivation for Spider-Man to operate above and beyond normal legal channels, the film assures that we can safely root for him despite his outsider status. The contrast between his treatment by the press and his true motivations (both noble and guilt-ridden) makes Spider-Man a more psychologically complex character than many traditional superheroes.

Unlike the unambiguous moral victories that characterized *Superman* and other DC comics, Marvel pioneered a different type of comic in the 1960s, known for "the tragic qualities of its characters" (Wright, 203). *The Fantastic Four*, for example, introduced a group of characters beset by human flaws and weaknesses. The Hulk was another variation of the new "alienated antihero," a superhero who expressed and embodied the anxieties of his young male readers. Fitting in with neither children nor adults, teenage readers could easily identify with these misunderstood outcasts. *The Hulk* also explicitly dramatized another aspect of growing up, providing an "allegory of pubescent metamorphosis. . . . The Hulk, for example, got big and hairy and his voice changed. Go figure" (Bukatman, 54). Acknowledging the adolescent appeal of *The Hulk*, Stan Lee and Steve Ditko took a chance and created a comic strip whose main character was more than just metaphorically adolescent. As Wright argues, "Spider-Man was the most brilliant concept for a comic book superhero since Superman" (210). Soon to follow were the mutant X-Men, popularized on the big screen in 2000.

As a new type of superhero, *Spider-Man* also provides a more complex version of masculinity than the traditional male hero, once again problematizing gender roles in similar fashion to its antecedents in fantasy and comic books. While initially a comment on the perils of the nuclear age, *The Hulk* soon turned explicitly to exploring the burgeoning crisis in American male identity. Alternating between his identity as a "hulky" green monster and mild Bruce Banner (described by Genter as an "effeminate intellectual" beholden to the bureaucracy), *The Hulk* dramatized the tensions of the postwar, white-collar male within the body of a single character. While the Hulk might be best seen as a reassertion of traditional masculinity, as an antidote to conflicting messages about appropriate gender traits, the sensitive male typified by Peter Parker explores a more androgynous ideal of masculinity that emerged after World War II and one that would increasingly be touted by psychologists and sociologists, particularly post-Vietnam (Ehrenreich, 127–8). (Also see *Big*, *Always*, and *Groundhog Day*.) But an acceptance of "new age male" qualities frequently requires a compensatory move. For example, the acceptance of the 1950s bachelor "playboy" model was assured through its obsession with women's bodies and (heterosexual) sex, thus counteracting the more feminine aspects of the image, and forestalling suspicions that risked linking bachelorhood and consumerism (shopping!) with homosexuality (Ehrenreich, 50). Just as less-than-macho male characters are easily accepted by audiences when they are "really" little boys or ghosts (*Big*, *Always*) a sensitive nice guy like Peter *can't possibly be* called a wimp because he's (really!) a manly superhero. As Bukatman notes: "The self-pity that underlies so many superhero titles since the 1960s (the *sensitive new age mutant* syndrome) indicates an awareness of emotional need but only within a hypermasculine context" (64). Thus the "soap opera" of Peter's conflicted personal life is simultaneously counteracted by a standard fantasy of adolescent male empowerment. (Like the duck/bunny illusion, viewers can choose where to focus their attention.)

Peter Parker resembles a number of other fantasy characters who demonstrate a sensitive, sometimes geeky side while simultaneously (or alternately) fulfilling a more traditional ideal of a male hero. As with Clark Kent and Harry Potter, Peter's eyeglasses at the beginning of the movie mark him as an underdog and a nerd. Eyes that need glasses represent a physical deficiency and therefore advertise weakness. Glasses, furthermore, are themselves fragile. They can easily be broken and must be removed before a superhero "performs," as Superman regularly does (note, of course, that his glasses are merely part of his *fake* identity). Upon becoming Spider-Man, Peter assumes a dual persona comprised of opposites: brains vs brawn, nerdy vs cool, weak vs strong, ordinary vs extraordinary. Wright notes that in the original comic books, Peter

Parker eventually stops wearing his nerdy glasses and assumes a James Dean appearance (212). Genter attributes this, in part, to the desire of illustrator Steve Ditko to promote a version of rugged individualism, which, as in *The Hulk*, expressed a rejection of middle-class conformity. In the movie, Peter's eyes are magically improved overnight following the spider bite. Although Pete sheds his glasses, his original nerdiness and passivity nevertheless provide the critical context against which the entire drama unfolds.

As with Clark Kent's failure to impress Lois Lane, Peter's mild-mannered demeanor fails to romantically captivate Mary Jane and makes him the target of bullies. But the beauty of a dual identity is that two sets of opposing qualities can be simultaneously valued. The audience shares in M.J.'s admiration for the astounding heroism and breathtaking stunts of Spider-Man. Meanwhile, we also know that Peter is a good guy and hope that Mary Jane realizes it. (Peter's positive qualities provide an obvious contrast to the other men in M.J.'s life: Flash, Harry, and her abusive father). In fact, M.J. never rejects Peter as a love interest so much as she remains oblivious to the very idea until the end of the film. But her declaration of love is bittersweet since Peter now knows that he cannot be with her as long as he remains Spider-Man. Exposing his true identity or even consorting with others while appearing as Spider-Man risks putting friends and loved ones in danger. This, apparently, is the burden of being so gosh-darn cool and powerful. "Physical strength only hides the emotionally complex inner subject. Power is not self-aggrandizing; it is rather a cross to be silently borne" (Bukatman, 64). So the modern superhero gets to be *both* the nice sensitive, caring guy *and* the stoic, strong silent type. And like many Western heroes (*Shane*, 1953, *The Man Who Shot Liberty Valance*, 1962, etc.), it is the superhero's burden to remain alone and romantically uninvolved.

The appeal of a character who can save the day even when the authorities can't is undeniable. This may have been part of the enormous popularity of the first *Superman* comics released in 1938. The Great Depression, the devastating effects of the Dust Bowl, and the menacing prospect of another war all conspired to create a climate of helplessness. Similarly, the events of 9/11 had hardly begun to fade from viewers' minds in 2002 when *Spider-Man* was released as a film. Set in New York City, the movie's promotional trailer had originally featured an action scene with Spider-Man and the Twin Towers, but this was pulled from theaters following their collapse. In the film, Spider-Man saves innocent people from tall buildings, prevents M.J. from plunging to her death from a great height, and rescues passengers from a cable car suspended over the

East River. It's hard to begrudge any compensatory emotions that *Spider-Man* might have evoked in the face of the nation's worst terrorist attack but, of course, the film did not intentionally reference this event as it was shot prior to 9/11. Movies have frequently featured the skyscrapers and monuments of New York as the *mise-en-scène* for adventure, disaster, or science-fiction scenarios. There's something thrilling about seeing King Kong climb the Empire State Building, the X-Men do battle atop the Statue of Liberty, or the "Men in Black" scale the World's Fair tower. Part of the appeal lies in our astonishment at seeing fantastic events appear in and around familiar and iconic landmarks.

The vertical heights of New York City have always been integral to Spider-Man and other superheroes. As Bukatman observes, superheroes logically gravitate to big cities, where the sheer density of the population assures abundant crime-fighting opportunities. Furthermore, the anonymity of the city provides the perfect setting for a culture of indifference and corruption where crime can flourish (Wright, 10). Spider-Man's credo serves as an antidote to such alienation and disconnection. Through his actions he fights not only crime but also cynicism, reinvesting the city with its iconic status as a place of hope – a place where anything can happen, where the sky's the limit. If the city of Metropolis provides Superman with the opportunity to illustrate this by literally "leaping over tall buildings in a single bound," New York is the perfect setting for Spider-Man's skills. As we saw in *Big*, Josh questions the fun of playing with a robot that turns into a building. "What's so fun about playing with a building? That's not any fun." Buildings are boring – unless you're Spider-Man, of course, in which case buildings become your playground. (Interestingly, Josh suggests that the robot should instead turn into a "bug.") Bukatman describes the city of comic-book superheroes as

> a multitude of fantasies projected in three dimensions. The superhero, in his costumed extravagance, muscular absurdity, and hyperkinetics, super-imposes the fantastic on the face of the utilitarian, bringing the city back to the fact of its fantasy. First of all, superheroes negate the negation of the grid – they move through space in three dimensions, designing their own vehicles, choosing their own trajectories. To be a superhero, you've got to able to move. Superhero narratives are sagas of propulsion, thrust, and movement through the city. (189)

Superheroes are thus action personified. And much of the pleasure of this movie derives from the sheer exuberant delight of following Spidey as he dizzily swoops through the skyscraper canyons of New York. He thus literally sews his karmic web, tying building to building as he pendulums across the city, collapsing the space between its far-flung edges and arriving out of thin air for miraculous rescues.

While the big city is the perfect venue for Spider-Man's flamboyant costume and acrobatic athleticism, its sheer size underscores Peter's quiet loneliness. Superheroes with secret identities benefit from the anonymity a large city affords, and this is particularly important for the habitually misunderstood Spider-Man, who breaks the law while serving justice. But being in trouble with the law is also part of Spider-Man's appeal. Besides linking him with so many other maverick live-action movie heroes, his outsider status is a metaphor for the misunderstood teenager. He's always getting into trouble, and no one seems to understand him. Like a teenager, Peter is always broke and chronically late, but Spider-Man is super-punctual and ever-present, arriving in the nick of time and popping up magically where crimes are being committed.

The dual-identity theme extends equally to *Spider-Man*'s villain, the Green Goblin, who emerges as a variation of Jekyll and Hyde and whose alternate personalities are simultaneously present and absent through the twin devices of mirrors and masks. (See Meyer for an in-depth Jungian perspective of these as archetypal "shadow" devices in *Spider-Man*.) Oedipally, Norman Osborn (Willem Dafoe) takes a fatherly interest in Peter, despite the fact that he's the biological father of Peter's best friend Harry (James Franco). Just as Luke battles his father in *Star Wars* and Harry battles a father stand-in in the *Harry Potter* series, Peter faces a menacing father figure and emerges triumphant. And as in *Star Wars*, *Harry Potter*, and so many other movies (including Westerns like the above-mentioned *Shane* and *The Man Who Shot Liberty Valence*), the hero and the villain are constructed as doppelgangers – two diametrically opposed sides of the same hero/villain. Osborn's adoption of the hideous Green Goblin mask is a grotesque answer to Spider-Man's elegant disguise, recalling once again the world of carnival and wrestling, where costumes serve as hyperbolic signifiers of good and evil. By killing his friend's father, Spider-Man provides the expected (yet satisfying) defeat of the villain but also unwittingly creates a new opponent when Harry swears vengeance. The pay-back device established at the outset now extends *Spider-Man*'s web into the next film, illustrating the potential of stories that become self-perpetuating franchises, and proving, yet again, that what comes around goes around.

CHAPTER 11

THE LORD OF THE RINGS (2001–3)
Tolkien's Trilogy or Jackson's Thrillogy?

In 1968, Stanley Kubrick's groundbreaking *2001: A Space Odyssey* helped to legitimize science-fiction film. Who knew that by the *actual* year 2001, sci-fi would be eclipsed by fantasy? Despite the popularity of *Harry Potter*, it was Peter Jackson's adaptation of J.R.R. Tolkien's, *The Lord of the Rings* that finally brought prestige to the much maligned fantasy genre. Tolkien is perhaps the most important figure in modern fantasy with his ability to invent and provide a coherent, meaningful vision. "It is Tolkien . . . who claims the name *Fantasy* for the genre in which he himself aspired to work. *The Lord of The Rings* is the paradigm of fantasy in our time" (Scholes, 17). By the time the *Rings* movies were released, audiences had already become well acquainted with variations on mythical and magical quest stories through the medium of sci-fi. The first "inkling" that fantasy film would emerge triumphant in the decades to come was the popularity of *Stars Wars* in 1977, a film that mixed science fiction with fairy-tale and mythical influences, thus paving the way for many more fantasy adventures. In a twist of fate reminiscent of the time-travel trope of fantasy films, an ostensibly "science-fiction" film may thus have helped set the stage for a successful movie version of *Rings* while the popularity of Tolkien's novels helped create a hospitable climate for *Star Wars* in the first place.

The *Rings* movies might never have been made if not for the popularity of science-fiction literature. As Delany argues, the popularity of Tolkien's work in the 1960s "could never have occurred without the stability of the SF editorial complex," a stable, distinct entity that had established itself over decades (69). For example, it was a science-fiction editor who first made Tolkien's books available in paperback – "a move no commercial general paperback editor would have been likely to make" (70). Thus, Tolkien, the dean of fantasy literature, penetrated a mass audience thanks to the legions of sci-fi fans who bought his paperbacks. Originally published in Great Britain as a single book and later split into three, the *Rings* trilogy earned a cult following with science-fiction fans, high-school and college students throughout the US. As noted throughout this volume, science fiction, fantasy, and horror form a continuum across genres – a complex that emerges from the modern, industrial context. Though *Rings* is set in a distant past (so far distant as to be an alternate reality), the story illustrates many of the same concerns found in science fiction, horror, and the shady blending of both.

Rings features two diametrically opposed forms of magic. The first is "Faerie," which characterizes the world of enchantment, filled with peril but capable of provoking great joy. But Tolkien saw magic as pernicious when used to manipulate others or the environment. He understood this latter type of magic to be a kind of machinery, capable of wreaking destruction in the same way that the machinery of the Industrial Revolution raped the land for materialistic ends. It is characterized by its "immediacy: speed, reduction of labour, and reduction also to a minimum (or vanishing point) of the gap between the idea or desire and the result or effect" (Tolkien 2000, 200). Just as many science-fiction and horror films focus on the dangers of rationality and technology, in *Rings* evil magic is a tool for exerting power over others. The One Ring is not merely a magic talisman, it is the epitome of technology at its most dangerous. Tolkien's story is thus the antithesis of traditional epics and fairy tales. Frodo's quest entails destroying rather than acquiring a coveted object. Instead of carrying the Ring back triumphal to a needy world, he must instead undertake, as Chance says, "an anti-quest, a non-battle, and a lonely trip to run an errand – to throw something away" (176). Chance almost makes Frodo's task sound trivial, recalling the "take out the garbage" trope in *Big* and *Galaxy Quest*. But his "chore" is none other than to dispose of that which threatens to turn the world itself into a giant garbage disposal, a wasteland created by Sauron's minions. The environmental destruction that emerges as the Orcs wield their mechanical advantage over the landscape links machinery with evil and sets it in harsh opposition to nature, romanticized through the sylvan calm of the Shire and the Ents' and Elven worlds. The Orcs' hellish existence evokes science-fiction dystopias and post-apocalyptic movies in which technology creates nightmarish landscapes ravaged by machinery and pollution and scorched by fire and smoke, as seen in *Blade Runner* (1982), *The Terminator* (1984), *Mad Max* (1979), and other films.

The discourses of sci-fi and horror converge in the Orcs and Uruk-hai, who follow in the tradition of Frankenstein's monster as examples of technology gone wrong. The Uruk-hai are not only horrific in appearance and brutality, their very origin is monstrous because they are "engineered" by Saruman (Christopher Lee – himself synonymous with the horror genre) – apparently no more than disgusting tools of oppression. As Lianne McLarty writes, the movies place a heavy emphasis on disgust as a code for evil (185-7). In one scene from *The Fellowship of the Ring* (2001), the Uruk-hai rise up almost unformed out of the boiling mud as if made from dirt and sewage, presenting a threat that emerges from the "twin towers" of horror and science fiction. On the one hand, the enemy monsters are horrific because they're disgusting and "animal-like." They grunt and snarl but barely speak, marking them as subhuman. But like machines they also lack distinct individuality. Despite the innovative special effects designed to allow individual figures to move with apparent autonomy (see below), the members of the evil army remain largely anonymous, with little distinct personal identity – each a mere cog in a fighting machine, each one interchangeable with another. Likewise, the Ring turns Gollum into a horror-style wraith, but the "technology" that depletes his subjectivity and "humanity" (or Hobbit-y) links him to Saruman's relentless and dehumanized fighters.

Saruman's army is a lumpy, decrepit-looking bunch whose violent proclivities extend to their "savage" relationship with food. Whereas the Hobbits' appreciation of food and drink signifies comfort and good cheer, Saruman's army is comprised of cannibals. Gollum's role is clarified in *The Two Towers* (2002) when we learn of his unappealing use of rabbits and fish. He eats them raw, practically alive (McLarty, 186). If the visuals of Gollum cracking open a live bunny rabbit while blood slobbers down his face aren't disgusting enough to cue some viewers, Sam (Sean Astin) makes it explicit, exclaiming that Frodo (Elijah Wood) will be "sickened" by the sight.

The *Rings* adaptation is heavily influenced by science-fiction/horror movies like *Godzilla* (1954, 1998) and *Jurassic Park* (1993), featuring scary beasts out of control. In fact, it was the idea of creating monsters that most excited director Peter Jackson about the project. Jackson had previously directed several gory "splatter" films and was eager to create Harryhausen-style monsters, but this time with sophisticated computer-generated imagery. He had actually been inspired to use advanced CGI upon seeing the dinosaurs in *Jurassic Park* (Thompson 2007, 22, 58–60). Much of the appeal of the horror genre is attributed to the allure of actually *seeing* the monster that we imagine and fear. The word "monster" as derived from Latin means to warn but it draws equally from its Indo-European roots meaning "to show" (McConnell, 232). Our desire to see the monster "de-monstrated," making visible the desires and fears of our sub-conscious, is one area where horror and fantasy film often overlap. And of course, science-fiction films depend upon showing us convincing detail to create their ostensibly science-based stories. Likewise, Tolkien's self-contained world is so saturated with detail that interpreting it for film required a heavy emphasis on its visual components, a challenge for Jackson and his crew.

While Tolkien would call this visualization a process of "sub-creation," David Bordwell defines it as "world-making," a trend already made popular by *2001*, *Star Wars*, and *Blade Runner* (58). In order to meet the "massive" challenge posed by one of the most famous self-contained worlds ever, Jackson and crew ended up creating new special-effects technology, such as the Massive program for creating realistic crowd scenes. As Kristen Thompson writes: " . . . the results will have a lasting impact on the way special effects are done" (2007, 279). Massive has since been used by *Harry Potter and the Order of the Phoenix* (2007), the *Narnia* movies, *The Golden Compass* (2007), and *Wall-E* (2008), but also non-fantasy movies such as *Leatherheads* (2008) (http://www.massivesoftware. com/film/).

Gollum posed one of the most serious visual problems for the special-effects team. Although Gollum's Hobbit-hood is almost completely eroded by the Ring, the character needed to be complex enough to make us believe that he was once like Frodo, thereby dramatizing the power of the Ring in a way that no verbal warnings could ever accomplish. He therefore needed to behave with all the subtlety of a live actor. And he needed to look and sound believable enough that his computer-generated origins wouldn't distract viewers from the absorbing and emotional story of his live-action cohorts. Finally, he had to satisfy fans of the books, who had their own visions of what Gollum should look like. The Gollum problem was solved in part through the motion-capture technique, which combined creative artists, model makers, and animators with live actor Andy Serkis, who also provided Gollum's voice (Sibley, 165). One of the biggest achievements was recreating the translucent quality of human skin, a digital-effects feat which garnered a special technical award from the Academy of Motion Picture Arts and Sciences in 2004 (Thompson 2007, 98). Elvis Mitchell of *The New York Times* described the effect: " . . . Gollum's translucent, waxy skin is a membrane that just barely contains his insides." Emaciated and shrunken, his skin a cadaverous film, Gollum hisses and slithers through the films. Noted film critic Roger Ebert (2002) cited Gollum as "one of the most engaging and convincing CGI creatures I've seen." The success of Gollum was one of many technical achievements that benefited from Jackson and crew's unprecedented attention to detail. The superb special effects and the dedication to visual details throughout the films are aspects that most critics and fans applaud, and their "careful, imaginative design, more than anything else, won over fans and made them more willing to excuse changes in the plot" (Thompson 2007, 86).

And yet, the movies' focus on monsters and the unusually violent and lengthy battle scenes imbue the trilogy with a swords-and-sorcery feel that, unfortunately, subverts a central aspect of the novels. Tolkien himself had criticized a plot summary from an earlier proposed film because it showed a "preference for fights" (2000, 271). Similarly, Janet Brennan Croft faults Jackson's version of the scene at Weathertop in *The Fellowship of the Ring* where Aragorn (Viggo Mortensen) fends off the Ringwraiths with "screams and rather meaningless slashings" (70). As Tolkien pointed out, the Ringwraiths are non-physical. Their "peril is almost entirely due to the unreasoning fear which they inspire" (2000, 272). It's worth pointing out that *Harry Potter's* Dementors owe much to Tolkien's Ringwraiths, but succeed better in imparting their wraith-like existence and fear-inspiring dread, particularly in the third film, *The Prisoner of Azkaban* (2004). In Jackson's production, the Ringwraiths provoke just another physical fight in a movie already saturated with violence. We can blame some of this on the difference between novels and film and the exigencies of commercial moviemaking. It is true that, throughout the film, Jackson had to somehow impart the dire nature of evil in a visually convincing way, and the sheer length of the story demanded compelling action sequences. While it was understood that the films would have to satisfy the demanding and ultra-loyal fans of the books, at the same time they needed to appeal to the enormous number of viewers required to justify the epic story and the high cost of special effects. The movies, therefore, would need to appeal equally to adults and teenage audiences worldwide. The tension between pleasing the devoted fans and appealing to young audiences who might not have read the books accounts for a number of choices made by the filmmakers.

Beyond the overemphasis on monsters and battles, Tolkien's notion of fantasy as a whole is subverted in the films. The exclusion of Tom Bombadil, widely noted among critics, is understandable since his story does not directly advance the plot. But it is also symptomatic of the way in which Tolkien's emphasis on nature and enchantment is minimized. Tolkien's story depends upon danger and evil, but the martial emphasis that dominates the films is disconcerting. Tolkien experienced firsthand the horrors of World War I and wrote much of the *Rings* trilogy during World War II. In a 1944 letter to his son, he writes that the "utter stupid waste of war, not only material but moral and spiritual, is so staggering to those who have to endure it" (2000, 75). The movies convey the horrors of war exceptionally well, but the glorification of violence is suspect, especially because identifying strongly with wise old Gandalf (Ian McKellen), the ancient and artful Elves, and the peaceful Hobbits is, arguably, what the original books were all about. As David Bratman so aptly says: "The book smells of elves; the movies reek of orcs" (30). He characterizes the battle between Saruman and Gandalf as "wizard-fu," a physical fisticuffs not found in the book (52). Gandalf actually "socks Denethor in the teeth" in the film version of *The Return of the King* (2003), whereas in the book this last Steward of Gondor is the object of Gandalf's pity (50). While the movies exude melancholy and suffering, they also risk effectively reversing a key point of the novels, falling prey to the fallacy expressed by Tolkien as he uses *Rings* to criticize World War II. This conflict he characterizes as "attempting to conquer Sauron with the Ring. And we shall (it seems) succeed. But the penalty is, as you will know, to breed new Saurons, and slowly turn Men and Elves into Orcs" (2000, 78). Here, Tolkien expresses the conviction that violence risks corrupting even those with good intentions. The dark side of the "karmic web" (which, as we have seeen, also operates in *Spider-Man*) is represented here by the evil Ring. It ensures that its owner will perpetuate a never-ending cycle of violence and destruction: once more, what comes around goes around.

Tolkien's novels are sensitive to and, ultimately, center on this paradox but the release of the movie versions (beginning in December 2001) confronted audiences still reeling from the events of 9/11 with a story that risked being taken as an argument for triumphant militarism. While some criticized the movies for making Aragorn, Frodo, and even Gandalf reluctant "modern" heroes, wracked with angst, this aspect of the movies at least serves to counter the pernicious idea that absolute good is inherent to some, while absolute evil belongs to "Others." By showing Frodo struggle with his temptation and Aragorn resist his role as King, the filmmakers retain Tolkien's original notion that intention and choice are crucial and that the temptation to control people and events may backfire.

Tolkien explains that the motive for the creation of the Elves' three Rings of Power was to prevent or slow decay, "the preservation of what is desired or loved, or its semblance – this is more or less an Elvish motive. But also they enhanced the natural powers of a possessor – thus approaching 'magic', a motive easily corruptible into evil, a lust for domination" (2000, 152). This is the muted heart of the entire story. The Elves created the first three rings to preserve beauty, thus dangerously skirting the perils of magic, but Sauron secretly created the One Ring for the sole purpose of domination. Tolkien employs an elemental image to distinguish the two motives: the Elven rings did not bestow invisibility, a power used by Sauron to "see all" and to spy on others in order to enslave them (152). Thus in *Rings*, invisibility is synonymous with power and deceit (unlike invisibility in *Harry Potter* or many ghost movies, where it may serve a number of other purposes).

While the creation of the rings in the first place was not evil, the important and problematic message is that "this frightful evil can and does arise from an apparently good root, the desire to benefit the world and others – speedily and according to the benefactor's own plans" (Tolkien 2000, 146). This idea is overshadowed, however, through the films' us–vs–them approach. J.E. Smyth is one of many who argue that *Rings* is racist in its portrayal of good characters as white and European, while the bad guys are routinely portrayed as dark and Eastern (Plate 20). (See also Cubitt; Fuchs; Kellner; Kim; and McLarty for related arguments.) Smyth explicitly links the films to Western imperialism, claiming that the filmmakers have "remade memories of Western imperialism as the only honorable alternative to an evil Eastern Empire" (20). Given their popularity and the coincidence of the films' release at this particular historical moment, such accusations are difficult to ignore. Tolkien resisted allegorical interpretations of his novels, but viewers will be hard put not to make their own connections. The coincidence of "*The Two Towers*" and the World Trade Center Twin Towers was not lost of viewers, some of whom circulated an on-line petition to change the name of the movie (Barry Keith Grant, personal email communication, 6 July 2009).

Rings has also been accused of being patriarchal and sexist, aspects of the original novels that only exacerbate accusations of male militarism in the movie versions (see Goldberg and Gabbard; and Kellner, for example). But the movies have also won praise for being *less* sexist than the novels by making three female characters, Galadriel (Cate Blanchett), Eowyn (Miranda Otto), and Arwen (Liv Tyler), more central to the story

PLATE 20 *The Lord of the Rings: The Fellowship of the Ring* (2001 New Line Cinema): Dark monsters. (Courtesy of Photofest.)

(McLarty; Thum). Of course, just as the films were designed to attract both young and old, they also needed both male and female viewers, and this was not a foregone conclusion given the all-male fellowship and the reliance on epic battles as both plot and spectacle. Erik Hedling points out that the movie trailers focused heavily on the romance between Arwen and Aragorn despite the fact that this was a minor aspect of the films (232). This was one tactic in marketing the films to women. Another was to reveal Eowyn's identity as a soldier immediately (rather than as a last-minute surprise, as in the book), thereby following a trend of movies featuring athletic and warrior women (*Alien* and *The Terminator*, for example). And of course, it is Galadriel who narrates the story of the Ring and who (arguably) seems as powerful and as wise as Gandalf himself (Thum, 240–1). Audience research shows that women were indeed interested in the female characters, but also in some of the attractive male actors, notably Viggo Mortensen and Orlando Bloom (Legolas) (Klinger, 77). Women cited both the intensity and variety of emotions they felt while watching the film (76), as well as the strength, courage, and traditional masculine qualities they enjoyed in the mostly male cast: "For some, these male figures appear as antidotes to the more cynical, less heroic present day, making nostalgia for mythic masculinities a prime ingredient in the pleasure derived from male characters" (79).

Regardless of whether or not most viewers find *Rings* to be sexist or racist, the ideological implications of the films will no doubt keep scholars and critics arguing for years. And the DVD provides so many extended scenes and so much additional information that attempting to delineate the boundaries of the "official" text becomes almost impossible. Kate Egan and Martin Barker argue that documentaries about the films and the many DVD extras have helped to position viewers' experience of the trilogy, encouraging audiences to draw on these sources to "complete" their understanding of the films (101). In one case, extras on the extended DVD of *The Return of the King* seemed designed to "rescue the books from potential error" by focusing heavily on the "reluctant heroes" who nevertheless rise to their positions of leaders and heroes (91). But add to these officially sanctioned texts the plethora of related websites with all their additional information (not to mention all the unofficial sites and chat rooms) and the locus of debate loses focus. While the trend in texts that extend beyond the screen might seem like a recent phenomenon, Tolkien, with seeming prescience, had actually provided a print version of this process before. Though Tolkien published *The Silmarillion* in 1977, decades after *Rings*, he created it as a companion to the novels while he was writing them. Richard Mathews refers to it as a kind of bible for Middle Earth (62). Since then, fans and scholars have been consulting it to expand their understanding of the story-world. Tolkien himself said that *The Silmarillion* was "essential" to understanding *Rings*, presaging, in his repeated response to his readers' concerns, the unprecedented involvement of fans with Jackson's team during the making of the film. Tolkien thus created a kind of "supertext" that included *The Hobbit* (1937), *The Silmarillion*, and the *Appendices* to *Rings* (included in the original publication of *The Return of the King* in 1955). Nevertheless, the extent to which the *Rings* movie franchise has expanded this process of "textual overflow" (Gray, 241) is unprecedented and points to a central aspect of the *Rings* phenomenon. And on this point everyone seems to agree: the impact of *Rings* on the media industry has been enormous. Thompson says that *Rings* "can fairly claim to be one of the most historically significant films ever made" (2007, 8). She also calls the trilogy the perfect franchise that has become "a small industry in itself" (7–9).

The paradox of using the technology of cinema to create fantasy has been broached in previous chapters, but in the *Rings* franchise it is sadly ironic in light of Tolkien's overriding anti-technology themes. *Rings* is not just a product of cinematic machinery, it has itself become a "massive" machine, generating untold profits through ancillary products including DVDs, CDs, games, toys, posters, figurines, etc., a fact widely remarked upon. Worse, Time Warner reaps the benefits – not the Tolkien estate (Wasko and Shanadi, 25). Movie execs have joked that *Rings* is now the one to rule them all, but in an era when a small handful of multi-national conglomerates control every aspect of the media (not to mention related non-media commodities), one has to think that Tolkien is rolling over in his grave.

Though many viewers are aware that movies are mega-commodities, sophisticated PR campaigns coupled with new fan-oriented materials like DVD extras attempt to erase the corporate machinery from the viewer's awareness. True, viewers can learn about the genius special effects and how various scenes were shot, but as Jonathan Gray points out, the focus is repeatedly on the labor of love required to make the film. Artistry as a higher good is emphasized and an almost Elvish craftsmanship is show-cased. According to this public-relations spin, Jackson is a visionary auteur whose artistic choices are framed in opposition to the wishes of the corporate and Sauron-like movie industry. Indeed, the entire cast and crew are characterized as a fellowship with a heroic and noble purpose. The project thus emerges magically and heroically unsullied by financial suasion, supposedly a testament to Tolkien's vision (Gray). Not only does this misrepresent the nature of this beast but, as Sue Kim argues, it obscures the conditions of production that relied on the cheap, temporary labor of mostly minority groups in New Zealand. In this respect, the production of *Rings* is merely a "creature" of the global economic trends of its time. Like the three Elven rings, the creation of the three movies was no doubt the result of considerable effort, expertise, and a sincere desire to create a work of art. But also like the Elven rings, it has inadvertently spawned something monstrous and powerful whose effects reach far beyond the movies themselves. Ironically, Jackson and company named their new special-effects workshop "Weta," after a small New Zealand cricket – a critter that, despite its initial humble status, is "practically indestructible and can grow to be one of the heaviest bugs in the world" (Sibley, 20). In thus naming their new company, Jackson and his colleagues perhaps unwittingly foretold the future.

If the material conditions of the movies' production belie their fantasy message, it is nonetheless true that the films succeed admirably in valuing teamwork and the interconnectedness of human action. As *Always* and *Spider-Man* illustrate, this impulse stands in constant tension with the notion of individuality and macho heroism. The Bush administration faced intense criticism for plunging unilaterally into the Iraq war, a strategy that became increasingly characterized as a simple bid for control of territory. To critics, Bush, and not Bin Laden, was Sauron (Gelder,

103). At the same time, many have wondered why President Bush never asked the nation to make sacrifices at home while lives and resources were being spent overseas. Regardless of who played Sauron in the contemporary "real" world, *Rings* addresses these criticisms in a palpable way, dramatizing a story of cooperation and sacrifice in the face of great danger. For many different reasons, this aspect of the story may therefore have appealed to viewers of the time either as an expression of wartime solidarity or as an *antidote* to the violence of war that the films seem to privilege. Tolkien eschewed an allegorical reading of *Rings*, but there is no denying that both the films' military triumphalism and their emphasis on solidarity and friendship speak to and reflect the historical moment of their release.

CHAPTER 12

THE CHRONICLES OF NARNIA: THE LION, THE WITCH AND THE WARDROBE (2005)
A Joyful Spell

Long before Harry Potter captured the imagination of millions of young readers, *The Chronicles of Narnia* (1950–6) captured the hearts of their parents and grandparents as children. C.S. Lewis strongly defended the value of fantasy for all ages, despite writing *Narnia* explicitly for children. Still, "a children's story which is enjoyed only by children is a bad children's story. The good ones last" (Lewis, 33). *Narnia* has indeed stood the test of time and still resonates with many adults as it draws on classic fantasies, fairy tales, and myths. Nevertheless, the series makes a point of mostly excluding grown-ups from its fantasy world, in part because, for Lewis, "adulthood" has tended to hinder the acceptance of all that fantasy has to offer. Thus, in the first story and movie, *The Lion, the Witch and the Wardrobe*, the magic portal will not lead just anyone to Narnia, and even the sympathetic Professor is denied entry. At the end of the second book, *Prince Caspian* (1951), Aslan tells Peter and Susan that they won't be returning to Narnia because they have grown too old. In the movie version (2008), it's because they've "learned what they needed to," implying to older viewers that one is never too old to be childlike and that *Narnia* is for adults as well as kids. Not coincidentally, the youngest of the children, Lucy (Georgie Henley), is the first to enter

Narnia and she remains the most faithful to Aslan (and hence Narnia) in both movies. This fits a pervasive model of folk tales described as "youngest-best stories" (Hartland). In such tales the youngest child is oppressed but emerges a hero because of wisdom that eludes the elder siblings. In Victorian fantasy, a more direct influence on Lewis, the youngest child represents the purest and most open-minded and is therefore the quintessential figure for experiencing the fantastic. Influenced by William Morris, Lewis was also an ardent fan of Victorian fantasy writer George MacDonald, whose (then heretical) use of theology in his fantasy stories steered Lewis toward a similar approach. In the biblical Gospels, a link can be found between *Narnia* and MacDonald's notion that children are privileged spiritually: "But Jesus said, Suffer little children, and forbid them not, to come unto me: for such is the kingdom of heaven" (Matt. 19:14); and, "Verily I say unto you, Whosoever shall not receive the kingdom of God as a little child, he shall not enter therein" (Mark 10:15) (quoted in Rabkin, 101).

While not literally orphans, the Pevensie children are *effectively* orphaned in *Lion* when their father goes off to war and their mother sends them away from London for their own safety. Just as orphans in other fantasies are relieved of parental supervision, the children's separation from their parents signals an escape from the rational and restrictive adult world. In fairy tales, orphans also invoke the fantasy trope of metamorphosis, at least in the figurative sense, reminding us that appearances are not always what they seem. An orphan could be anyone, really. And so, in fairy tales the humble hero may turn out to be a prince or princess by birth, or may possess special attributes that distinguish him from his peers (as in *Harry Potter*). In *Lion*, the children eventually return to England as normal children, but first fulfill the formula when all four are crowned Kings and Queens of Narnia. Bruno Bettelheim argues that becoming a king or queen at the end of a fairy tale signifies complete independence for the character. But at the same time, it provides the feeling of safety and fullness experienced in the total dependency of childhood (127). Thus, the coming-of-age story combines a child's desire to be safe with the childlike capacity for wonder, adventure, and autonomy. In the William Morris fantasy *News from Nowhere* (1890), a character explains: "It is the child-like part of us that produces works of imagination. When we are children time passes so slow with us that we seem to have time for everything" (quoted in Rabkin, 95). Narnia provides ample "time for everything" as the children live an entire lifetime before returning to England, as if no time had passed at all.

Lion features many themes and motifs emblematic of fantasy, including fantastical creatures and an evil witch, but Lucy's passage through the wardrobe has itself become as iconic as Alice falling down the rabbit hole. The device of a portal into fantasy can be found in scores of books and movies. As Clute and Grant note, "few fantasy texts lack them" (776). Portals are not limited to pure fantasy but often show up in science fiction, as implied by the title of the film (and television show) *Stargate* (1994). In horror, the portal is more likely to be a gateway *from* rather than *into* the beyond (776), as in *Poltergeist*. Whereas in *Lion*, Lucy enters a closet holding furry clothes, *Monsters, Inc.* riffs on the idea that clothes in a child's closet are really furry monsters. Through its lovable furry beasts, the movie spoofs on horrific monsters but also the doors that allow entry, as the film involves a factory that circulates "monster doors" to children's bedrooms. Some portals may be metaphorical, taking the form of a wish or even a book, as in *The Neverending Story* (1984) or *The Princess Bride*. Whereas windows (*The Wizard of Oz*) and mirrors (*Through the Looking Glass and What Alice Found There*) are associated with looking and reflecting, they (along with the twin devices of sleeping and waking) remind us of watching a movie and suggest at least the possibility that the fantasy may be entirely psychological or subjective. Doors, on the other hand, suggest physically entering another world and are therefore powerful symbols for stories seeking to combine a primary world with a separate, self-contained secondary world. If the invisible rabbit in *Harvey* allows characters to overcome space and time as well as any objections, the wardrobe functions as just such an invitation. Lucy literally puts the contemporary world behind her when she steps through the wardrobe, and viewers are simultaneously invited to leave behind rational and cynical objections to the wonders of *Narnia*.

In the film adaptation of *Prince Caspian* (2008), the characters *seem* like children, but their immature bodies conceal a lifetime of ruling Narnia, suggesting – as so many fantasies and fairy tales do – that appearances may be deceptive. The point is made explicitly when they are at first not taken seriously by Trumpkin the Dwarf (Peter Dinklage). Unfortunately, they elect to prove their merit in a duel, one of many in this thinly plotted second movie (and book). In the first movie, appearances deceive when the beauty of the White Witch (Tilda Swinton) signals not goodness, but deception, a reversal also of our tendency to associate white with goodness and black with evil. And while beavers and other animals may look like those of the ordinary world, the children discover that many are human-like and can talk!

Talking beasts are one of the oldest traditions in fantasy. In a later book in the *Narnia* series, *The Magician's Nephew* (1955), the issue of talking animals is especially vivid, and critics like Ann Swinfen have noted its allegorical similarity to the book of Genesis (22). Here, and elsewhere in the series, animals that *can't* talk are not treated with the same compassion and respect as talking animals. But even worse, non-talking animals appear to be essentially damned (also see Newkirk). In *Caspian* we see a hint of this trend when a non-talking bear attacks Lucy. He is killed in self-defense and the children in the book actually eat him (albeit reluctantly). It will be interesting to see how the movies handle this as the series progresses. An "unspoken" irony of *Lion* is that the children take coats from the wardrobe, donning the fur of animals to keep warm, a fact ignored by their animal friends.

Talking animals become a point of contention in *Wicked*, Gregory Maguire's 1995 revisionist novel expanding on the world of *The Wizard of Oz*. Professor Dillamond the Goat is the only animal professor at Shiz University, but he soon becomes the "scapegoat" for the Wizard's discrimination against all animals. Uncomfortable with Dillamond's research on the profound similarities between animals and humans, the Wizard attempts to send all animals "back to the farm," and Dillamond is mysteriously murdered. While in many children's stories, talking animals merely substitute for people, in *Narnia* and *Wicked*, speech creates the divide between human and beast. Just as *Planet of the Apes* (1968) broaches the topic from a science-fiction perspective, *Wicked* interrogates the concept through its fairy-tale allegory, turning Elphaba (the Wicked Witch) into an animal rights activist and creating parallels between animals and other oppressed minority groups.

In *Narnia*, like so many horror films, lack of speech is most often associated with the beastly or monstrous. Frank McConnell explores this aspect of movie monsters in horror and science-fiction hybrids such as *Frankstein*, where the monster wishes desperately to speak, but "definitively" fails, proving him less than human. The classic movie monster is "form without language," a trope reversed in some science-fiction films such as Kubrick's *2001*, where the computer HAL is only "language without form" (236–7) – simulating humanity with its voice as it commits murder (much like Frankenstein's monster). Like *Rings*, *Narnia* uses Massive special-effects technology to create monsters whose evilness is signalled visually through their ugliness, but also through their brutish snarling and grunting, introduced most dramatically in *Lion* during the final battle scenes.

But language is a paradox at the heart of fantasy. It can be used to cast spells and tell wondrous tales, and it can be used to lie and deceive, or to tell the truth. At the beginning of *Lion*, Lucy's siblings accuse her of lying about Narnia's existence (or at least pretending). Soon after, Edmund (Skandar Keynes) utters the real lie, pretending that he has never visited Narnia, and the plot is driven forward by the power of this deception. The White Witch also wields language – like magic – to manipulate others for her own ends. Although she magically produces drinks and snacks, she need only employ ordinary language to seduce Edmund into betraying Lucy, casting the simplest spell, flattery, to suggest that he is "fit to be king" of Narnia. Language is thus both a sign of human-ness and an essential human weakness. For a clever villain, language is a vehicle for betrayal (in the Christian tradition, the cleverest of villains is Satan; in indgenous American cultures, the trickster). Zipes describes villains in traditional wonder tales as being "those that use words and power intentionally to exploit, control, transfix, incarcerate, and destroy for their own benefit" (2006, 51).

The lies told by Edmund and the White Witch incite the central narrative conflict of the film, ensuring that the Witch will pursue the children, and that the children will pursue Edmund, whom the Witch soon imprisons. Edmund's sin is atoned for by the lion Aslan (voiced by Liam Neeson), who sacrifices himself, only to be resurrected by the deep magic that eludes the Witch. And here the movie tells us where words will do no good. We only *see* Aslan speaking to Edmund from afar, and when they return to the group, Aslan says to the children: "What's done is done. There is no reason to bring up the past with your brother." By not revealing his words, the scene helps to preserve a sense of Aslan's mysterious power, which lies as much in his numinous presence as it does in any speech he might give. At the same time, Aslan intimates that while Edmund is officially forgiven, words will not undo the damage his betrayal has caused. Nevertheless, despite nearly succumbing to evil, Edmund is redeemed and now takes his place with his siblings as defenders of Narnia so that the story ends happily (and the series can continue).

As the villain of the piece, the White Witch dominates the film and recalls Hans Christian Andersen's Snow Queen, but also draws on a tradition of casting powerful females as wicked witches. In Europe fear of magic was often "projected" onto women, and "witch" was a label consciously or subconsciously applied as a method of scapegoating (Russell and Magliocco, 9773). The resiliency of the evil witch motif in literature also points to an ambivalence about femininity in patriarchal societies. "The male view of the archetypal feminine is tripartite: she is the sweet, pure virgin; she is the kindly mother, she is the vicious, carnal hag" (9774). This ambivalence appears in *Lion*, the movie, where Edmund appears more troubled than the other children by his parents' abandonment of them. The movie opens with him trying to retrieve a photo of his absent father as the family flees to a bomb shelter. Edmund's mother (Judy McIntosh) chastises him: "Edmund, get away from there! What do you think you're doing?" Later Edmund complains about having to leave London: "If Dad were here, the war would be over, and we wouldn't have to go." His mother yet again admonishes him, telling him to obey his older brother. The mother as nag ("hag") helps to instill in Edmund a feeling of powerlessness and adds to the sibling rivalry that infuses the first part of the movie. These scenes (not found in the book) help motivate Edmund's bad attitude toward his siblings and his willingness to believe in the Witch. He has both a desire for autonomy (he'll be a king and his siblings will serve him!) and a desire for maternal comfort as the White Witch nourishes him with food and drink and, instead of chastising him, calls him a *good* boy (while also noting that she would like a child of her own). The Witch then points Edmund to her castle and reveals, in none too subtle fashion, that he will soon be nestling in the cleavage of two monstrously mammalian mountains.

Lewis believed in the power of a good story to enthrall us, to work a positive spell on listeners or readers. The original meaning of the word "spell" in Old English was "story." Hence the Gospels are the "good story," the God spell (Dickerson and O'Hara, 55). Lewis understood the connection between these concepts, arguing that the meaning and effect of a good story enchant and thereby enrich the reader. Lewis was no fan of movies, because he believed that they tend to accentuate "excitement" and "danger" at the expense of the enriching aspects of the best oral and print stories (Lewis, 5, 16). But he had a keen sense of the visual, claiming that a "mental image" was his usual starting point for his stories (45, 53), and he believed that when reading or hearing a story, the mental images we create "speak" for themselves. In advising how to write for children, he wrote, "Let the pictures tell you their own moral" (41). Lewis's vehement rejection of the idea that overt moral messages should be the basis of fiction (for children *or* adults), however, has been questioned by many critics, who object to the didacticism of his work.

For Lewis, good fantasy, like myth, casts a spell by *transcending* language. Like Tolkien, Lewis saw danger in magic, but also saw in it the expression of the *inexplicable* (Shakel, 175), akin to Tolkien's "enchantment" and distinguished in Narnia by the difference between the Witch's machinations and the influence of deep magic, which subtends the entire world. Fantasy literature relies on language as its vehicle and also commonly features it as a thematic component. But for Lewis good fantasy works its spell through transcending language, much as myth does. For Lewis, "myths exist apart from words" (Dickerson and O'Hara 33). Like Jung, Lewis saw mythic symbols as defying definitive meaning, expanding rather than limiting our imaginative comprehension of the world. Lewis "presents myth as a vehicle for truth even more powerful than are language and propositional speech – indeed, even as an embodiment of truth" (33).

As friends and colleagues at Oxford, Lewis and Tolkien founded the "Inklings," an informal literary group that met to discuss and debate ideas about fantasy literature. Both Lewis and Tolkien rejected the idea that fantasy was childish, but unlike Lewis, Tolkien also rejected those fantasies that mixed secondary worlds with contemporary elements. Indeed, Tolkien's notion of escape into Faerie was in part a reaction to the dehumanizing effects of contemporary technology. He saw no benefit in replacing horses with cars, and accordingly places his fantasies in worlds of nature. For Tolkien, who was not sympathetic to the *Narnia* stories (1966, 352), the electric lamp is just one of many examples of so-called "progress," and has no place in fantasy: "The electric street-lamp may indeed be ignored, simply because it is so insignificant and transient. Fairy-stories, at any rate, have many more permanent and fundamental things to talk about" (2000, 80). And yet one of the compelling "mental images" that Lewis devised was a modern-street lamp (albeit not elec-trified) in the otherwise ancient world of Narnia. An explanation for the street-lamp's anomalous presence can be found in *The Magician's Nephew*. It is here that we learn that long before the Pevensie children traveled through the wardrobe, two children, Polly and Diggory, had used magic rings to travel to an alternate universe in the woods. While there, they accidentally awakened the evil Queen Jadis of Charn. Jadis then followed the two fleeing children back to London, where she created much havoc. In the process, she broke off a piece of a street lamp, which she still had in her hand when she returned to the fantasy world. When Aslan appeared, she threw the iron bar at him and it grew into a new lamppost, coinciding with the birth of Narnia, and explaining how a London street-lamp exists in the middle of the Narnian woods (Plate 21). In the first movie, however, it represents the anomalous intrusion of the primary world into the magical world in the same way that Edmund's flashlight does in *Caspian* (another bit of modern "light"). Just as the train provides a connection between the mundane and magical worlds in *Potter*, so here

PLATE 21 *The Chronicles of Narnia: The Lion, the Witch and the Wardrobe* (2005 Walt Disney Pictures): The modern world intrudes. (Courtesy of Photofest.)

the lamp signals the potential interaction of the contemporary and the fantasy world. The lamp functions as a further transition from the wardrobe to the magical world and provides a landmark that lights the way back at the beginning of the film for Lucy, but also at the end of the film, when the "adult" Pevensie kings and queens have long forgotten about the wardrobe.

The anomalous mixture of the contemporary with the mythical in *Narnia* is not a flaw, as Tolkien thought, but for Lewis was integral to the story. Just as Dorothy and other fantasy characters experience the wonder of discovering a glorious "other world," the Pevensie children (and Lucy in particular) experience wonder and joy upon entering Narnia. Many readers/viewers enjoy this same feeling as they vicariously share in the characters' amazement at finding a snowy wood at the back of a mundane piece of household furniture. Readers must imagine this in their minds' eye, while viewers of the movies are treated to the visual incarnation of Narnia. *Lion* succeeds admirably in this regard, with its magical snowy woods, and the charming and believable Mr Tumnus the faun (James

McAvoy) providing the perfect introduction to this magical, mythical place. Director Andrew Adamson, who also directed *Shrek*, manages to combine some of *Shrek*'s humor and whimsy with action and drama. Much like *The Wizard of Oz* and the *Potter* films, *Lion* intersperses its lightheartedness with scary scenes: the rabid wolves, the evil witch, and her entourage of hideous creatures. High production values and computer imagery recall the landscape of *Rings* (also shot in New Zealand) and lend the film some of that trilogy's epic scope, helping to sustain the viewer's sense of awe even after the children have accepted Narnia's existence. The movie also succeeds on an emotional level when Aslan sacrifices himself to atone for Edmund's betrayal. The scene in which the White Witch's monstrous minions strap Aslan to the Stone Table and then shave and kill him is emotionally intense (perhaps too intense for children).

Aslan's sacrifice and resurrection in *Lion* have been well explored as an allegory for Christ's death and resurrection, even though Lewis himself disdained pure allegory. Like Tolkien's perception of danger in magic, both he and Lewis saw allegory as a betrayal of the creative gift. Like the Ring, it "dominates the gift, thereby enslaving it and depriving it of much of its power" (Pearce, 122). But Lewis admits, "The whole Narnian story is about Christ" (123), calling his efforts a "supposal" rather than an "allegory," because not everything in the books represents something in the real world (Downing, 64). Regardless of this attempt at nuance, Christian aspects of *Lion* provoke everything from celebration to apathy or revulsion in those who notice them (although many, especially kids, don't). In addition to seeing Aslan as Christ because of his sacrifice and resurrection for Edmund's "sin," we can also point to his power to resuscitate those like Mr Tumnus who have been turned into statues by the White Witch. To do so, Aslan breathes life into them, the same process he uses in *The Magician's Nephew* when he creates Narnia and all its inhabitants through his divine breath, recalling Genesis. Aslan has great power, yet he never forces the children to act on his behalf, nor does he directly save them from the White Witch. The children must all have "faith" in Aslan, as Lucy does from the beginning. And although they are given "gifts" to help them defeat the Witch, the children must act of their own volition. All of this is easy to read as Christian allegory with its emphasis on sacrifice, sin, faith, and free will. But some aspects of *Lion* are common to secular coming-of-age stories, as Peter (William Mosely) learns to summon his courage and become a leader, and Edmund puts aside his petty jealousies to take Peter's side in battle. When Mr Beaver (Ray Winstone) first reads the "prophecy" (another religious allusion), foretelling the defeat of the White Witch by two sons of Adam and two daughters of Eve, Peter objects: "I think you've made a mistake; we're not heroes!" Susan (Anna Popplewell) then pipes up: "We're from Finchley!" But by the end of the film, all four children from Finchley will be heroes, just as so many "ordinary" children become heroes in fairy tales and other fantasies. We may choose to focus on the children's maturation and call to action as an expression of Christian philosophy, or we can choose to focus on *Lion*'s value as a secular coming-of-age story – or both (once again recalling the rabbit/duck phenomenon). As Russell W. Dalton notes, even if it's taken as Christian allegory, the story virtually *requires* that the children become the agents of change, if only for dramatic reasons. After all, it wouldn't be the compelling, popular story it is if Aslan could just fix everything in a trice, like a "deus ex machina" (133). Furthermore, *Lion* reflects Christian values that are also secular. Regardless of one's religious bent, most readers/viewers can agree on the value of friendship, loyalty, honesty, and bravery – all traits celebrated in other fantasies such as *Wizard*, *Rings*, and *Potter*.

With Aslan, Lewis was hoping to instill in the reader a sense of the "numinous," a term that combines fear and "holy dread" with joy and wonder (Downing, 65). This is why Tumnus tells Lucy that Aslan is not a "tame" lion, although she knows he's a "good" lion. Aslan works fantasy's "deep" magic when he invokes in the reader/viewer the same wonder and awe experienced by the characters, regardless of whether this is experienced as an explicitly Christian or religious feeling, or a more secular version of the phenomenon enjoyed by many fans of fantasy. Unfortunately, the movie doesn't *quite* succeed here. At times "Aslan is just a big, well-digitized stuffed animal" (Alleva). While the special effects create a very credible creature, Aslan's "awe"-someness is somewhat reduced by Liam Neeson's gentle, coddling tone. The king of the forest (if not all of Narnia and humankind) needs to intimidate, a failure we notice at once in the juxtaposition of "cowardly" with "lion" in *Wizard*. Bert Lahr's superbly burlesque but emotional performance works so hilariously *precisely* because it exposes the most powerful beast of all to be just a cuddly pussy cat. By contrast, the "Lion-King" on the Island of Misfit Toys in the beloved television Christmas classic *Rudolph the Red-Nosed Reindeer* (1964) may not be as "realistic" or important to the story as Aslan, but his authority works quite "awesomely" in that movie's context, with his deep voice solemnly ordering the characters to continue their quest to help *all* the misfits of the world.

Another television Christmas classic, *How the Grinch Stole Christmas* (1966) (adapted for the big screen in 2000, with Jim Carrey), lovingly portrays the Grinch's attempt and failure to steal Christmas from Who-ville. In *Lion*, however, it is the much more evil White Witch who has grinchily succeeded in banishing Christmas from Narnia for a hundred years. In *Lion*, Christmas becomes a placeholder for the loss that Narnia has suffered and a promise of the eventual return of happier times, just as it signifies the joyous Christian birth moment in the midst of the darkest night of winter. In *Lion*, Father Christmas (James Cosmo) plays a minor role, but he personifies all of the goodness and joy suppressed by the Witch. In Hollywood, light snowfall bears a heavy burden as a visual signifier of Christmas, invoking Lucy's enchantment when she first arrives in Narnia. But Narnia's snow soon connotes the frozen statues of the Witch's victims, reminiscent of Phil's petrified life in *Groundhog Day*. As with Aslan, Christmas may be taken as a religious or secular allusion. When "Santa" finally does arrive, he brings gifts, but not the traditional toys a modern child expects at Christmas. Instead, the gifts are the classic talismans, weapons, and potions of fairy tales – the very devices necessary for the children to complete their mission. As the youngest and most "wondrous" child, Lucy receives not just a weapon for the final battle, but an elixir that will magically resurrect the wounded. But Father Christmas does not *just* bring gifts. He gives children what so many Hollywood Christmas movies offer their audiences. From *Miracle on 34th Street* to the many *Christmas Carol* versions and *The Santa Clause*, Christmas has become synonymous with wonder, joy, and belief in something beyond the mundane and the material. As Lucy gleefully exclaims to her oldest sibling after meeting the iconic bearded gentleman, "Told you he was real!"

Imagination is not just important for Lewis; it is actually "shaped" by joy, as it was for Coleridge ("willing suspension of disbelief") (Filmer, 15). In *Lion*, the arrival of Christmas functions quite neatly as the turning point in a film where the acceptance of fantasy is not about "frozen statues" (allegory), but about the possibility of "re-birth," "recovery," and renewal (fantasy). True, Hollywood versions of Christmas manage to reject but still champion the "joy" of material goods, but to the extent that the films invoke childlike wonder, they have helped Christmas to emerge as a powerful, secular symbol for family togetherness and playful make-believe. Father Christmas thus serves *Lion* well as a concise symbol of two things valued so highly by Lewis and by many lovers of fantasy – joy and imagination.

CHAPTER 13

HARRY POTTER I–VI (2001–9)
Words are Mightier than the Sword

A lone street-lamp in the middle of a snowy wood marks Lucy's introduction to Narnia, and the same beacon lights us into the first *Harry Potter* movie. The film opens on a shot of a street-lamp, but here the anomaly of modern technology in a magical world is the inverse of Narnia's. Instead of an ordinary character intruding into a magical world, a wizard alights in the mundane. Zooming out, we see rows of streetlights shining on suburban houses, lawns, and cars. Dumbledore (Richard Harris) wields his wand and suddenly the lamps dim, deepening this "dark and stormy night."

Magic, thunder, lighting, and dramatic music portend a supernatural adventure. Welcome to *Harry Potter and the Sorcerer's Stone* (2001).

Sorcerer's Stone (or *Philosopher's Stone*, as it was known outside the US), along with *The Fellowship of the Ring*, made 2001 a watershed year for fantasy film. *Rings* might have been "the perfect franchise," as Thompson (2007) deemed it, but *Harry Potter* is still a contender as one of the most lucrative movie franchises in history. By 2007, it had brought in at least $15 billion, with the first five movies accounting for roughly $4.5 billion worldwide (Harris et al.). Moreover, the franchise's box-office record was broken with the release of *Half-Blood Prince* in 2009, which earned $104.2 million worldwide on its first day (CBS). This is pretty impressive for a "children's" movie.

There's no doubt that *Potter* owes a debt to Tolkien. Like *Rings*, *Potter* features wizards, magic, and fantastical creatures. Both series focus on a battle between good and evil, dramatizing the perils of absolute power. And both *Rings* and *Potter* feature characters of humble origins (orphans) who accomplish heroic tasks against all odds. They offer moral and philosophical lessons about friendship, sacrifice, loyalty, and redemption. And, in both stories, the villainous quest for immortality becomes synonymous with *immorality*. In *Potter*, not even Dumbledore can escape death. Only the phoenix, Fawkes, can be resurrected, and then only because his regenerative power is part of his very essence. Crucial to both is the essential fantasy idea that magical power is neither inherently good nor bad. Magic *per se* is neutral and practical, an extension of the user's choices and intentions.

Rowling denies having been heavily influenced by Tolkien (Nel), but it is clear that she has drawn from much of the same "cauldron of story." Nevertheless, the differences between the two series make for quite different reading and viewing experiences and reflect the many other generic influences that inform Rowling's story-world. Despite a number of whimsical moments confined mostly to the Hobbits and Gimli the Dwarf, *Rings* is a more serious, adult fantasy that young people may enjoy while *Potter* is primarily a children's series that adults also enjoy. In fact part of the appeal of the series, particularly the earlier installments, is their humor and whimsical approach to magic, despite the fact that the stories gradually "mature" along with Harry himself. *Potter*'s many fairy-tale elements inform a variation of Joseph Campbell's ancient monomyth: an orphan leaves home to face many trials, learns that he is born to greatness, and returns home victorious. Cartmell and Whelehan argue that *Potter* is largely based on *Star Wars*, which itself famously drew on Campbell's work (44). They cite, for example, the similarity in the protagonist's discovery of his unique gift, his two sidekicks – one male and one female (Ron and Hermione/Han Solo and Princess Leia) – Voldemort's betrayal of his mentor (which echoes Darth Vader's betrayal of Obi-Wan Kenobi), and the use of wands (made somewhat less vulgar than the easily aroused light sabers of the *Star Wars* franchise). But Rowling's strongest influences may be more literary. The *Potter* series is just another in a long line of British boarding-school novels stretching back to *Tom Brown's School Days* (1857) and to the work of Enid Blyton (1897–1968), coupled with the strong satirical streak that Philip Nel correctly connects to Roald Dahl and Jane Austen.

Rowling's fun with names hearkens to the importance Tolkien placed on etymology and nomenclature but is also reminiscent of Dahl's "caricature tag names," which Richard Seiter traces to Charles Dickens (192). Most of the names in *Potter* provide commentaries on characters' personality, origins, or their role in the story, and many of them do so humorously. This intertextual play is part of the fun of this fantasy, as in Dahl's *Charlie and the Chocolate Factory* (1964), where a gluttonous child is onomatopoetically named Augustus Gloop, and in *Potter*, where the similarly gluttonous but bullying sidekicks whom Malfoy (Tom Felton) commands are named Crabbe and Goyle, suggesting a pair of irritable gargoyles (played by Jamie Waylett and Josh Herdman, respectively). This playfulness gratifies fans and critics alike by offering a richness of reference and resonance with its precursors. Like *Shrek*, the *Potter* series succeeds at subtly building up a rich semiotic field. Such layering appeals to a variety of audiences, including fans who revisit the texts over and over again. For example, younger reader/viewers may not immediately grasp that Dumbledore's "pensieve" recalls the word "pensive" and also combines the French word for "think" with the humorous notion that brains (particularly older forgetful ones) often *seem* like sieves. (Interestingly, "pensieve" is an anagram of Pevensie, the children's last name in the *Narnia* series.) Plays on spelling can be lost in a visual medium like film, but they can be foregrounded, as with signs for Knockturn Alley in the second film, an allusion to the roughness of the neighborhood and to the nocturnal fantasy world where we dream up the kit and caboodle of wizardry.

Viewers share Harry's amazement at the wizarding world as they peel back layers of the contemporary *mise-en-scène* to uncover a fantasy realm. Nel points out that this combination of the contemporary and fantastical has antecedents in the work of E. Nesbit (1858–1924), the prolific British children's writer. Nesbit popularized fantasies that departed from the separate "secondary world" model adopted by Tolkien, instead penning magical adventures that occur in the contemporary, real world (Natov, 128). In this same vein, the *Potter* movies excel at creating a feeling of lighthearted awe as we discover a world much like our own but full of "enchanting" variations. It's the same feeling we get when Dorothy first arrives in Oz or when Lucy arrives in Narnia – a sense of paradise lost and regained. Unlike Dorothy, but like Lucy, Harry (Daniel Radcliffe) finds his true home only by *leaving* his so-called home. Hogwarts is Harry's true home from the moment in the first film when Professor McGonagall (Maggie Smith) tells the students that their school "houses" will become like their families. This is confirmed when the students leave Hogwarts at the end of the year and Hermione (Emma Watson) remarks on how strange it feels to be going home. Harry replies, "I'm not going home.

Not really." In the second film Harry tells Dobby the House Elf (voiced by Toby Jones) that Hogwarts is his home and, when he and Ron (Rupert Grint) arrive there, Ron says the magic words: "Welcome home." (Prior to this, a meter at the Weasleys' house flips back to the "home" position to indicate that Ron and his brothers are now safely back. On the dials are photos of the children which only register smiles when returned to the home position.)

Though Hogwarts becomes Harry's true home, he is continually surprised by its strangeness and the frequent *uncanny* emotion of exhilaration and fright that he experiences there. His world seems both familiar and unfamiliar, evoking Freud's notion of the "uncanny" as a feeling of being simultaneously home/not home (similar to that experienced by Dorothy in Oz, and the children in Narnia). This is a world both wonderful and perilous. A chess game whose men magically take orders from the players at first seems wondrous. But it turns creepy when the knights actually demolish one another (foreshadowing the life-sized version the students will soon play). Thus in *Potter*, games may be deadly serious, but at the same time deadly serious things may be funny. The tension between horror and the wondrous whimsy of a child's fantasy remains nicely balanced. Lightning, fog, ghosts, spiders, ominous music, and a host of other ghoulish signifiers create horror and suspense, on the one hand, and humor and delight, on the other. Nearly Headless Nick is horrific and a bit gross, but he's also funny – a funniness reinforced by the casting choice of Monty Python's John Cleese. When he greets the students, he doffs his *head* instead of a hat. This horror/humor trope is established early in the first movie when the Dursleys (Richard Griffith and Fiona Shaw) attempt to isolate Harry in a secluded lighthouse. A dark and stormy night sets the Gothic mood as the front door is bashed open and a menacing giant looms over the group. But seconds later, the tone shifts and we see it's only the mild Hagrid (Robbie Coltrane), who blithely apologizes, "Sorry 'bout that!" Hagrid's enormity and force present a humorous contrast to his kindness and overblown sentimentality for children and animals. Over the course of the films, frightening dragons are similarly played first as scary, then as adorable, and then as fearsome again (as Harry learns during the Triwizard Tournament in the fourth film).

The metaphorical parallels between the real and fantastical worlds expand as the series progresses. The stereotypical teenage automobile fantasy is transformed into a wild adventure in the second movie, *Harry Potter and the Chamber of Secrets* (2002), when Harry and Ron end up "borrowing" the Weasleys' car to get to school. Echoes of *Chitty Chitty*

Bang Bang (1968) combine with a more problematic outcome as they crash the magically flying car and land Ron in trouble with his mother (Julie Walters). Of all the films, this one is the most insistent on showing Harry and pals as typical teenagers flouting the rules and either getting away with it, being punished (detention, etc.), or suffering the direct and unpleasant consequences of their actions. When a spell backfires and strikes Ron instead of Malfoy, Ron ends up vomiting slugs. Curiously, rather than go to the infirmary, Harry suggests they go see Hagrid. Why? Because Ron has broken a rule and they know that Hagrid won't report them. But Hagrid is unable to help, saying there's nothing to do but wait as Ron repeatedly barfs into a bucket, curiously reminiscent of what can happen when young people "overdo" something they're not supposed to do in the first place. When the trio drink polyjuice potion, effectively "experimenting with drugs," we witness another scene of hurling in the toilet prior to the revelation that Hermione has turned into a cat. With its puking, "boneless" arm, and mandrake roots that cry like babies and later develop acne, *Chamber* delights in the (pre)adolescent gross-out humor established in the first film. In that movie, besides vomit- and earwax-flavored candy, we are treated to troll "bogies" and giant three-headed dog slobber. It's all played for fun, just as the students' misspoken spells result only in cartoon-style explosions.

The third film, *Harry Potter and the Prisoner of Azkaban* (2004), marks a transition from the more lighthearted tone of the first two under the direction of Alfonso Cuarón The visuals of the film mirror the more serious turn of events in the story: " . . . the tone and color palette have shifted, the bright, flat lighting giving way to a somber and dangerous feel, evocative of horror films" (Dargis and Scott). The Dementors turn a romantic/fairy-tale concept into a trope of horror. Instead of a kiss bringing a person back to life, their lips suck the life and drain the hope from their victims. If hope is at the heart of fantasy, then the Dementors represent fantasy's ultimate monster.

Despite its darker tone, *Azkaban* continues to humorously explore differences and connections between the wizarding and the ordinary world. What might a wizard use for transportation? Maybe a broom, or a Muggle car that flies. Or, it could be the Knight Bus, a triple-decker equipped with beds and a chandelier, traveling at ultra-high speeds and capable of changing its shape or even slowing time's passage. When the bus hurtles through London, unseen but narrowly missing ordinary traffic, we imagine that our own mundane world might likewise conceal fantastic phenomena. As Cara Lane reminds us, "muggles (including the film's viewers) could recognize the magic that surrounds them if they could open themselves to thinking in new ways." Compared to the first two movies, *Azkaban* more fully realizes the aspects of contemporary culture that inform the wizard world, reaffirming, as Lane writes, that "the film speaks to real life rather than offering an alternative fantasy." For example, Harry reads a book under the covers of his bed, just like readers of the *Potter* novels might. (But of course Harry uses a wand instead of a flashlight.) Whereas in the first film, the students wear uniforms beneath their robes, this movie clothes them in contemporary Muggle garb. Professor Lupin (David Thewlis) dons classic professorial tweed, and the Minister of Magic (Robert Hardy) sports a pin-striped robe, reminding us that style is an element of both our worlds. And, in a moment of catharsis and humor, Hermione surprises us by decking Malfoy with a very real-world punch, rather than using her wand (Lane). This is the *Harry Potter* version of the celebrated scene in *Raiders of the Lost Ark* where Indiana Jones appears to be threatened by a classic swashbuckling swordfight, but suddenly surprises us by changing the rules and simply pulling out a gun to shoot his opponent.

The fourth film, *Harry Potter and the Goblet of Fire* (2005), directed by Mike Newell, ends with the death of a Hogwarts student, a mark of the series' definitive transition to more serious matters (the first of the series to receive a PG-13 rather than a PG rating). With the Triwizard Tournament, the fourth film still offers up the riddles and game-like fun of the earlier ones but ratchets up the intensity with numerous scary scenes of Death Eaters and Lord Voldemort (Ralph Fiennes) himself. Still, the tension between magic and the mundane continues to infuse this movie, where an old boot serves as a "portkey" to the Quidditch World Cup, an event which nicely parallels the real world of sports entertainment.

The fifth film, *Harry Potter and the Order of the Phoenix* (2007), directed by Peter Yates, is darker still, both in content and in style. Many reviewers praised it for just this reason, some going so far as to classify it as a political thriller (Andrews; Dargis and Scott). But by the end of the film, Voldemort appears much more like any run-of-the-mill movie baddie where it all comes down to a physical fight. As Hermione opines in *Chamber*, fear of the name only increases fear of the thing itself – and in this movie "he who must not be named" gets named an awful lot. Voldemort loses his mystique and becomes more mundane, a flaw in the *Potter* tradition, but perhaps inevitable as the wondrous and "numinous" qualities becomes more familiar as the series progresses.

Harry Potter and the Half-Blood Prince (2009) continues in the same vein as *Phoenix*, conveying a darker feeling than the first few films and focusing on the more sinister aspects of the wizarding world. Directed by Yates and penned by Steve Kloves (who wrote all but the fifth movie install-ment), *Half-Blood Prince* thus combines the more adult tone that Yates had brought to *Phoenix* with Klove's knack for humor and his continued attention to the personal intrigue of Hogwarts' maturing students. Although the emphasis on the adolescents' burgeoning love lives at times seems a bit "half-hearted," *Half-Blood Prince* nevertheless dramatizes an essential element of fantasy: while the wizard world may celebrate wonder and whimsy in a way that no muggle world could, it also reflects real life in its insistence on the complexities (and pettiness) of adult relationships and on the serious responsibilities that all coming-of-age characters face. By combining story elements that resonate not just with children but with adolescents and adults, and which deftly combine horror with humor, the *Potter* series successfully bridges what sometime seem like separate worlds (whether generational or generic).

Potter's hybrid (shall we say "half-blood") nature also extends to the series' emphasis on riddles and mysteries. Thus *Potter* is not just a fantasy, but a kind of detective story. The contemporary appeal of extravagant mystery stories was demonstrated by the success of *The Da Vinci Code* (2003) and *Angels & Demons* (2009), which provided complicated, non-magical adventures for adults. In *Potter*, the centrality of riddles is embodied by the villain himself. In *Chamber*, for example, we learn that the young Voldemort's name was originally Tom Marvolo Riddle, an anagram for "I am Lord Voldemort." Over the course of the series, the puzzles are interwoven with the metamorphical character of a world in which nothing can be taken as what it seems.

Because *Potter* is set in the present, humor and controversy arise naturally from the contemporary milieu. Like *Rings* and *Narnia*, *Potter* has been accused of everything from sexism and elitism to devil worship. (For excellent scholarly critiques, see anthologies such as Anatol; Heil-man; and Whited.) The issues of class and race inform our distaste for Harry's arrogant classmate Draco Malfoy, while racism underlies much of Voldemort's villainy. Some critics applaud Hermione's struggle to free the House Elves from slavery, but others argue that she is marginalized and ridiculed for her actions (Mendlesohn, 180). The House Elves certainly echo pernicious stereotypes about slavery in the real world. For example, it seems that that they don't want to be free in the first place and have no agency to effect liberation except with express permission ("manumission") from their masters (181). Indeed, racial prejudice permeates the entire premise of the series as the fantasy is predicated upon a segregated Muggle/wizard world. Those who are part-Muggle and part-wizard have to "pass" as Muggles when in the presence of

Muggle relations. And unlike superheroes, who routinely help those without superpowers, wizards never attempt to solve Muggle problems. This system of apartheid has actually been ordained by the Ministry of Magic itself. Wizards are strictly forbidden to use magic to either help or harm Muggles and they are barred from using magic where Muggles may detect it. Muggles, like the Dursleys, are clearly seen as inferior and narrow-minded, but we begin to wonder if wizards may be just as bigoted. The term "Muggle" is never used by those without magical ability – it's a pejorative used by others to characterize a people and a world without magic. Voldemort and Malfoy are certainly detestable bigots for whom the two worlds are separate and decidedly *not* equal, but *Potter* does not condone the segregated world. As a fantasy, it permits a more oblique and therefore less threatening dramatization of a difficult issue.

In fact, fantasy itself is championed by the Muggle/wizard dichotomy. Muggles are not just incapable of magic in a practical sense, they are also deficient in imagination, the primary, metaphorical root of magic. Although there is disdain on both sides, the wizard and Muggle worlds are revealed to be similar in many ways. Both are highly flawed societies where the inhabitants are subjected to each other's pettiness, prejudice, and corruption.

While the existential differences of the worlds are profound, the practical distinctions often revolve around a constellation of oppositional ideas. Magical artifice is juxtaposed with rationality, science, and technology. William Morris, the nineteenth-century fantasy writer, described men as being "shackled to an inexorable, *mechanical struggle*" (Rabkin, 86, my italics). How interesting that collapsing that phrase yields the word describing Rowling's vision of humanity: a Mechanical strUGGLE = a Muggle. While a kind of natural magic exists in both *Rings* and *Potter*, Tolkien saw a certain type of magic to be nearly synonymous with machinery, where both are the enemy of Faerie or Enchantment. Magic is bad when conceived of as "external plans or devices (apparatus) instead of development of the inherent powers or talents – or even the use of these talents with the corrupted motive of dominating: bulldozing the real world, or coercing other wills. The Machine is our more obvious modern form though more closely related to Magic than is usually recognized" (Tolkien 2000, 146). The magic in *Potter* appears to be the type that Tolkien disdains, but it serves a positive function here by reflecting our own Muggle existence. Much of the humor in *Potter* derives from the substitution of magic, with all of its trappings and flourishes, for the mundane practicality of everyday technologies. But, as in *Rings*, magic is a privileged realm. Anyone can learn to drive a car, but only those with the gift can learn to disapparate or use a wand. Again, we can see this talent as analogous to a healthy imagination and an open mind, or we can see it as a kind of spiritual capacity, as Dickerson and O'Hara suggest (236). That is, magical ability denotes an internal wisdom unavailable to Muggles and suggests that magic is not so much a power external to the character as a resource developed from within. As with Spider-Man or Luke Skywalker, the gift is special and must be developed properly. Of course, the *craft* of wizardry also involves its own technologies like potions and charms, devices that hearken back to our earliest pre-histories.

The primeval melds with the bucolic countryside in *Potter*, serving mostly as a backdrop to the narrative and, along with its medieval buildings, helping to establish Hogwarts' fairy-tale feel. The dark forest provides a handy venue for scary adventures, evoking woods in many tales from *Little Red Riding Hood* to *The Wizard of Oz*. As with the rest of the wizarding world, it's filled with fantastical creatures. Sometimes frightening and often familiar from myth, folklore, and fairy tales, many of these creatures are sentient and some can talk. As we have seen, the difference between talking and muteness is a major issue in the *Narnia* world, signifying capacities like judgment and choice.

In *Potter*, some characters can use magic to transform themselves physically, most often by taking the shape of an animal. "Animagi" transformation may be voluntary and (like invisibility) may be used for either good or evil. The benevolent aspect of this type of magic is introduced at the very beginning of the first movie, as a skulking black cat turns out to be Professor McGonagall, who secretly awaits the safe arrival of the orphan Harry. By contrast, in *Azkaban*, Ron's pet rat Scabbers proves to be none other than Voldemort's minion, Peter Pettigrew (Timothy Spall). Pettigrew's shape-shifting is clearly malevolent, as he has been disguising himself in order to spy on Harry (thus "ratting him out"). Unlike voluntary transformations, involuntary ones are generally an abuse of magic associated with curses (except when used to counteract other evils). Thus in *Azkaban*, we also learn that the difference between an animagus and a werewolf depends upon whether the person has chosen the transformation. In the next installment, "choice" emerges as a concept central to Harry's moral education, and one that subtends issues of magic, power, and slavery.

Enchantment lies at the heart of the fantasy world, endowing animals with speech and causing inanimate objects to take on lives of their own. Their primal nature is distinct from what Tolkien describes as the "vulgar devices of the laborious, scientific, magician." It is of the same type that Lewis employs in *Narnia* and "lie(s) near the heart of Faerie: the desire of men to hold communion with other living things" (Tolkien 1966, 39, 43). This is what truly distinguishes the wizarding from the Muggle world – an enchantment that infuses the very fabric of existence.

Just as words have a privileged relation to physical reality through spells, ideas about the world become one with material reality in the fantasy realm. For example, a book *about* monsters is *itself* monstrous, viciously attacking those who attempt to open its pages (first seen in *Azkaban*). The conflation between humans, animals, and objects is often a source of humor. (*The Flintstones* cartoon series, 1960–6, for example, featured animals or Stone-Age items serving as modern household appliances. The trunk of a wooly mammoth became a vacuum cleaner, shower, or dishwasher, and brontosauruses worked like steam shovels.) Making fun of magic itself, though he objected to it, can serve Tolkien's purpose of *recovery*, the notion that we can be made to see the primary world with fresh eyes. When a fantasy's photos and paintings self-animate, we re-conceptualize their definitions and boundaries. Animated paintings or photos are not very different from television or computer screens, but they seem magical in *Potter* because their movement is "framed" by real-world contexts like the portraiture and still lifes in which they are embedded. Harry's invisible ink correspondence with Tom Riddle in *Chamber* resembles email or text-messaging but seems magical because it is "bound" by the conceptual confines of a physical book.

Just as re-spelling Tom Marvolo Riddle yields the name that must not be spoken, verbalization is the key to transformation by spells. In *Potter* magic spells provide hidden information, thinly disguising their Latin derivations. While language is critical to Tolkien, Lewis, Le Guin, and other fantasy authors, the importance of speech in *Potter* becomes magnified in the films because we are able to *hear* the words and not just read them. Likewise, we see the actors' gestures and body movements as they wield their wands. Thus both spells and wands become extensions of the agency of the human body. McClintock writes that the sword is the perfect weapon for medieval fantasies because it becomes the logical extension of a human arm, as compared to a mechanical projectile device like a gun (34). The wand, often wielded in very sword-like manner in the *Potter* films, is an extension of both the human arm and the human voice as it casts a spell ("words" being an anagram of "sword") (Plate 22).

The magic spells that the characters employ in *Potter* are rooted in ancient language and they demand a performance of voice and gesture

PLATE 22 *Harry Potter and the Prisoner of Azkaban* (2004 Warner Bros.): The wand – extension of word and deed. (Courtesy of Photofest.)

suffused with a sense of ritual. Words thus accumulate meaning and power, in part, through repetition over time. But words can also be deprived of their potency when taken out their normal context. Harry realizes this as he increasingly tries to control the effect of language by saying "Voldemort" aloud in casual conversation, thus robbing the name of its ritual mystery. Much of the power struggle in the series rests on the characters' attempts to appropriate language for their own uses. And yet, in the real world, we are never fully in control of our speech, as Hagrid's slips of the tongue suggest ("I should not have said that, I should NOT have said that"). In addition, multiple meanings and shifting contexts mean that "our" utterances are never really our own, but belong to a larger web of meaning. And yet through the device of magic, the *Potter* series offers a fantasy antidote – precise language that can yield precise results through the ritualistic performance of spells.

But the power struggle remains as our words may be misinterpreted, suppressed, or intentionally used against us. Hagrid's inability to master his own tongue serves as a comic counterpoint to other characters who attempt to willfully *misuse* speech and writing for their own ends. For example, *Goblet* introduces the journalist Rita Skeeter (Miranda Richardson), who consistently files sensational and often completely false reports. And in *Phoenix*, the repeated attempts at censorship by Dolores

Umbridge (Imelda Staunton) and the smear tactics used by the Ministry of Magic both become central to the conflict in that film.

The magic spells used throughout the series emphasize the power of speech, but also relate to the theme of racism that underlies the story's continuing conflict. What is the relationship, for example, between verbally casting a spell and Malfoy insulting Hermione in *Chamber* by calling her a "mudbloood"? Does merely insulting someone with racial epithets have the potential to injure that person in the same way that malicious spells do? It seems so, as Hermione exhibits a physical reaction to Malfoy's insults, demonstrating that words have the power to directly affect the physical world through the human body. Not only does *Potter* tie conventions of fantasy to contemporary concerns about hate speech, bigotry, and race but, by setting contemporary issues in a fantasy setting, the books and films are able to explore sensitive issues without offending their audiences. Unlike the characters in the movie, children and adult viewers of the films can sit in a crowded theater and hear the term "mudblood" without inadvertently promulgating the use of racial epithets. This is a danger in the real world, as reported by Judith Butler, who describes how her attempts to discuss racial epithets in a college class resulted in a renewed use of the terms by certain students. "No matter how vehement the opposition to such speech is, its recirculation inevitably reproduces trauma . . . the critical discourse on them becomes precisely the instrument of their perpetration" (1997, 37–8). The power of words to wound or to heal suffuses the *Potter* stories, but fictional terms like "mudblood" act like protective "spells" to shield us from the potential harm of propagating hateful speech. Hermione is not so lucky. As Butler describes it, name-calling "puts you in your place" by, paradoxically, attempting to take you out of your place in the social network (4). Hermione is "put in her place" by Malfoy's insults, which declare that she has "no place" at Hogwarts. Butler writes that such insults are often experienced as a "slap in the face," literally and figuratively throwing the victim off-balance. Thus, both spells and name-calling or hate speech may have an immediate effect on the receiver and are what J.L. Austin calls illocutionary utterances. They "do what they say, and do it in the moment of that saying. . . . As utterances, they work to the extent that they are given in the form of a ritual, that is, repeated in time, and, hence, maintain a sphere of operation that is restricted to the moment of utterance itself" (Butler 1997, 3). When a judge says "I sentence you," the effect is immediate and real, just as magic spells have an instantaneous effect, and just as Malfoy repeatedly provokes Hermione to tears or anger by simply insulting her.

A victim of racial prejudice herself, Hermione empathizes with the House Elves and creates an organization which she names the Society for the Promotion of Elfish Welfare, or S.P.E.W. In the book version of *Goblet*, it seems as if the otherwise meticulous Hermione has inadvertently allowed language to undercut the seriousness of her cause with an acronym that reflects poorly on the organization. Indeed critics have chastised Rowling for appearing to mock Hermione's efforts (Heilman and Gregory, 245; Mendlesohn 180). The problem of the House Elves is downplayed in the movie versions, and in *Goblet*, Hermione's organization is deleted altogether. It's a pity because we might equally note that the meaning of the acronym escapes this simplistic definition. S.P.E.W. derides not Hermione's organization, but the practice of name-calling associated with bigotry that her organization opposes. After all, a person doesn't just "say" racial epithets, he or she more likely "spews" them. Retaining the House Elves but downplaying Hermione's crusade in the films not only weakens Hermione's character, it also dilutes the racial issues raised by the apparent acceptance of the House Elves' enslavement, an injustice that helps to illuminate what is at stake in the central conflict.

Although the *Potter* stories give us the satisfaction of first hating, and then vanquishing despicable characters, it is important to note that the problem of otherness is not just positioned as a function of any one individual's moral failing. Bigotry is not external to, but actually *built into*, the creation of Hogwarts itself, as represented by the House of Slytherin. Malfoy and his housemates' legacy is historical, acquired from their fathers and forefathers. When he insults mudbloods, Malfoy demonstrates his desire to make "linguistic community with a history of speakers" (Butler 1997, 52), his pure-blooded ancestry.

As with most Hollywood movies, the complexity of the problem risks being resolved only at the personal level rather than through any sort of systematic change – accentuated here by the personalization of the films' conflict as a one-on-one battle between Harry and Voldemort. At heart, Harry's struggle is against his own potential —he could easily have been "interpellated" (to quote Althusser), that is, verbally "hailed" or recognized by the sorting hat as a member of Slytherin. When the hat vacillates, Harry makes the choice to reject *that* community, calling on the strength of love left to him by his mother.

Harry is the chosen one not because he was born special (as in a fairy tale when the lowly hero is ignorant of his royal blood), but because his mother sacrificed her life for him out of love. Farah Mendlesohn criticizes the stories for their insistence on heredity as the key to characters' social status and says that Harry's choice of Gryffendor "is actually between two heredities or destinies. It is not a free choice" (171). While there is much to this argument, we can as easily read his dilemma as a powerful critique offered up by the series (born, as it is, in England, with its history of royalty and distinct class divisions). The hold that our racial and economic heritage has on our identities and choices is certainly powerful. When it comes to race, Harry is no less a product of his heritage than Voldemort. Harry and Voldemort (as Tom Riddle) are both part-Muggle, and both grew up as abused orphans. We are reminded that Harry risks turning into Voldemort, perpetuating a cycle of hate and violence because of similar circumstances. But that is exactly why we need Harry to make the right choices. As Terri Doughty remarks, Harry "is proof that the cycle need not be continued" (248).

Ron Weasley serves as a classic contrast to Harry. He's one of the good guys but he shows how easy it is to accept the status quo. When he mocks Hermione's efforts to save the elves, repeating the ridiculous notion that they don't want to be free, or when he makes generalizations about giants, he provides an illustration of how "nice" people unintentionally perpetuate pernicious behavior by making assumptions about the naturalness of things as they are. That is why Ron is not the hero. His goodness derives from his loyalty to the one who *chooses* to be good – Harry. Harry must choose, and that is the function of the hero. In this way, *Potter* attributes the propagation of attitudes (whether good or bad) to the generations that came before but also dramatizes the momentous, heroic struggle to break free.

The tension between freedom and struggle is what Hall points to in the novels as a conflict between "Structure and Chaos" (159). Chaos, of course, is exactly what the narrative seeks to contain – to make sense from the senselessness of evil. It is against such chaos that we find comfort and contrast in the hierarchical world of wizards and the structured, tradition-filled world of Hogwarts (even while learning that some traditions are better than others). Hogwarts not only thrives on its rules and traditions, it serves as a model for resolving the structure/chaos struggle because its mission is to teach students to master not just their environment but their own personal development. That this takes place in a school is important despite the fact that much of the learning takes place outside the classroom. This is a tradition of the boarding-school novel, but is also the necessary microcosm of the larger structure/chaos world, a rubric of fantasy stories that play off a highly structured world and an alternate arena free from restriction in order for the fantasy/development to occur.

Some parents may be disturbed by the fact that Harry and friends routinely break school rules, while others like Hall criticize the wizarding world for its unfairness, corruption, and an inconsistent application of justice. It may seem surprising that a world of magic is not a utopian paradise, but far from being an indictment of the series, this is part of its strength. It is all part of a larger ambivalence about magic, ultimately acknowledging that magic cannot provide the solution to all problems or final answers to moral questions. When Harry, Hermione, and Ron resort to illegal actions or violate school rules, they never do so because they're willfully rebellious; they only respond to problems or threats that others have created. Over and over, Harry is wrongly accused, his actions misunderstood. This is a common element of children's stories because it mimics life from a child's perspective (Natov, 125). The fact that Harry is often unfairly blamed for a number of incidents resonates with kids who feel unfairly punished under arbitrary adult rules or because of adults' inability to prevent injustice. The persistent "absence of the rule of law" is integral to the intrigue and emotional appeal of Harry's circumstances and is not, therefore, a flaw in the story.

Harry's dilemma resonates with adults too, who often face arbitrary and unjust rules. The challenge that the series presents is for characters to avoid using power for personal gain even though the system may be flawed. Viewers experience the vicarious thrill of flouting or supervening rules when they don't make sense or have outlived their relevance. As we have seen, Spider-Man and other superheroes routinely operate outside the law when no legal entity can or will save the day. Likewise, cop and crime movies feature heroes who circumvent the authorities and save the day in spite of – and not because of – laws which too often prove ineffective or corrupt. In this sense, Hogwarts functions more as a vocational school, while Harry's struggle against Voldemort outside the classroom provides the moral education that supplements his practical training. Harry's mission at the tradition-bound Hogwarts is thus to propagate the correct traditions, acknowledging "the hero's paradoxical struggle to maintain tradition and to subvert it for evolution to occur" (Natov, 130). This is part and parcel of why Harry "must break the very rules at Hogwarts needed to maintain order and basic values" (130). In the same way, by "breaking the rules" of the physical world, fantasy films violate norms but simultaneously propose a new version of "order," a fresh perspective on the traditions that have shaped our world.

CHAPTER 14

CONCLUSION
Imagine That!

From *The Wizard of Oz* to *Harry Potter*, fantasy films have shown an affinity for orphan characters. How fitting since, until recently, the fantasy genre has been something of an orphan itself. Unmoored from literary conceptions of high art and, for the most part, not even considered worthy of pop-culture study (while sci-fi and horror films have enjoyed plenty of critical scrutiny), fantasy has lurked at the fringes of conventional, respectable society. If this were a movie, little orphan fantasy would struggle to gain acceptance while being deprived of material privileges (production budgets and special effects) and it would wrestle to find its "true identity," only to overcome obstacles (often with helpers), and ultimately emerge victorious. Little orphan fantasy would then be applauded for bringing "boons" and benefits to the larger society. The helpers are fans, critics, and scholars, and even technology. The obstacles include myopic critics who have dismissed fantasy out of hand, as well as the many weak films that have hurt the genre's reputation. But, of course, this fantasy has yet come to a conclusion, and the subtext to the story is rich and far more complicated than any fairy tale. Perhaps there is no "coming of age" for the fantasy genre. As a lover of many fantasy films, however, I believe in happy endings. While not all fantasy is worthwhile, a number of fantasy works have indeed "come of age" and deserve our time and attention.

This book has only skimmed the surface of a vast terrain, leaving many gaps and omissions, both in films left un-discussed and many more strands in the weave of critical perspectives. Hollywood would have trouble wrapping up all the loose ends in this little movie, given the eclectic nature of fantasy. Can *Groundhog Day* and *Lord of the Rings really* belong to the same genre? Yes! Fantasy films make explicit what is implicit in our enjoyment of all mainstream films – the need to relax imaginatively, the need to get away from the rat race.

True, nobody works harder than the "rat" Phil Connors, who toils endlessly in *Groundhog Day*, an effort that eventually pays off for him – a useful message indeed. But Phil's cosmic sentence to hard labor occurs precisely because he takes an exclusively instrumental perspective. He wonders how Rita, the television "producer," can be "productive" for him – what will be her "output?" And so Phil spends the entire movie trying to get Rita to "put out." Only after realizing that he has missed the point – of enjoying life – is he released from his "life" sentence. Fantasy films (like all mainstream movies) are first and foremost designed to entertain. As a form of play, a type of ritual fun, fantasy may therefore not have a useful purpose *per se*, at least as far as most audiences are concerned. If this seems anathema to our sense of work ethic, it's because it is! A movie invites us to temporarily leave our cares behind, and that may *be* its ultimate "purpose."

Leisure is not simply the absence of work or mere idleness, as many assume. It is, at its best, a celebration of oneself and one's place in the world. It is this sense of leisure, or celebration and festival (see Pieper), that is completely lacking in Phil, and it is this quality which provides a central impulse to so many fantasy stories. Harvey, the invisible rabbit, is the spectral inverse of the workaday world. It is not that work isn't essential. Work is necessary, but it is not sufficient. This is the invisible thread that links a film like *Groundhog Day* to *The Lord of the Rings*. The healthy work of the Hobbits and the craftsmanship of the Elves are essential to the values of Middle Earth, but they are not the same as the oppressive, mechanical drudgery of the Orcs. The opening scene in the Shire establishes productive village life and the bucolic countryside, but also shows the Hobbits in full festival mode. Productive work integrated with joyful celebration is precisely what is at stake in *Rings* and what is lost or tarnished at the end of the books. (In true Hollywood fashion, however, the movie version deletes the scourge of the Shire, and returns us to its unsullied state.)

But questions remain. Can fantasy really contribute to a vision of life with room for work *and* leisure, where both are valued *equally*? Does going to the movies constitute leisure or wasted time? And if leisure is conceived of as a break from work, do we take it only so that we may be *more* productive at work? The mainstream movie industry exemplifies the very productive work of our modern "information" society. And we, as film viewers, must work in order to make money to pay for the privilege of watching what Hollywood produces. The more we work, the more we need leisure, and thus the more leisure and work remain polarized in our culture. Leisure is not fully conceptualized or valued outside of this form of "vicious cycle." This is amply illustrated in *Harvey*, where the very idea of leisure is pathologized and cannot be conceived of *except* as a tippler's figment of imagination or as a spectral presence. Leisure and play *are* valued, however, in the context of childhood, as seen in so many fantasy movies.

C.S. Lewis hoped that fantasy would take its place in helping to spark the imagination of those in whom it is dead or sleeping. And if anything contrasts fantasy to science fiction and horror, it is the vanquishing of despair and restlessness through imagination and hope. Tolkien and Lewis conceived of fantasy in this spiritual, celebratory sense. Those who don't value or have no capacity for the leisure and adventure inherent in fantasy are, in this sense, Muggles all. But just as Peter Parker can't "force" his web-making, neither can you force leisure. In *Groundhog Day* Phil tries desperately to force "play" with Rita in the snow, a contradictory impulse which only serves to "alienate" her.

While the imaginative experience is essential for both viewer and critic alike, any analysis of film necessarily focuses on one or more interpretative strategies that may foreground some aspects of at the expense of others. Most of us don't go to the movies to "interpret" them, but to enjoy them. But viewers *do* interpret films, whether consciously or not, and what fulfills one, another finds trivial, what excites one person offends someone else. The variety of responses elicited by the *Harry Potter* films is a case in point and underscores the difficulty of pinning down definitive meaning. But it also reminds us why fantasy films may be particularly rich: they excel in employing multi-faceted symbols that engage viewers on many levels.

To critics who suggest that fantasy is inferior because it is a "cowardly" escape from reality, we might paraphrase the Cowardly Lion and ask: "What do they got that we ain't got?" If "we" is defined as those who produce, consume, and enjoy fantasy films, I hope this book has helped in some small way to answer that. Fantasy films are no better or worse than other mainstream films. And if "they" includes both non-fantasy films and those who categorically elevate those films above fantasy, I say this: There has never been much risk in praising, engaging with, or analyzing realist and/or "serious" movies. The same has not been true for fantasy film. So, Courage!

Dorothy is heroic in part because she has dared to use her imagination. She lets it take her someplace extraordinary and faces a terrifying, fantastic adventure. Her comrades the Tin Man and Scarecrow embody one of the central dialectics of fantasy film, reason and rationality vs imagination and emotion. Having unified them, Dorothy returns home and completes the circuit: merging the twin faces of fantasy, of heart and mind – but also reality and illusion. Just as the Tin Man always had a heart, the Scarecrow a brain, and the Lion courage, Dorothy and the audience have always had the ability to unite these dichotomies because imagination is not opposed to reason and never has been. Fantasy vs reality is a false division, and just as Dorothy never "really" left home, elements of fantasy have never really been absent from mainstream films. They've been there all along, lurking "behind the curtain" of realist and mimetic conventions that promote the illusion of reality. Who put the "ape" in apricot? (to paraphrase the Cowardly Lion). Well, who put the "fan" in fantasy? Nobody. Or everybody. The fantasy fan was always there, from the earliest days of storytelling. Fantasy has always been with us, in our own collective back yard.

REFERENCES

American Film Institute. "10 Top 10."http//
www.afi.com/10TOP10/fantasy.html
(accessed October 18, 2009).

Aleiss, Angela. "Animated Features of a Different Hue." *The Los Angeles Times*, Jan.
24, 1999:18.

Alleva, Richard. "No Tame Lion," *Common-
weal*, 133.1, Jan. 13 (2006): 22.

Altman, Rick. *Film/Genre*. London: BFI,
1999.

Anatol, Giselle Liza, ed. *Reading Harry Potter:
Critical Essays*. Westport, CT: Praeger,
2003.

Andrews, Nigel. "Potter Has Now Left the
Playground," *Financial Times. London*,
July 12, 2007: 15.

Armitt, Lucy. *Fantasy Fiction: An Introduction*. New York: Continuum, 2005.

Attebery, Brian. *Strategies of Fantasy*. Bloomington: Indiana University Press,
1992.

Bakhtin, Mikhail. *Rabelais and His World*, trans. Hélène Iswolsky. Bloomington:
Indiana University Press, 1984.

Barker, Martin. "The Functions of Fantasy: A Comparison of Audiences for *The
Lord of the Rings* in Twelve Countries," *Watching The Lord of the Rings:
Tolkien's World Audiences*. Eds Martin Barker and Ernest Mathijs New
York: Peter Lang, 2008.

Barker, Martin and Ernest Mathijs, eds. *Watching The Lord of the Rings: Tolkien's
World Audiences*. New York: Peter Lang, 2008.

Barron, Neil, ed. *Fantasy and Horror: A Critical and Historical Guide to Literature, Illustration, Film, TV, Radio and the Internet*. Lanham, MD: Scarecrow Press, 2000.

Barthes, Roland. *Mythologies*, trans. Annette Lavers. New York: The Noonday Press, 1993.

Beggan, James K. and Scott T. Allison. "The Playboy Rabbit is Soft, Furry and Cute: Is This Really the Symbol of Masculine Dominance of Women?" *Journal of Men's Studies*, 9.3 (2001): 341–70.

Bell, Elizabeth, Lynda Haas, and Laura Sells, eds. *From Mouse to Mermaid: The Politics of Film, Gender, and Culture*. Bloomington: Indiana University Press, 1995.

Bellin, Joshua David. *Framing Monsters: Fantasy Film and Social Alienation*. Carbondale: Southern Illinois University Press, 2005.

Benson, Sheila. "Spielberg's 'Always': Where's the Fire?" *L.A. Times*, Dec. 22, 1989: 1.

Bettelheim, Bruno. *The Uses of Enchantment: The Meaning and Importance of Fairy Tales*. New York: Vintage Books, 1989.

Biltereyst, Ernest Mathijs and Philippe Meers. "An Avalanche of Attention: The Prefiguration and Reception of *The Lord of the Rings*." *Watching The Lord of the Rings: Tolkien's World Audiences*. Eds Martin Barker and Ernest Mathijs New York: Peter Lang, 2008.

Bordwell, David. *The Way Hollywood Tells It: Story and Style in Modern Movies*. Berkeley: University of California Press, 2006.

Bordwell, David, Janet Staiger, and Kristin Thompson. *The Classical Hollywood Cinema*. New York: Pantheon Books, 1988.

Bratman, David. "Summa Jacksonia: A Reply to Defenses of Peter Jackson's *The Lord of the Rings* Film, after St Thomas Aquinas," *Tolkien on Film: Essays on Peter Jackson's The Lord of the Rings*. Ed. Janet Brennan Croft. Altadena, CA: The Mythopoeic Press, 2004.

Breatnach, Deasun. "The Puca: A Multi-functional Irish Supernatural Entity." *Folklore*, 104.1/2(1993): 105–10.

Bronfen, Elisabeth. *Home in Hollywood: The Imaginary Geography of Cinema*. New York: Columbia University Press, 2004.

Brosnan, John. *Movie Magic: The Story of Special Effects in the Cinema*. New York: Plume Books, 1976.

Buckingham, David. *After the Death of Childhood: Growing Up in the Age of Electronic Media*. Malden, MA: Polity/Blackwell, 2000.

Bukatman, Scott. *Matters of Gravity: Special Effects and Supermen in the 20th Century*. Durham, NC: Duke University Press, 2003.

Burgin, Victor, James Donald, and Cora Kaplan, eds. *Formations of Fantasy*. London: Routledge, 1986.

Butler, Judith. *Gender Trouble: Feminism and the Subversion of Identity*. New York: Routledge, 1990.

Butler, Judith. *Excitable Speech: A Politics of the Performative*. New York: Routledge, 1997.

Byne, Eleanor and Martin McQuillan. *Deconstructing Disney*. London: Pluto Press, 1999.

Caillois, Roger. *Man, Play and Games*, trans. Meyer Barash. Urbana: University of Illinois Press, 2001.

Campbell, John W. "Professional Wrestling: Why the Bad Guy Wins," *Journal of American Culture*, 19.2 (Summer 1996): 127.

Campbell, Joseph. *The Hero with a Thousand Faces*. Princeton: Princeton University Press, 1973.

Carroll, Noël. "Why Horror?" in *Horror: The Film Reader*. Ed. Mark Jancovich. New York: Routledge, 2001.

Cartmell, Deborah, and Imelda Whelehan. "Notes on Harry Potter," *Books in Motion: Adaptation, Intertextuality, Authorship*. Ed. Mireia Aragay. Amsterdam/New York: Rodopi, 2005.

CBS " 'Potter' Enchants Fans with $58m Open: Newest Film Breaks Franchise Record for Single-Day Earnings." http://www.cbsnews.com/stories/2009/07/16/entertainment/main5166191.shtml

Chance, Jane. "Tolkien's Women (and Men): The Films and the Book," *Tolkien on Film: Essays on Peter Jackson's The Lord of the Rings*. Ed. Janet Brennan Croft. Altadena, CA: The Mythopoeic Press, 2004.

Clemens, Justin and Dominic Pettman. *Avoiding the Subject: Media, Culture and the Object*. Amsterdam: Amsterdam University Press, 2004.

Clute, John and John Grant. *The Encyclopedia of Fantasy*. New York: St Martin's Press, 1997.

Cook, David A. *A History of Narrative Film*, 4th edition. New York: Norton, 2004.

Corliss, Richard. "Bill Murray's Déjà Voodoo," *Time*, 141.7, Mar. 15, 1993: 61.

Croft, Janet Brennan. "Mithril Coats and Tin Ears: 'Anticipation' and 'Flattening' in Peter Jackson's *The Lord of the Rings* Trilogy," *Tolkien on Film: Essays on Peter Jackson's The Lord of the Rings*. Ed. Janet Brennan Croft. Altadena, CA: The Mythopoeic Press, 2004.

Cubitt, Sean. "The Fading of the Elves: Eco-Catastrophe, Technopoly, and Bio-Security," *From Hobbits to Hollywood: Essays on Peter Jackson's Lord of the Rings*. Eds Ernest Mathijs and Murray Pomreance. Amsterdam: Rodopi, 2006.

Dalton, Russell W. "Aslan is on the Move: Images of Providence in *The Chronicles of Narnia*," *Revisiting Narnia: Fantasy, Myth and Religion in C.S. Lewis' Chronicles*. Ed. Shanna Caughey. Dallas, TX: Benbella Books, 2005.

Dargis, Manohl and A.O. Scott. "Harry Potter and the Four Directors," *The New York Times*, July 15, 2007: AR 11.

Davis, Amy M. *Good Girls & Wicked Witches: Women in Disney's Feature Animation*. Eastleigh, UK: John Libbey Publishing, 2006.

Delany, Samuel R. "The Gestation of Genres: Literature, Fiction, Romance, Science Fiction, Fantasy . . . ," *Intersections*. Eds George E. Slusser and Eric S. Rabkin. Carbondale: Southern Illinois University Press, 1987.

Dickerson, Matthew and David O'Hara. *From Homer to Harry Potter: A Handbook on Myth and Fantasy*. Grand Rapids, MI: Brazos Press, 2006.

Dighe, Ranjit S. *The Historian's Wizard of Oz: Reading L. Frank Baum's Classic as a Political and Monetary Allegory*. Westport, CT: Praeger, 2002.

Doane, Mary Ann. *The Emergence of Cinematic Time: Modernity, Contingency, The Archive*. Cambridge, MA: Harvard University Press, 2002.

Doughty, Terri. "Locating Harry Potter in the Boys' Book Market," *The Ivory Tower and Harry Potter*. Ed. Lana A. Whited. Columbia: University of Missouri Press, 2002.

Dowling, Collette. *The Cinderella Complex: Women's Hidden Fear of Independence*. Pocket Book, 1982.

Downing, David C. *Into the Wardrobe: C.S. Lewis and the Narnia Chronicles*. San Francisco: Jossey-Bass, 2005.

Durbin, Karen. "A New, if Not Improved, Use of Stereotypes," *The New York Times*, June 21: 2.13.

During, Simon. *Modern Enchantments*. Cambridge, MA: Harvard University Press, 2002.

Dyer, Richard. "Entertainment and Utopia," *Movies and Methods: An Anthology*, Vol. II. Ed. Bill Nichols. Berkeley: University of California Press, 1985.

Ebert, Roger. "Always," *Chicago Sun Times* 22 Dec.1989 http://rogerbert.suntimes.com/apps/pbcs.dll/articl?AID=/19891222/REVIEWS/912220301/1023 (accessed October 18, 2009)

Ebert, Roger. "Lord of the Rings: The Two Towers," *Chicago Sun Times*, Dec. 19, 2002. http://rogerebert.suntimes.com/apps/pbcs.dll/article?AID=/20021218/REVIEWS/212180301/1023 (accessed October 18, 2009)

Egan, Kate and Martin Barker. "The Books, the DVDs, the Extras, and Their Lovers," *Watching the Lord of The Rings: Tolkien's World Audiences*. Eds Martin Barker and Ernest Mathijs. New York: Peter Lang, 2008.

Ehrenreich, Barbara. *The Hearts of Men: American Dreams and the Flight from Commitment*. New York: Anchor Books, 1983.

Filmer, Kath. *Scepticism and Hope in Twentieth-Century Fantasy Literature*. Bowling Green, OH: Bowling Green State University Popular Press, 1992.

Fowkes, Katherine A. *Giving up the Ghost: Spirits, Ghosts, and Angels in Mainstream Comedy Films*. Detroit, MI: Wayne State University Press, 1998.

Fowkes, Katherine A. "Melodramatic Specters: Cinema and *The Sixth Sense*," *Spectral America: Phantoms and the National Imagination*. Ed. Jeffrey Andrew Weinstock. Madison: University of Wisconsin Press, 2004.

Frank, Alan. *Science Fiction and Fantasy Handbook*. Totowa, NJ: Barnes and Noble Books, 1982.

Friedman, Lester. *Citizen Spielberg*. Urbana: University of Illinois Press, 2006.

Friedman, Lester and Brent Notbohm. *Steven Spielberg Interviews*. Jackson: University Press of Mississippi, 2000.

Fuchs, Cynthia. " 'Wicked, Tricksy, False': Race, Myth, and Gollum," *From Hobbits to Hollywood: Essays on Peter Jackson's Lord of the Rings*. Eds Ernest Mathijs and Murray Pomerance. Amsterdam: Rodopi, 2006.

Genter, Robert. "With Great Power Comes Great Responsibility: Cold War Culture and the Birth of Marvel Comics," *Journal of Popular Culture*, 40.6, Dec. (2007): 953.

Gelder, Ken. "Epic Fantasy and Global Terrorism," *From Hobbits to Hollywood: Essays on Peter Jackson's Lord of the Rings*. Eds Ernest Mathijs and Murray Pomerance. Amsterdam: Rodopi, 2006.

Gilbey, Ryan. *Groundhog Day*. London: BFI, 2004.

Giroux, Henry A. *Disturbing Pleasures: Learning Popular Culture*. New York: Routledge, 1994.

Goldberg, Johan. "A Movie for All Time: Tomorrow and Tomorrow and Tomorrow, *Groundhog Day* Scores," *National Review*, 57.2 (2005): 35–7.

Goldberg, Ruth and Krin Gabbard. "What Does the Eye Demand: Sexuality, Forbidden Vision and Embodiment in *The Lord of the Rings*," *From Hobbits to Hollywood: Essays on Peter Jackson's Lord of the Rings*. Eds Ernest Mathijs and Murray Pomerance. Amsterdam: Rodopi, 2006.

Gordon, Andrew. "You'll Never Get Out of Bedford Falls: The Inescapable Family in American Science Fiction and Fantasy Films," *Journal of Popular Film and Television*, 20 (Summer 1992): 2–9.

Gray, Jonathan. "Bonus Material: The DVD Layering of *The Lord of the Rings*," *The Lord of the Rings: Popular Culture in Global Context*. Ed. Ernest Mathijs. London: Wallflower Press, 2006.

Greenberg, Harvey, "The Wizard of Oz: Little Girl Lost - and Found," *The Movies of Your Mind*. New York: Saturday Review Press, 1975.

Griffin, Sean. *Tinker Belles and Evil Queens: The Walt Disney Company from the Inside Out*. New York: New York University Press, 2000.

Gunning, Tom. "Primitive Cinema: A Frame-Up? Or the Trick's on Us," *Cinema Journal*, 2 (Winter 1989): 3–12.

Hall, Susan. "Harry Potter and the Rule of Law: The Central Weakness of Legal Concepts in the Wizard World," *Reading Harry Potter: Critical Essays*. Ed. Giselle Liza Anatol. Westport, CT: Praeger, 2003.

Harmetz, Aljean. *The Making of the Wizard of Oz*. New York: Hyperion, 1977.

Harris, Mark,Tanner Stransky, and Adam Markovitz. "J.K. Rowling," *Entertainment Weekly* Nov. 30, 2007: 34.

Hartland, E. Sidney. "The Outcast Child," *Folk-lore Journal*, 4 (1886): 308–49. http://www.jstor.org/stable/1252856

Hartwell, David G. "Introduction: The Return of Fantasy," *Fantasy and Horror: A Critical and Historical Guide to Literature, Illustration, Film, TV, Radio and the Internet*. Ed. Neil Barron. Lanham, MD: Scarecrow Press, 1999.

Hedling, Erik. "Framing Tolkien: Trailers, High Concept and the Ring," *The Lord of the Rings: Popular Culture in Global Context*. Ed. Ernest Mathijs London: Wallflower Press, 2006.

Heilman, Elizabeth E., ed. *Critical Perspectives on Harry Potter*. New York: Routledge, 2003.

Heilman, Elizabeth E. and Anne E. Gregory. "Images of the Privileged Insider and Outcast Outsider," *Critical Perspectives on Harry Potter*. Ed. Elizabeth E. Heilman. New York: Routledge, 2003.

Hornstein, Lillian Herlands. "'Though This Be Madness': Insanity in the Theater," *College English*, 7 (1945): 7–9.

Hume, Kathryn. *Fantasy and Mimesis: Responses to Reality in Western Literature*. New York: Methuen 1984.

Irwin, W.R. *The Game of the Impossible: A Rhetoric of Fantasy*. Urbana: University of Illinois Press, 1976.

Jackson, Rosemary. *Fantasy: The Literature of Subversion*. New York: Methuen, 1981.

James, Caryn. "Ghosts Must Catch the Spirit of the Time," *The New York Times*, July 29, 1990: sec. 2, 17.

Kauffmann, Stanley. "Fantasy and Fandom," *New Republic*, 208.11 (1993): 24–5.

Kawin, Bruce. "Children of the Light," *Shadows of Magic Lamp*. Eds George Slusser and Eric S. Rabkin. Carbondale: Southern Illinois University Press, 1985.

Kelley, Karol. "A Modern Cinderella," *Journal of American Culture*, 17.1 (1994): 87–92.

Kellner, Douglas. "*The Lord of the Rings* as Allegory: A Multiperspectivist Reading," *From Hobbits to Hollywood: Essays on Peter Jackson's Lord of the Rings*. Eds Ernest Mathijs and Murray Pomerance. Amsterdam: Rodopi, 2006.

Kempley, Rita. "Always: Love in the Afterlife," *The Washington Post*, Dec. 22, 1989: D1.

Kim, Sue. "Beyond Black and White: Race and Postmodernism in the *Lord of the Rings* Films," *Modern Fiction Studies* 50.4 (Winter 2004): 875–907.

Kinder, Marsha. "Back to the Future in the 80s with Fathers & Sons, Supermen & PeeWees, Gorillas & Toons," *Film Quarterly*, 42.4 (Summer 1989): 2–11.

King, Geoff. *New Hollywood Cinema: An Introduction*. New York: Columbia University Press, 2002.

Klinger, Barbara. "What Do Female Fans Want? Blockbusters, *The Return of the King*, and U.S. Audiences," *Watching the Lord of The Rings: Tolkien's World Audiences*. Eds Martin Barker and Ernest Mathijs. New York: Peter Lang, 2008.

Kline, Stephen. "The Making of Children's Culture," *The Children's Culture Reader*. Ed. Henry Jenkins New York: New York University Press, 1998.

Kratz, Dennis M. "The Development of the Fantastic Tradition through 1811," *Fantasy and Horror: A Critical Guide to Literature, Illustration, Film, TV, Radio, and the Internet.* Ed. Neil Barron. Lanham, MD: Scarecrow Press, 1999.

Kroeber, Karl. *Romantic Fantasy.* New Haven: Yale University Press, 1988.

Kuipers, Giselinde and Jeroen DeKloet. "Global Flows and Local Identifications? *The Lord of the Rings* and the Cross-National Reception of Characters and Genres." *Watching The Lord of the Rings: Tolkien's World Audiences.* Eds Barker, Martin and Ernest Mathijs. New York: Peter Lang, 2008.

La Valley, Albert J. "Traditions of Trickery: The Role of Special Effects in the Science Fiction Film," *Shadows of the Magic Lamp: Fantasy and Science Fiction in Film.* Eds George Slusser and Eric S. Rabkin. Carbondale: Southern Illinois University Press, 1985.

Lane, Cara. "The Prisoner of Azkaban: A New Direction for Harry Potter," *Film & History,* 35.1 (2005): 65–8.

Laplanche, Jean and J.-B. Pontalis. "Fantasy and the Origins of Sexuality," *Formations of Fantasy.* Eds Victor Burgin,James Donald, and Cora Kaplan. London: Routledge, 1986.

Lawrence, John Shelton and Robert Jewett, *The Myth of the American Superhero.* Grand Rapids, MI: William B. Eerdmans Publishing, 2002.

Le Guin, Ursula K. *The Language of the Night.* New York: Putnam, 1949.

Lewis, C.S. *On Stories and Other Essays on Literature.* Orlando, FL: Harcourt, 1982.

Loy, David R. and Linda Goodhew. *The Dharma of Dragons and Daemons: Buddhist Themes in Modern Fantasy.* Somerville, MA: Wisdom Publications, 2004.

McClintock, Michael W. "High Tech and High Sorcery: Some Discrimination between Science Fiction and Fantasy," *Intersections.* Eds George E. Slusser and Eric S. Rabkin. Carbondale: Southern Illinois University, 1987.

McConnell, Frank. "Born in Fire: The Ontology of the Monster," *Shadows of the Magic Lamp.* Eds George Slusser and Eric S. Rabkin. Carbondale: Southern Illinois University Press, 1985.

McDonald, Tamar Jeffers. *Romantic Comedy: Boy Meets Girl Meets Genre.* London: Wallflower Press, 2007.

McLarty, Lianne. "Masculinity, Whiteness, and Social Class in *The Lord of the Rings,*" *From Hobbits to Hollywood: Essays on Peter Jackson's Lord of the Rings.* Eds Ernest Mathijs and Murray Pomerance. Amsterdam: Rodopi, 2006.

Marcus, Daniel. *Happy Days and Wonder Years: The Fifties and the Sixties in Contemporary Cultural Politics.* New Brunswick, NJ: Rutgers University Press, 2004.

Mathews, Richard. *Fantasy: The Liberation of the Imagination.* New York: Routledge, 2002.

Mendlesohn, Farah. "Crowning the King: Harry Potter and the Construction of Authority," *The Ivory Tower and Harry Potter.* Ed. Lana A. Whited. Columbia: University of Missouri Press, 2002.

Meyer, Michaela D.E. "Utilizing Mythic Criticism in Contemporary Narrative Culture: Examining the 'Present-Absence' of Shadow Archetypes in Spider-Man," *Communication Quarterly*, 51.4 (Fall 2003): 518–29.

Mikos, Lothar, Susanne Eichner, Elizabeth Prommer, and Michael Wedel. "Involvement in *The Lord of the Rings*: Audience Strategies and Orientations," *Watching The Lord of the Rings: Tolkien's World Audiences*. Eds Martin Barker and Ernest Mathijs. New York: Peter Lang, 2008.

Mitchell, Elvis. "The Lord of the Rings: The Two Towers (2002). Film Review: Soldiering on in Epic Pursuit of Purity," *The New York Times*, Dec. 18, 2002. http://movies.nytimes.com/movie/review?res=9E01E 3DB153DF93BA25751C1A9649C8 B63&scp=3&sq=Lord%20of%20the %20Rings%20The%20Two%20Towerrs&st=cse (accessed October 18, 2009)

Morris, Nigel. *The Cinema of Steven Spielberg: Empire of Light*. London: Wallflower Press, 2007.

Morris, Tom and Matt Morris. *Superheroes and Philosophy: Truth, Justice, and the Socratic Way*. Chicago: Open Court Press, 2005.

Nathanson, Paul. *Over the Rainbow: The Wizard of Oz as Secular Myth of America*. Albany, NY: State University of New York Press, 1991.

Natov, Roni. "Harry Potter and the Extraordinariness of Being Ordinary," *The Ivory Tower and Harry Potter*. Ed. Lana A. Whited. Columbia: University of Missouri Press, 2002.

Naficy, Hamid. *Home, Exile, Homeland: Film, Media, and the Politics of Place*. New York: Routledge, 1999.

Neal, Steve and Frank Krutnik. *Popular Film and Television Comedy*. New York: Routledge, 1990.

Nel, Philip. "Is There a Text in This Advertising Campaign? Literature, Marketing, and Harry Potter," *The Lion and the Unicorn*, 29.2 (2005): 236–67.

Newkirk, Ingrid. "Would the Modern-Day C.S. Lewis be A PETA Protestor?" *Revisiting Narnia: Fantasy, Myth, and Religion in C.S. Lewis' Chronicles*. Ed. Shanna Caughey. Dallas, TX: Benbella Books, 2005.

Nicholls, Peter. *Fantastic Cinema: An Illustrated Survey*. London: Ebury Press, 1984.

O'Connor, Anahad. "The Claim: Some People Dream Only in Black and White," *The New York Times*, Dec. 1, 2008: D5.

Pieper, Josef. *Leisure: The Basis of Culture*. South Bend, IN: St Augustine's Press, 1998.

Pearce, Joseph. "Narnia and Middle-Earth," *Revisiting Narnia: Fantasy, Myth, and Religion in C.S. Lewis' Chronicles*. Ed. Shanna Caughey. Dallas, TX: Benbella Books, 2005.

Polan, Dana B. "Eros and Syphilization: The Contemporary Horror Film," *Planks of Reason: Essays on the Horror Film*. Eds Barry Keith Grant and Christopher Sharrett. Lanham, MD: Scarecrow Press, 2004.

Pols, Mary. "Norbit Doubles Up on Nasty: Murphy Squanders His Talent in Mean-spirited Comedy," *Contra Costa Times*, Feb. 9, 2007: 1.

Pratten, J.D. "Professional Wrestling - Multimillion Pound Soap Opera of Sports Entertainment," *Management Research News*, 26.5 (2003): 32.

Propp, Vladimir. *Morphology of the Folktale* ed. Louis A. Wagnertrans. Laurence Scott. Austin: University of Texas Press, 1968.

Prince, Stephen. "The Emergence of Filmic Artifacts: Cinema and Cinematography in the Digital Era," *Film Quarterly*, 57.3 (Spring 2004): 24–53.

Rabkin, Eric S. *The Fantastic in Literature*. Princeton: Princeton University Press, 1976.

Rawlins, Jack P. "Confronting the Alien: Fantasy and Antifantasy in Science Fiction Film and Literature," *Bridges to Fantasy: Essays From the Eaton Conference on Science Fiction and Fantasy Literature*. Eds George E. Slusser, Eric S. Rabkin, and Robert Scholes. Carbondale: Southern Illinois University Press, 1982.

Rickitt, Richard. *Special Effects: The History and Technique*. New York: Billboard Books, 2007.

Rose, Mark. "Fantasy and History," *Genre at the Crossroads*. Eds George Slusser and Jean- Pierre Barricelli. Three Rivers, MA: Xenos Books, 2003.

Rushdie, Salman. *The Wizard of Oz*. London: BFI, 1992.

Russell, Jeffrey and Sabina Magliocco. "Witchcraft: Concepts of Witchcraft," *Encyclopedia of Religion* Vol. 14, 2nd edition. Ed. Lindsay Jones. Detroit, MI: Macmillan Reference, 2005.

Sandler, Kevin S. "Gendered Evasion: Bugs Bunny in Drag," *Reading the Rabbit: Explorations in Warner Bros. Animation*. Ed. Kevin S. Sandler. New Brunswick, NJ: Rutgers University Press, 1998.

Sartin Hank. "From Vaudeville to Hollywood, From Silence to Sound: Warner Bros. Cartoons of the Early Sound Era," *Reading the Rabbit: Explorations in Warner Bros. Animation*. Ed. Kevin S. Sandler. New Brunswick, NJ: Rutgers University Press, 1998.

Schakel, Peter J. *Imagination and the Arts in C.S. Lewis: Journeying to Narnia and Other Worlds*. Columbia: University of Missouri Press, 2002.

Scholes, Robert. "Boiling Roses: Thoughts on Science Fantasy," *Intersections*. Ed. George E. Slusser and Eric S. Rabkin. Carbondale: Southern Illinois University Press, 1987.

Segal, Robert A. *Myth: A Very Short Introduction*. Oxford: Oxford University Press, 2004.

Seiter, Richard D. "The Bittersweet Journey from Charlie to Willy Wonka," *Children's Novels and the Movies*. Ed. Douglas Street. New York: Frederick Ungar Publishing, 1983.

Selcer, Richard. "Home Sweet Movies," *Journal of Popular Film & Television*, 18.2 (Summer 1990): 52–64.

Setoodeh, Ramin and Jennie Yabroff. "Princess Power," *Newsweek*, 150.22, Nov. 26, 2007: 66.

Shippey, Tom. *J.R.R. Tolkien: Author of the Century*. London: HarperCollins, 2001.

Sibley, Brian. *The Lord of the Rings: The Making of the Movie Trilogy*. New York: HarperCollins, 2002.

Simon, John. "Frail Fantasy, Forceful Fiction," *National Review*, 45.7 (1993): 4.

Singer, Irving. *Reality Transformed: Film as Meaning and Technique*. Cambridge, MA: MIT Press, 1998.

Slusser, George and Eric S. Rabkin, eds. *Shadows of the Magic Lamp: Fantasy and Science Fiction in Film*. Carbondale: Southern Illinois University Press, 1985.

Slusser, George E. and Eric S. Rabkin, eds. *Intersections: Fantasy and Science Fiction*. Carbondale: Southern Illinois University Press, 1987.

Slusser, George E.,Eric S. Rabkin, and Robert Scholes, eds. *Bridges to Fantasy: Essays from the Eaton Conference on Science Fiction and Fantasy Literature*. Carbondale: Southern Illinois University Press, 1982.

Smyth, J.E. "The Three Ages of Imperial Cinema from the Death of Gordon to *The Return of the King*," *Tolkien on Film: Essays on Peter Jackson's The Lord of the Rings*. Ed. Janet Brennan Croft. Altadena, CA: The Mythopoeic Press, 2004.

Sobchack, Vivian. *Screening Space: The American Science Fiction Film*. New Brunswick, NJ: Rutgers University Press, 1987.

Sobchack, Vivian. "The Virginity of Astronauts: Sex and the Science Fiction Film," *Alien Zone: Cultural Theory and Contemporary Science Fiction Cinema*. Ed. Annette Kuhn, London: Verso, 2003.

Stableford, Brian. "From Baum to Tolkien, 1900-1956," *Fantasy and Horror: A Critical and Historical Guide to Literature, Illustration, Film, TV, Radio and the Internet*. Ed. Neil Barron. Lanham, MD: Scarecrow Press, 1999.

Stam, Robert. *Film Theory: An Introduction*. Malden, MA: Blackwell, 2000.

Swinfen, Ann. *In Defense of Fantasy: A Study of the Genre in English and American Literature since 1945*. London: Routledge, 1984.

Stein, Murray. *Jung's Map of the Soul: An Introduction*. Chicago: Open Court Press, 1998.

Sutton-Smith, Brian. *The Ambiguity of Play*. Cambridge, MA: Harvard University Press, 2001.

Taylor, Philip M. *Steven Spielberg* London: B.T. Batsford Ltd., 1992.

Todorov, Tzvetan. *The Fantastic: A Structural Approach to a Literary Genre*, trans. Richard Howard. Ithaca, NY: Cornell University Press, 1975.

Tolkien, J.R.R. *The Tolkien Reader*. New York, Ballantine Books, 1966.

Tolkien, J.R.R. *The Letters of J.R.R. Tolkien*. Ed. Humphrey Carpenter. Boston: Houghton Mifflin, 2000.

Thompson, Kristin. *Storytelling in the New Hollywood: Understanding Classical Narrative Technique*. Cambridge, MA: Harvard University Press, 1999.

Thompson, Kristin. *The Frodo Franchise: The Lord of the Rings and Modern Hollywood*. Berkeley: University of California Press, 2007.

Thompson, Kristin and David Bordwell. *Film History: An Introduction,*3rd edition. New York, McGraw-Hill, 2009.

Thum, Maureen. "The 'Sub-creation' of Galadriel, Arwen, and Eowyn: Women of Power in Tolkien's and Jackson's *Lord of the Rings*," *Tolkien on Film: Essays on Peter Jackson's The Lord of the Rings*. Ed. Janet Brennan Croft. Altadena, CA: The Mythopoeic Press, 2004.

Valenti, Peter L. "The 'Film Blanc': Suggestions for a Variety of Fantasy: 1940–45," *Journal of Popular Film 6.4* (Winter 1978): 295–303.

Villarreal, Phil. " 'Big,' a Film With Heart and Soul, Proved Tom Hanks' Potential," *Arizona Daily Star*, June 3, 2007.

Waggoner, Diana. *The Hills of Faraway: A Guide to Fantasy*. New York: Atheneum, 1978.

Warner, Marina. *From the Beast to the Blonde*. New York: The Noonday Press, Farrar, Straus and Giroux, 1994.

Wasko, Janet. *Understanding Disney*. Malden, MA: Polity, 2001.

Wasko, Janet and Govind Shanadi. "More than Just Rings: Merchandise for Them All," *The Lord of the Rings: Popular Culture in Global Context*. Ed. Ernest Mathijs. London: Wallflower Press, 2006.

Whited, Lana A., ed. *The Ivory Tower and Harry Potter: Perspectives on a Literary Phenomenon*. Columbia: University of Missouri Press, 2002.

Wood, Juliette. "Filming Fairies: Popular Film, Audience Response and Meaning in Contemporary Fairy Lore." *Folklore* 117.3 (2006): 279–96.

Wood, Robin. "The American Nightmare: Horror in the 70s," *Horror: The Film Reader*. Ed. Marc Jancovich. London: Routledge, 2001.

Wood, Robin. "Ideology, Genre, Auteur," *Film Genre Reader III*. Ed. Barry Keith Grant. Austin: University of Texas Press, 2003.

Worland, Rick. *The Horror Film: An Introduction*. Malden, MA: Blackwell Publishing, 2007.

Worley, Alec. *Empires of the Imagination: A Critical Survey of Fantasy Cinema from Georges Méliès to The Lord of the Rings*. Jefferson, NC: McFarland, 2005.

Wright, Bradford J. *Comic Book Nation*. Baltimore, MD: Johns Hopkins University Press, 2001.

Zipes, Jack. *Fairy Tale as Myth, Myth as Fairy Tale*. Lexington: University Press of Kentucky, 1994.

Zipes, Jack. *Happily Ever After: Fairy Tales, Children, and the Culture Industry*. New York: Routledge, 1997.

Zipes, Jack. *Sticks and Stones: The Troublesome Success of Children's Literature from Slovenly Peter to Harry Potter*. New York: Routledge, 2001.

Zipes, Jack. "Jack Zipes Discusses Standards of Beauty Expressed in Fairy Tales." Transcript of interview with Susan Stamberg and hosts Steve Inskeep and Renee Montagne, *Morning Edition*, Washington, DC, NPR, July 6, 2004.

Zipes, Jack. *Why Fairy Tales Stick: The Evolution and Relevance of a Genre*. New York: Routledge, 2006.

INDEX